SPOKEN
SPANISH

THIRD EDITION

SPOKEN SPANISH
for students and travelers

Manuel Durán
Yale University

Gloria Durán
Hartford College for Women

Charles E. Kany

D. C. HEATH AND COMPANY
Lexington, Massachusetts Toronto

International Standard Book Number: 0–669–00879–6

Library of Congress Catalog Card Number: 77–75690

PREFACE

Much time has gone by since the first edition of *Spoken Spanish for Students and Travelers,* but it has nevertheless shown a remarkable staying power. Because of this, it was felt that an updated edition should be published.

The purpose of the book is to offer easy but adequate conversational Spanish to students of the language (in colleges and high schools, and in adult education courses) and to travelers in general. The book may be considered a basic conversational text not only for beginners with no knowledge of Spanish, but also for those who already possess a foundation. A skeleton grammar is appended for the benefit of those who may wish to consult it. To this end, footnoted references will be found throughout the text corresponding to explanatory paragraphs in the Appendix.

The dialogues have been carefully selected to meet the ordinary requirements of the traveler in his daily life and have been slanted particularly toward Spanish America.

It is well known that in some instances words and meanings may differ from one Spanish-speaking country to another and that American Spanish has been enriched by many local Indian words unfamiliar in Spain. In such cases of variation we have tried to select the word or words most widely used and therefore most readily understood throughout the Spanish-speaking world. In all cases, however, the various forms are footnoted.

As for the prices of goods and services that appear in the dialogues, it should be remembered that inflation is a way of life in many Spanish American countries and that these prices do not actually prevail.

"Material preliminar" is an elementary introduction for those who have never studied Spanish. Parts 2, 3, and 4 begin more complex dialogues which take the reader by train and car to Mexico City. There, sightseeing and daily life form the subject matter of the dialogues. Part 5 continues the trip— by plane to Guatemala and by boat to Buenos Aires.

The English translation is given primarily for the benefit of the student of Spanish, but it may also be used by Spanish-speaking students who wish to acquaint themselves with conversational usage in (American) English.

An entirely new section has been added on medical emergencies. There are also new sections on dealing with the police, real estate agents, a pharmacist, a beautician, etc. New vocabulary envisions women's, as well as men's, potential requirements when traveling.

Manuel Durán

Gloria Durán

CONTENTS

4 En la ciudad de México

5 La América, Central y del Sur

LA AMÉRICA DEL SUR

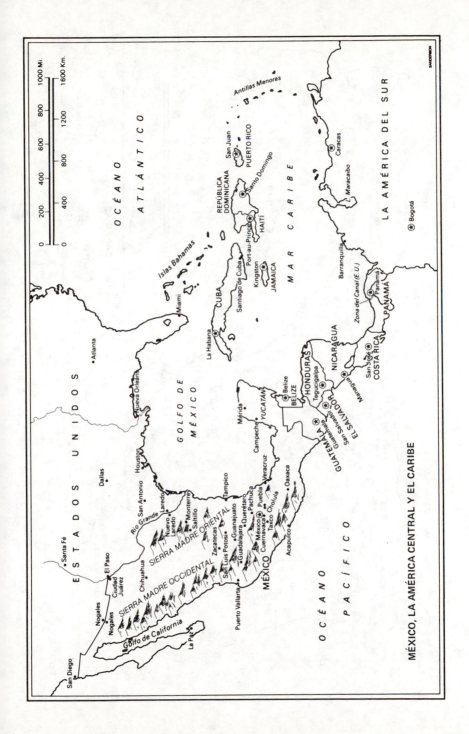

MÉXICO, LA AMÉRICA CENTRAL Y EL CARIBE

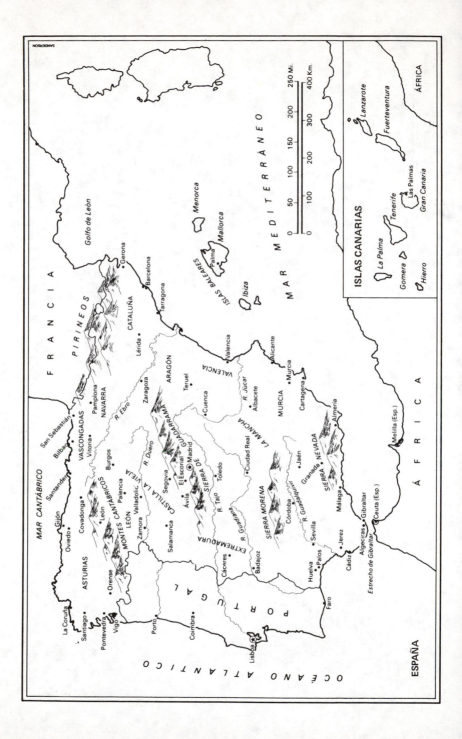

SPOKEN SPANISH

PRONUNCIATION

The *approximate*[1] English equivalents are as follows:

I. Vowels (all are short and clear):

a   as in *a*h!

e   as in th*ey* (without the final *i* glide sound of English). Under certain conditions more like *e* in m*e*t: especially before double *r*.

o   as in *o*pen (without the final *u* glide sound of English). Under certain conditions more like *o* in n*o*rth: especially before double *r* and when syllable ends in a consonant.

i (y) as in mach*i*ne

u   as in r*u*le; silent in **gue, gui** unless written **ü**

II. Consonants (those not mentioned here are *approximately* as in English):

b and **v** have the same sound. After a pause and after **m**

---

[1] Only approximate sounds can be discussed here. Imitation should be practiced.

or **n,** the sound is approximately like *b* in *b*oy. Otherwise, upper and lower lips are brought together and the breath passes between them, as is done in blowing dust.

c   before **o, a, u** as in cat but softer, almost like English **g**

c   before **e, i** as in *th*in in Spain (except Andalusia), as in *s*in in Spanish America

ch   as in *ch*in

d   after a pause or **n** and **l** is approximately like *d* in *d*o but tongue touches lower edge of upper front teeth. Elsewhere **d** is like *th* in *th*ough, but less interdental and softer than the English sound.

g   before **a, o, u** after a pause and after **n** like *g* in *g*o. Elsewhere more relaxed, softer almost to the point of disappearing; before **i, e** like the Spanish **j.**

h   is silent

j   is like *ch* in German Ba*ch*. Press back of tongue against soft palate and force breath through, as in expectorating. In Spanish America it is much more relaxed and often a mere aspiration like *h* in *h*im.

l   farther forward in mouth than in English

ll   in most of Spain approximately as in mi*lli*on but the **ll** begins the syllable; elsewhere, as in Spanish America, it is generally like *y* in *y*es; in Argentina it is like *s* in plea*s*ure.

ñ   approximately as in ca*ny*on, but the **ñ** begins the syllable.

p   as in English but softer, almost like English *b*

qu like English *k*

r is pronounced with one flip of tongue against roots of upper front teeth. But when initial in word or after **l** or **n** it is like **rr.**

rr is trilled several times

s as in *see*. When preceding **m, n, d, b, v, g,** and **l,** as in ro*s*e.

t approximately as in English, but tip of tongue touches edge of upper front teeth and the sound is softer, with no breath escaping immediately after it; almost like English *d*

x before a consonant is like *s*; before a vowel it is like *x* in e*x*tra (not like *x* of e*x*ist).

y initial in word or syllable is like *y* in *y*es, but more intense; in Argentina it is like *s* in plea*s*ure.

z same as **c** before **e** and **i**

III. **A diphthong is a combination of a strong vowel (a, e, o)** and a weak vowel (**i, u**) or of two weak vowels (**i, u**). It forms one syllable, but each vowel is pronounced, the strong vowel receiving the stress (of two weak vowels, the second takes the stress): **au, ei, ie, ay, ui,** etc.

A triphthong is the combination, in a single syllable, of a strong vowel between two weak vowels: **iai, iei, uay, uey,** etc.

IV. **Accent**

1. If a vowel bears a written accent, stress that syllable; otherwise:

2. Stress last syllable if word ends in a consonant except **n** or **s.**

3. Stress next to last syllable if word ends in a vowel or **n** or **s.**

V. Syllabification

1. A single consonant goes with the following vowel: **ca-sa, a-vión. Ch, ll,** and **rr** are considered single consonants.

2. Combinations of **b, c, f, g, p** with a following **l** or **r** (and **tr** and **dr**) go with the following vowel: **o-bra, mo-no-pla-no, pa-dre,** etc.

3. Other combinations are divided: **sol-da-do, per-der, con-tra, cos-tar,** etc.

1

Material preliminar

Preliminary Material

Vocabulario útil

Useful Vocabulary

■ **Pidiendo informes**   *Asking for Information*

dispense usted	*excuse (me)*
¿dónde está	*where is*
el aeropuerto?	*the airport?*
el autobús?	*the bus?*
el avión?	*the plane?*
el banco?	*the bank?*
el correo?	*the post office?*
el hotel?	*the hotel?*
el museo?	*the museum?*
el restaurante?	*the restaurant?*
el retrete?	*the toilet?*
el tren?	*the train?*
la calle?	*the street?*
la estación?	*the station?*
la plaza?	*the square?*
la iglesia?	*the church?*
la catedral?	*the cathedral?*
¿dónde hay	*where is*
un mapa?	*a map?*
un médico?	*a doctor?*
un policía?	*a policeman?*
un directorio de teléfonos?	*a telephone directory?*

■ **Contestaciones**   *Answers*

está aquí	*it is here*
está allí	*it is there*

está lejos	*it is far*
no está lejos	*it is not far*
está cerca	*it is near*
no está cerca	*it is not near*
está a la derecha	*it is to the right*
está a la izquierda	*it is to the left*
no lo tenemos	*we don't have one*
no sé	*I don't know*

Practice combining questions and answers.

dígame usted por favor	*tell me please*
¿dónde está	*where is*
el baño?	*the bathroom?*
el comedor?	*the dining room?*
el cine?	*the cinema, movie?*
el taxi? or el libre?	*the taxi?*
el teatro?	*the theater?*
el teléfono?	*the telephone?*
la entrada?	*the entrance?*
la salida?	*the exit?*
mi cuarto?	*my room?*
mi llave?	*my key?*

adelante	*forward, ahead*
al final	*at the end*
en frente	*opposite*
siga usted	*keep going*
todo derecho ⎫ todo seguido ⎭	*straight ahead*

Está a cinco minutos a pie,
  en autobús.
	*It's five minutes on foot,
	  by bus.*

Usted tiene que tomar un taxi.	*You have to take a taxi.*
gracias	*thanks*
muchas gracias	*many thanks*
de nada	*you're welcome (lit. "of nothing")*

Practice as follows:
  — Dígame usted, por favor, ¿dónde está el baño?

— Está aquí (allí, lejos, cerca, etc.). Siga usted todo derecho.
— Muchas gracias.
— De nada.

■ **Pidiendo refrescos**   *Ordering Refreshments*

usted tiene	*you have*
¿tiene usted?	*do you have, have you got?*
tengo	*I have*
no tengo	*I do not have*
déme usted	*give me*
tráigame usted, por favor	*bring me, please*
pan	*bread*
sopa	*soup*
cigarrillos	*cigarettes*
un vaso de	*a glass of*
agua	*water*
agua caliente	*hot water*
agua fría	*cold water*
agua mineral	*mineral water*
cerveza fría	*cold beer*
leche caliente	*hot milk*
leche fría	*cold milk*
leche pasteurizada	*pasteurized milk*
leche descremada	*skim milk*
té helado	*iced tea*
vino blanco	*white wine*
vino dulce	*sweet wine*
vino tinto	*red wine*
un yogurt ⎱ leche búlgara ⎰	*yogurt*
una taza de	*a cup of*
café caliente	*hot coffee*
chocolate caliente	*hot chocolate*
té caliente	*hot tea*
¿cuánto es?	*how much is it?*
es caro	*it's expensive*

no es caro	*it's not expensive*
es barato	*it's cheap*
no es barato	*it's not cheap*
es demasiado	*it's too much*

■ ¿Qué hora es?   *What Time Is It?*

1	uno, una	5	cinco	9	nueve
2	dos	6	seis	10	diez
3	tres	7	siete	11	once
4	cuatro	8	ocho	12	doce

¿qué hora es?	*what time is it?*
es la una	*it is one o'clock*
son las dos, etc.	*it is two o'clock, etc.*
es la una y cuarto	*it is a quarter past one*
es la una y veinte	*it is twenty past one*
son las dos y media	*it is half past two*
son las tres y diez	*it is ten minutes after three*
son las diez menos diez ⎱ faltan diez para las diez ⎰	*it is ten minutes to ten*
es tarde, temprano	*it's late, early*
¿a qué hora	*what time*
regresa el médico?	*does the doctor come back?*
sale el tren?	*does the train leave?*
sale el avión?	*does the plane leave?*
llega el autobús?	*does the bus arrive?*
llega el barco?	*does the boat arrive?*
empieza el teatro?	*does the theater begin?*
empieza la comida?	*does dinner begin?*
termina el cine?	*does the movie end?*
termina el concierto?	*does the concert end?*
sale, llega, empieza, termina	*it leaves, arrives, begins, ends*
a las siete	*at seven*
a las ocho y media	*at half past eight*
a las once en punto	*at eleven sharp*

a las dos menos cinco   *at five minutes to two*
(or cinco para las dos)

■ Frases útiles   *Useful Phrases*

debo	*I must*
tengo que	*I must, have to*
comprar	*buy*
dar	*give*
decir	*say*
descansar	*rest*
despertarme	*wake up*
dormir	*sleep*
entrar	*go in, enter*
escribir	*write*
llamar	*call*
salir	*go out, leave*
se puede (?)	*one can, can one?*
bailar	*dance*
comer	*eat*
desayunar	*have breakfast*
fumar	*smoke*
ir	*go*
jugar	*play*
pasear	*walk*
pedir	*ask for*
preguntar	*ask (a question)*
tomar	*take (drink or eat)*
ver	*see*
¿qué tiempo hace?	*what's the weather like?*
hace buen tiempo	*the weather is good*
hace mal tiempo	*the weather is bad*
hace calor	*it is hot*
hace frío	*it is cold*
hace mucho calor	*it is very hot*
hace mucho frío	*it is very cold*
llueve	*it is raining*
no llueve	*it is not raining*

Conversaciones

Conversations

■ **Los saludos**   *Greetings*

— Buenos días.
  Good morning (or How do you do?).

— Buenos días.
  Good morning (or How do you do?).

— ¿Cómo está usted?
  How are you?

— Muy bien, gracias. ¿Y usted?
  Very well, thank you. And (how are) you?

— Así, así. Estoy un poco enfermo (–a).[1]
  So, so (or Fair). I'm slightly ill.

— ¡Cuánto lo siento!
  I'm sorry (lit. "how much I feel it").

— Muchas gracias.
  Thank you (lit. "many thanks").

— Adiós. Hasta luego.
  Good-bye. See you later (lit. "till later").

— Hasta mañana.
  See you tomorrow.

— Buenos días.
  Good morning.

---

[1] **enfermo, -a** = **malo, -a**.

— Buenos días, señor.
> *Good morning.*

— ¿Es usted norteamericano (–a)?
> *Are you an American?*

— Sí, señor. ¿Y usted?
> *Yes. And you?*

— Soy español (–a).
> *I'm Spanish.*

— ¿Habla usted inglés?
> *Do you speak English?*

— No, señor. Hablo español.
> *No. I speak Spanish.*

— Yo hablo inglés. No hablo español.
> *I speak English. I do not speak Spanish.*

— ¡Qué lástima![2]
> *What a pity!*

— Buenas tardes, señora.
> *Good afternoon.*

— Buenas tardes, señorita.
> *Good afternoon.*

— ¿Es usted inglesa?
> *Are you English?*

— No, señora; soy española. Mi marido es inglés. ¿Y usted?
> *No; I'm Spanish. My husband is English. And you?*

— Mi padre es mexicano. Mi madre es francesa. Hablo español y francés.
> *My father is Mexican. My mother is French. I speak Spanish and French.*

---

[2] § 6c.

■ **La presentación**   *The Introduction*

— Le presento[3] a mi amigo (amiga) ——.
May I introduce my friend.

— Tanto gusto *or* Mucho gusto en conocerle (conocerla).
How do you do?

— El gusto es mío.
How do you do? (lit. "the pleasure is mine")

— Permita usted que me presente: Carlos Terán, a sus órdenes.
Allow me to introduce myself: my name is Carlos Terán.

— Ramón Rodríguez, para servirle.
Mine is Ramón Rodríguez.

— (Despidiéndose) He tenido un verdadero gusto.
(Taking leave) Nice to have met you (lit. "it's been a real pleasure").

— El gusto ha sido mío.
And you (lit. "the pleasure was mine").

NOTAS

1. **buenas tardes** (used after midday till evening), *good afternoon, good evening*; **buenas noches**, *good evening, good night.*

2. **¿cómo está usted? = ¿cómo le va?** (*how goes it?*) **= ¿qué tal?** In familiar usage: **¡hola!** *hello*; **¿qué hay?** or **¿qué pasa?** *what's new?* or *what's up?* In Mexico one hears the familiar and popular **¿qué hubo? ¿qué húbole?** and **¿qué pasó?**

3. **así, así = regular = pasándolo = pasándola** (Mex.): **así no más** is common in Spanish America.

4. **adiós = ¡ que le vaya bien!** **adiós** is used also as a greeting.

5. **hasta luego = hasta la vista = hasta lueguito** (Chile, Arg., etc.). In familiar usage: **¡chao!** (Arg., Chile); **¡nos veremos!** and **¡nos vemos!** (Mex.; cf. our "I'll be seeing you").

---

[3] **le presento = permítame presentarle**; for **a** see § 11.

6. **¡a sus órdenes!** (*at your service*) is a common reply; **vale** (Spain) *O.K.*

7. Other adjectives of nationality are: **francés (francesa)**, *French*; **alemán (alemana)**, *German*; **ruso (rusa)**, *Russian*; **portugués (portuguesa)**, *Portuguese*. See also § 70. This and similar references will be made throughout the book to indicate corresponding paragraphs in the Appendix.

8. Note the frequent use of **señor, señora, señorita** (*Mr.*, *Mrs.*, *Miss*) in direct address, where in English the corresponding form is often either omitted or followed by the person's name.

9. Note that the adjective agrees in gender with the person qualified. A woman says "**soy norteamericana, española, francesa,** etc." See §§ 12, 13, 6a. In Spanish America **americano** usually means *Spanish American*. In Mexico an American is colloquially referred to as **gringo, -a**; in South America **gringo** is applied to any foreigner, particularly the fair-haired, and has no contemptuous connotation there.

10. **yo** is used only for emphasis.

11. The older spellings **México** and **mexicano** are official in that country, though the words are always pronounced **Méjico** and **mejicano** and are so spelled in Spain.

Un encuentro

A Meeting

— ¡Hola, amigo!
  Hello, there (friend).

— ¿Cómo le va?
  How are you? (or How goes it?)

— Mejor que ayer, gracias a Dios.
  Better than yesterday, thank Heaven.

— Me alegro.[1]
  That's good (lit. "I'm glad").

— ¿Qué hay de nuevo?
  What's new?

— Tengo que[2] aprender el español.[3]
  I have to learn Spanish.

— Pero ya lo habla usted muy bien.
  But you speak it very well already.

— ¡Qué va! Quiero hacer un viaje.
  Nonsense! I want to take a trip.

— ¿A dónde? si no es indiscreción (preguntarlo).
  Where, if I may ask?

— A México y a la América del Sur.
  To Mexico and South America.

— ¡Feliz usted!
  Aren't you lucky!

---

[1] **me alegro** = **lo celebro**. [2] **tengo que** = **necesito**. § 55a. [3] § 4c.

— Al contrario. Ahora tengo que estudiar el idioma.
> *On the contrary. Now I must study the language.*

— Pero ¿no lo estudió[4] usted en la escuela?
> *But didn't you study it in school?*

— Sí, hace muchos años.[5]
> *Yes, many years ago (lit. "it makes many years").*

— ¿Cuántos años hace?
> *How many years ago?*

— Cinco o seis.
> *Five or six.*

— ¿Y lo ha olvidado[6] usted?
> *And you've forgotten it?*

— Lo he olvidado todo.
> *I've forgotten everything.*

— Todo no. Todavía sabe usted algo.
> *Not everything. You still know something.*

— Es favor que me hace.
> *You're just being nice.*

— No es favor. Es la verdad.
> *Not at all. It's the truth.*

— Gracias. Es usted muy amable.
> *Thank you. You're very kind.*

NOTAS

1. Other words suggested by **ayer**: **hoy**, *today*; **mañana**, *tomorrow*; **pasado mañana**, *the day after tomorrow*; **anteayer** (**antier**), *the day before yesterday.*

2. For **¡qué va!** a Spaniard might use **¡ca!** or **¡quiá!**, but neither is common in Spanish America; **¡qué esperanza!** (Arg. and elsewhere).

[4] Preterite of **estudiar**, *to study.* § 59, § 40c.   [5] **hacer**, *to do, make.* §57c   [6] **olvidar**, *to forget.* § 60.

3. **hacer un viaje por barco, por ferrocarril,** or **por tren, en avión, en automóvil,** *to travel by boat, by train, by plane, by car*; *to take a walk, a step,* etc., **dar un paseo, un paso.**

La despedida

Taking Leave

— Buenas tardes.
  Good afternoon.

— Muy buenas.
  Good afternoon.

— ¿Qué es de su vida?
  How are you getting on (lit. "what is of your life")?

— Sin novedad (or Nada de particular).
  The same as usual (or Nothing new).

— ¿Estudiando mucho?
  Studying much?

— Sí, repasando la gramática.
  Yes, reviewing (the) grammar.

— Pues me alegro. ¿Ya está para[1] irse?
  Well, that's good. Are you about to leave?

— Casi. Primero voy[2] a México.
  Almost. First I'm going to Mexico.

— ¿Cómo piensa[3] usted ir: por tren, en avión o en automóvil (Mex. carro)?
  How do you expect to go: by train, by plane, or by car?

— No sé[4] todavia. Tengo un amigo (una amiga) que quiere[5] llevarme en su coche.
  I don't know yet. I have a friend who wants to take me in his (her) car.

[1] § 38.   [2] **ir**, *to go*. § 67, 9.   [3] **pensar (ie)**, *to think*. § 64, I.   [4] **saber**, *to know*. § 67, 16.   [5] **querer (ie)**, *to want, wish; to love*. § 64, I and § 67, 15.

— ¿Por qué no va usted con él (ella)?
  Why don't you go with him (her)?

— Porque quiero ir por otra ruta.
  Because I want to go by another route.

— ¡Ah, vamos!
  Oh, I see.

— Yo voy por tren, él (ella) va en coche, y nos vemos[6] en México.
  I'm going by train, he (she) is going by car, and we'll meet in Mexico.

— Desde allí ¿siguen[7] ustedes juntos?
  Will you go on together from there?

— Sí, seguimos juntos en avión hasta Guatemala.
  Yes, we'll go on together by plane to Guatemala.

— Pues, ¡feliz viaje!
  Well, I hope you have a nice trip.

— Muchas gracias.
  Thank you (very much).

NOTAS

1. Some idioms with **pensar**: **pensar de**, *to think of, have an opinion about*; **pensar en**, *to think of, meditate on*; **pensar** + inf,. *to intend, expect*; **¿qué piensa usted de esto?** *what do you think of this?* **pienso en ella**, *I think of her*; **pienso irme**, *I expect to go away.*

2. Some idioms with **seguir**: **siga usted**, *go on, continue*; **siga usted comiendo**, *go on eating*; **siga usted derecho**, *go straight ahead*; **siga** (traffic signal), *go.* § 41.

[6] ver, *to see*; **vemos** is present tense used for a future. § 67, 23; § 40a.   [7] **seguir** (i), *to follow, go on.* § 64, III.

2

El viaje por tren

The Train Trip

Oficina de información

Information Bureau

— Dispense usted. ¿A qué hora sale el tren para México?

    Excuse me. What time does the train leave for Mexico?

— Hay dos trenes diarios.[1] Uno que sale a las ocho de la mañana, y otro a las tres de la tarde.

    There are two trains a day. One that leaves at eight in the morning, and another at three in the afternoon.

— ¿Cuál de los dos es el rápido (or expreso)?

    Which of the two is the express (or the fast train)?

— El (tren) de las ocho. El otro es el ordinario.

    The eight o'clock (one). The other is the local.

— ¿A qué hora llega a México?

    What time does it arrive in Mexico?

— Llega a las once de la mañana; es decir, si no llega con retraso.[2]

    It arrives at eleven in the morning; that is, if it's not late.

— ¿Ese tren lleva coche cama y (coche) comedor?

    Does that train have a sleeper and a diner?

— Sí, señor. También un coche directo.

    Yes, sir. Also a through coach.

— ¿De modo que no tengo que trasbordar?[3]

    Then I don't have to change?

— No, señor; es decir, si no quiere hacer escala.[4]

    No, sir; that is, if you don't want to stop over.

---

[1] **diario, -a,** *daily* = **al día,** *a day.*   [2] **con retraso** = **atrasado,** *late.*   [3] **tra(n)sbordar** = **cambiar de tren,** *to change trains.*   [4] **hacer escala** = **detenerse,** *to stop (over).*

— En este viaje no quiero hacer ninguna escala.

I don't want to stop over anywhere on this trip.

— Muy bien. Puede[5] usted sacar su boleto en la ventanilla número diez.

O.K. You can get your ticket at window number ten.

— Gracias. Ah, se me olvidaba.[6] ¿Me hace usted el favor de un horario or itinerario)?[7]

Thank you. Oh, I nearly forgot. Could you give me a timetable?

— Con mucho gusto. Tome usted.

Certainly. Here you are.

— Muchas gracias.

Thank you.

NOTAS

1.   Except for such set expressions as **oficina de información** *information* is generally **informes**: **pedir informes**, *to ask for information.*

2.   **dispensar** means *pardon/excuse*, while **perdonar** means *pardon/forgive.*

3.   Other kinds of train: **mixto** (=**ordinario**), *carrying passengers and freight*; **tren de carga (mercancías)**, *freight train.*

4.   The opposite of **atrasado** is **adelantado**.

5.   **coche cama** = **pullman** (Mex.) = **coche dormitorio** (Span. Am.); (**coche**) **comedor** = **restorán** or **restaurante**; **vagón** or **coche** = **carro** (Span. Am.).

6.   Other vocabulary for traveling connections: **enlazar con**, **conectar con** (Mex.), **entroncar con** (Span. Am.), *to connect with.*

7.   **billete** is used for **boleto**, particularly in Spain; **tiquete** should be avoided.

---

[5] **poder (ue)**, *to be able to, can.* § 64, I; § 67, 13,   [6] **olvidar: se me olvidaba**, *I nearly forgot* or *it nearly slipped my mind* (lit. "it was forgetting itself to me"). [7] **guía de ferrocarriles** *f.*, *railroad guide.*

El despacho de boletos

The Ticket Office

— ¿Es éste el despacho de boletos?
 Is this the ticket office?

— Sí, señor. A sus órdenes.
 Yes, sir. What can I do for you?

— Un boleto para México.
 A ticket to Mexico City.

— ¿De qué clase: de primera o de segunda?
 What class: first or second?

— De primera.
 First.

— ¿De ida, o de ida y vuelta?[1]
 One way or round trip?

— ¿Por cuánto tiempo vale[2] el boleto de ida y vuelta?
 How long is the round-trip ticket good for (or valid)?

— Vale por tres meses.
 It's good (or valid) for three months.

— Entonces no me conviene, porque pienso quedarme cuatro
o cinco meses.
 *Then it won't do, because I expect to stay (or remain) four
 or five months.*

— Como usted quiera.[3]
 O.K. (or Just as you like).

---

[1] **de ida** = **sencillo.**   [2] **vale** (from **valer**) = **es válido, bueno, valedero.**   [3] **como usted
quiera** = **como usted guste** (from **gustar**). § 45*b*.

— ¿Cuánto vale el pasaje de primera?

How much is the first-class fare?

— Trescientos cincuenta pesos. En los boletos de ida y vuelta hay rebaja del veinte por ciento.

Three hundred and fifty pesos. There is a reduction of twenty percent on round-trip tickets.

— Siento[4] no poder aprovecharme de la tarifa especial.

I'm sorry I won't be able to take advantage of the special rate.

— Aquí tiene usted su boleto y su vuelto.

Here's your ticket and your change.

— Gracias. ¿Dónde saco mi boleto de coche cama?

Thank you. Where do I get my Pullman ticket?

— En la ventanilla de al lado.[5]

At the next window.

— Muchas gracias.

Thank you.

— De ese lado no. De éste.[6] A la derecha.

Not on that side. This side. To the right.

— ¿Donde está toda esa gente?

Where all those people are?

— Allí mismo. (A todos) ¡Favor de hacer cola!

Right there. (To all) Get in line please!

NOTAS

1.   **despacho de boletos** = **la taquilla** (Spain) = **la boletería** (Span. Am.); **boleto de ida**, *one-way ticket*; **de ida y vuelta** = **de viaje redondo** (Mex.).

2.   **el vuelto** (Span. Am.) = **la vuelta** (Spain), *change.*

---

[4] **siento** = **lamento**, *I am sorry.*   [5] **de al lado** = **siguiente**, *following*; **la casa de al lado**, *the house next door.*   [6] **este**, *this* (near speaker); **ese**, *that* (near person spoken to). § 26, § 27.

3. The **peso** is the monetary unit in Mexico, Colombia, Argentina, Chile, Uruguay; **dólar** in Cuba, Puerto Rico, and the Dominican Republic; **boliviano** in Bolivia; **colón** in El Salvador and Costa Rica; **sucre** in Ecuador; **quetzal** in Guatemala; **lempira** in Honduras; **córdoba** in Nicaragua; **balboa** in Panama; **sol** in Peru; **bolívar** in Venezuela.

4. **hacer cola** = **formarse** (Mex.): **hagan ustedes cola** = **fórmense**, *get in line* (command). § 41.

El coche cama

The (Pullman) Sleeper

— ¿(Me hace usted el favor de) una cama baja hasta México?
(Could you give me) a lower berth to Mexico City?

— ¿En qué tren piensa usted salir?
What train are you thinking of leaving on?

— En el (tren) de esta noche, el que sale a las 20 (veinte) horas.[1]
On tonight's (train), the one that leaves at eight o'clock (at 8:00 P.M.).

— Desgraciadamente no me queda ni una cama baja en ese tren.
Unfortunately I don't have a single lower berth left on that train.

— ¿Ni alta tampoco?
Nor an upper either?

— Un momento. Voy a ver.
Just a moment. I'll see.

— No me gustan las altas. Me cuesta trabajo[2] subir.
I don't like uppers. It's hard for me to climb in (lit. "it costs me work").

— Es fácil subir con la escalera.
It's easy with the ladder.

— Es que[3] soy muy gordo (–a).
But I'm quite stout.

---

[1] **veinte horas,** *eight P. M.*   [2] **costar (ue),** *to cost.* § 64, I.   [3] **es que,** *it's because, the fact is that, but,* etc. (lit. "it is that").

— Bueno, me quedan dos altas, la 6 (seis) y la 12 (doce).
¿Cuál prefiere usted?

> *Well, I have two uppers left, six and twelve. Which do you*
> *prefer?*

— Tomaré la 12. Está en medio del coche. Allí molesta
menos el ruido.

> *I'll take twelve. It's in the middle of the coach. There's less*
> *bother from the noise there.*

— Muy bien. La doce alta en el coche 52 (cincuenta y dos).
¿La aparto (or reservo) o la toma usted ahora?

> *Fine. Upper twelve in coach fifty-two. Shall I reserve it or*
> *will you take it now?*

— La tomo ahora. ¿Cuánto vale?

> *I'll take it now. How much is it?*

— Ciento veinte pesos. Es coche directo. No tiene usted que
trasbordar.

> *One hundred twenty pesos. It's a through coach. You won't*
> *have to change.*

— Muy bien. Le doy[4] tres billetes de a cincuenta.

> *Fine. I'll give you three fifty-peso bills.*

— Y le devuelvo[5] treinta pesos.

> *And I'll give you thirty pesos change.*

NOTAS

1. Other vocabulary: **sección** *f.*, *section*; **gabinete** *m.*,
drawing room.

2. **me cuesta (mucho) trabajo** = **me es (muy) difícil.**

3. **de a** expresses rate: **dos timbres (sellos, estampillas) de**
a cinco centavos, *two five-cent stamps*, etc.

4. **volver (ue)**, *to return*; **devuelvo el libro**, *I return the*
book; **vuelvo a casa**, *I return home.* § 64, I.

[4] **dar**, *to give.* § 67, 4.   [5] **devolver (ue)**, *to return* (something).

En la sala de equipajes

In the Baggage Room

— Cargador, haga el favor de llevar todo esto a la sala de equipajes.

> *Porter, would you carry all this to the baggage room.*

— (Llegando) ¿Quiere usted facturar su baúl?

> (*Arriving*) *Do you want to check your trunk?*

— No, señor. No tengo baúl. Tengo estas tres maletas, este paquete y esta sombrerera.

> *No. I don't have a trunk. I have these three suitcases, this package, and this hatbox.*

— Muy bien. Vamos a pesarlo todo.

> *O.K. Let's weigh it all.*

— ¿A cuántos kilos[1] tengo derecho?

> *How many kilos am I allowed?*

— Tiene derecho a treinta kilos. Vamos a ver. Todo esto pesa quince kilos.

> *You're allowed thirty kilos. Let's see. All this weighs fifteen kilos.*

— De modo que no hay exceso.

> *So there's no overweight.*

— Y no paga usted nada. Aquí tiene las contraseñas.

> *And you pay nothing. Here are your checks.*

---

[1] **kilo** *kilogram*$=2\frac{1}{4}$ *pounds.*

— Gracias. ¿Puede enviar mi equipaje al hotel?
  Thank you. Can you send my luggage to the hotel?

— ¡Cómo no! Con mucho gusto.
  Sure. (We'll be) glad to.

— Entonces aquí le dejo mi dirección.
  Then I'll leave my address here for you.

— No pierda[2] usted las contraseñas (or los talones).
  Don't lose the checks (or stubs, tags).

— No se preocupe.
  Don't worry.

— Además, las maletas llevan sus iniciales.
  Anyhow, your bags have your initials on them.

— Eso es. Todas menos este paquete.
  That's right. All except this package.

— Ya tiene que subir al tren.
  You'll have to board the train now.

— Es verdad. Faltan sólo cinco minutos.
  Right. I only have five minutes.

— Hay que[3] darse prisa.
  You'll have to hurry.

NOTAS

1. **la sala de equipajes** = **el despacho** or **cuarto de equipajes**; **el agente de equipajes**, *the baggage man.*

2. **el cargador** is the general Spanish American word; **changador** (Arg.) = **el mozo** or **mozo de estación** (Spain); **portero** (Pullman), *porter.*

3. **facturar** = **chequear** (Mex.) = **registrar** (in some places, though, **registrar** generally means *to search, examine*).

[2] **perder (ie)**, *to lose.* § 64, I.   [3] **hay que** = **es preciso** or **necesario.** § 56*b.*

4.   **la maleta**=**el velís** (Mex.) or **la petaca** (Mex.)=**la valija** (Arg. and other countries).

5.   **¡cómo no!** (Span. Am.)=**por supuesto** (used more in Span. Am. than in Spain)=**claro**=**no faltaba más**.

6.   **con mucho gusto**=**con todo gusto** (Mex.).

7.   **la dirección**=**las señas** (Spain).

8.   **darse prisa**, to hurry up=**apresurarse**=**apurarse** (Span. Am.). **Dése prisa**=**apresúrese, apúrese** (Span. Am.), *hurry up*!

En la consigna

In the Check Room

— Quisiera dejar este equipaje aquí.
  I'd like to leave this luggage here.

— Muy bien. Aquí estamos para servirle.
  O.K. We're here to serve you.

— ¿A qué hora se cierra[1] el depósito?
  What time does the check room close?

— Aquí se cierra a las once de la noche.
  We close here at eleven P.M.

— Y después ¿no puedo recogerlo (or retirarlo)?
  And can't I get it after that?

— Sí, señor. Después de las once lo puede usted recoger en la sala de equipajes.
  Yes, sir. After eleven you can get it in the baggage room.

— Perfectamente. ¿Cuánto se paga[2] por bulto?
  All right. How much do I pay apiece?

— Cinco pesos por veinticuatro horas.
  Five pesos for twenty-four hours.

— ¿Lo pago ahora o al retirarlo?[3]
  Do I pay now or when I get it?

---

[1] **cerrar (ie)**, *to close*, § 64, I; **se cierra**, *it is closed* or *it closes* (lit. "closes itself").
§ 53a.   [2] **pagar**, *to pay*; **se paga**, *is paid, one pays*. § 53c.   [3] **al** + inf. § 49a.

— Ahora, si me hace el favor.
  Now, please.

— Tome usted.
  Here you are.

— Aquí tiene usted las contraseñas.
  Here are your checks.

— ¿Qué hago si pierdo las contraseñas?
  What shall I do if I lose the checks?

— En ese caso tiene usted que declarar el contenido de las maletas y presentar la llave.
  In that case you'll have to indicate the contents and present the key.

— Menos mal que tengo dos llaves para cada maleta.
  It's a good thing I've got two keys for each bag.

— Pues ¡cuidado con perder las dos!
  Well, be careful not to lose both of them!

— Las[4] de esa maleta no me sirven[5] para nada.
  The ones for that bag are worthless.

— ¿Por qué? Ah, sí; ya veo. La cerradura[6] está rota.[7] ¡Caramba!
  Why? Oh, yes; I see. The lock is broken. Hey!

— ¡Cuidado con ésa!
  Be careful of that one!

— Gracias por la advertencia.
  Thanks for the advice (or tip).

NOTAS

1. **consigna = depósito de equipajes de mano.**

---

[4] **las = las llaves,** *the ones.*   [5] **servir (i),** *to serve, be of service,* § 64, III.   [6] **la cerradura = la chapa** (Span. Am.).   [7] **romper,** *to break;* **roto,** *broken.*

2.   The opposite of **cerrar** is **abrir**: **la tienda se abre a las diez**, *the store opens at ten*.

3.   Like **¿qué hago?** *what shall I do?*: **¿qué hacemos?** *what will we do?* **¿qué le digo?** *what will I tell him?* § 40a.

4.   **no sirvo para nada**, *I'm no good at anything*; **él no sirve para eso**, *he's no good at that*.

En el andén

On the (Railway) Platform

— Tengo que apresurarme. Faltan sólo cinco minutos. (Entrando) Dispense usted, señor. ¿Llega el tren a tiempo?
> *I've got to hurry. I've only got five minutes. (Entering) Excuse me. Will the train arrive on time?*

— El número seis trae diez minutos de retraso.
> *Number six is ten minutes late.*

— Pero aquel tren, el número ocho, parece que trae cinco minutos de adelanto.
> *But that train (over there), number eight, seems to be five minutes early (or ahead of time).*

— No es el tren de hoy; es el de ayer.
> *It's not today's train; that's yesterday's.*

— ¿El de ayer?
> *Yesterday's (lit. "the one of yesterday")?*

— Sí, y no trae cinco minutos de adelanto sino veintitrés horas cincuenta y cinco minutos de retraso.
> *Yes, and it's not five minutes early, but twenty-three hours and fifty-five minutes late.*

— ¡Caray! ¡Ojalá que el nuestro no llegue[1] con tanto retraso!
> *Wow! I hope ours won't be that late!*

— Tenemos suerte. Ya no tarda. Allí viene.
> *We're lucky. It won't be long. There it comes.*

---

[1] **llegar:llegue,** subjunctive. § 42, § 63, 2.

— ¿Dónde estará el coche número 52?
Where will coach number 52 be?

— Más adelante. Tenemos tiempo todavía.
Farther forward. We still have time.

— ¿Va usted a México también?
Are you going to Mexico City too?

— Sí, pero tengo que hacer escala en Mazatlán primero.
Yes, but I have to stop over at Mazatlán first.

— Lo envidio. Me gustaría[2] hacer lo mismo.[3]
I envy you. I'd like to do the same.

— Ya puede usted subir. Nos veremos en el tren.
Now you can get on. I'll see you on the train.

— Así lo espero. Hasta luego.
I hope so. See you later.

— (Portero) ¡Vámonos![4]
(Porter) All aboard!

NOTAS

1. **andén** = **plataforma**; **boleto (billete) de andén** *platform ticket, visitor's ticket.*

2. **apresurarme** = **darme prisa** = **apurarme** (Span. Am.).

3. Some expressions of time: **estar atrasado (adelantado)** *to be slow (fast)*: **mi reloj está adelantado,** *my watch is fast.*

4. **ojalá que** = **ojalá y** (Mex.) = **yo quisiera**: **¡ojalá que venga!** or **¡ojalá y venga!** *I wish he would come.*

5. **arribar** is often used in Spanish America instead of **llegar.**

6. For *you*, direct object, **le** is frequently used in Spain instead of **lo** or **la** (feminine). § 31.

---

[2] gustaría, conditional.   [3] **lo mismo** = **la misma cosa.**   [4] irse, *to go away*: **vámonos,** *let's go.* § 61a.

7.   **me gusta** *I like* (lit. "it pleases me"); **me gustaría,** *I would like*; **me gusta viajar,** *I like to travel*; **me gustan las flores,** *I like flowers*.

8.   **nos veremos** is an idiom (lit. "we'll see each other"; future of **ver,** *to see*): **¿a qué hora nos vemos?** *what time shall we meet?*

9.   **¡vámonos!** is Mexican; **¡pasajeros al tren!** would be the equivalent in Spain.

En el tren

On the Train

— No saque[1] usted la cabeza por la ventanilla.
   Don't stick your head out of the window.

— ¿Ni por la portezuela tampoco?
   Not out of the door either?

— No, señor. Está prohibido[2] asomarse.
   No. You're not allowed to lean out.

— Muy bien. ¡Caramba, se me ha metido[3] una ceniza (or carbonilla) en un ojo!
   O.K. Ow! A cinder's got into my eye!

— Pues, vamos a cerrar la ventanilla.
   Well, let's close the window.

— Tiene usted razón. Hay corriente y entra mucho polvo.
   You're right. There's a draft and a lot of dust is coming in.

— Y bajemos la cortinilla. El sol molesta.
   And we'll lower the shade. The sun is annoying.

— Muy bien. Además este coche (or vagón) tiene aire acondicionado (or refrigeración).[4]
   Fine! Besides, this coach is air-conditioned (or has air conditioning).

---

[1] **sacar**, *to stick out, pull out.* § 41, § 63, 1.   [2] **prohibir: está prohibido = es prohibido = se prohibe.** §§ 51*b*, 52, 53*a*.   [3] **meter**, *to put in*; **meterse**, *to get in.*   [4] **tiene aire acondicionado = tiene clima artificial = está acondicionado.**

— Eso es. Su boleto, por favor.
> *Right. Ticket, please!*

— ¡Ah, conque usted es el conductor!⁵
> *Oh, so you're the conductor!*

— Para servirle (or A sus órdenes).
> *Yes, sir (lit. "at your service").*

— Pero ¿dónde he puesto⁶ el boleto?
> *Now where have I put my ticket?*

— ¿No lo encuentra⁷ usted?
> *Can't you find it?*

— Un momento, por favor. Ah, sí. Me lo he guardado en este bolsillo.⁸ Aquí lo tiene usted.
> *Just a minute, please. Oh, yes. I've put it away in this pocket. Here you are.*

— Muchas gracias.
> *Thank you.*

— ¿Dónde está el comedor: adelante o atrás?
> *Where's the diner: forward or back?*

— Está adelante. Ya puede usted ir a almorzar.
> *It's forward. You may go to lunch now.*

— Gracias. En seguida voy. Tengo hambre.
> *Thanks. I'm going in a minute. I'm hungry.*

NOTAS

1. **sacar (comprar) boletos** *to get (buy) tickets.*

2. **ventana** *f.*, *window*; but the window of a coach, car, or a ticket window, etc., is **ventanilla** (lit. "small window").

3. **puerta** *f.*, *door*; but the door of a coach, car, etc., is **portezuela** (lit. "small door").

⁵ **conductor** = **revisor** = **inspector**. ⁶ **poner**, *to put*. §67, 14. ⁷ **encontrar (ue)**, *to find*. §64, I. ⁸ **bolsillo** (Spain) = **bolsa** (Span. Am.).

4.   **¡caramba! ¡caray!** are common interjections denoting surprise or anger; they may be translated in a variety of ways according to individual feeling and verbal habits.

5.   **carbonilla** is a diminutive of **carbón** *m.*, *coal, charcoal*.

6.   **cortina** *f.*, *curtain, shade*; but the curtain of a coach, car, etc., is **cortinilla** (lit. "small curtain or shade").

7.   A *person who takes tickets or money*, as on a bus if it is a different person from the driver, is **cobrador**; a *driver* of a bus, etc., is **conductor** (Spain), **motorista** (Span. Am.).   A bank teller would be a **cajero**.

8.   Note that English "can" is often not expressed in Spanish: **no lo veo**, *I can't see it*; **no lo encuentro**, *I can't find it*; **¿lo oye usted?** *can you hear it?* etc.

En el (coche) comedor

In the Diner

— ¿Hay sitio para una persona?
   Is there room for one person?

— Sí, señor. Aquí puede usted sentarse.
   Yes, sir. You may sit right there.

— No puedo ir de espaldas (or hacia atrás). Me mareo.[1]
   I can't ride backwards. I get sick.

— Entonces siéntese aquí, por favor.
   Then sit here, please.

— Gracias. ¿Es cubierto a precio fijo[2] o es a la carta?
   Thank you. Is it table d'hôte or à la carte?

— Lo que usted guste.[3] Aquí tiene usted la lista.
   Whatever you wish. Here is the menu.

— Bueno. Tráigame primero sopa bien caliente.
   Fine. First bring me soup, good and hot.

— Bien. Ya está. ¡Cuidado con quemarse!
   All right. Here you are (lit. "here it is already"). Be careful not to burn yourself.

— Después un filete bien cocido (poco cocido).
   After that a tenderloin steak well done (medium).

— ¿Con papas[4] fritas y ensalada de lechuga?
   With French fries and (lettuce) salad?

[1] **marearse,** *to get seasick* or *carsick*. [2] **cubierto a precio fijo = comida corrida** (Mex.).
[3] **guste = quiera.** § 46. [4] **papas** (Span. Am.) = **patatas** (Spain).

— Eso es. Mire que aquí falta el cuchillo, y el tenedor no está limpio. Y otro vaso, por favor.

>*Right. (Notice) the knife is missing and the fork isn't clean. And another glass, please.*

— En seguida le traigo todo. Cuchara y servilleta las tiene ¿verdad? ¿Qué desea beber?

>*I'll bring you everything right away. You have a spoon and a napkin, right? What would you like to drink?*

— Agua mineral helada, y después café solo.[5]

>*Cold mineral water, and later black coffee.*

— ¿Algo más, señor? Ya está todo.

>*Anything else, sir? Everything's here.*

— La cuenta, por favor.

>*The bill, please.*

— Aquí la tiene. Gracias, señor. ¡Que le vaya bien!

>*Here you are. Thank you, sir. Good-bye.*

— Adiós.

>*Good-bye.*

— Por ahí no. Por ahí se va a la cocina.

>*Not that way, sir. That's the way to the kitchen (lit. "that way one goes to the kitchen").*

— Dispense usted. Me he equivocado. Ya sé el camino.

>*Excuse me. I (have) made a mistake. Now I know the way.*

— Por ahí tampoco. Por ahí se va al tocador de señoras. Por aquí.

>*Not that way either. That's the way to the ladies' room. This way.*

— Gracias. Me confundo cuando veo entrar y salir a tantos pasajeros.[6]

>*Thanks. I get confused when I see so many passengers coming in and going out.*

---

[5] **café solo** = **puro** = **tinto** (Colombia).   [6] §49c.

— ¡Qué gentío! ¡Qué cantidad bárbara de gente!
What a crowd! What an awful lot of people!

— (Mejor dicho, ¡qué cantidad de gente bárbara!)
(Rather, what a lot of awful people!)

NOTAS

1.   **un filete** also suggests: **bistec (bisté, biftec)** *m., steak =*
bife (Arg.); **a la parrilla,** *grilled, broiled*; **churrasco** (Arg. and Chile)
m., (broiled) steak.

2.   In Argentina and Chile one hears also **adición** *f.* (from
the French**),** and the waiter is often called **garzón** (French, **garçon)**
instead of **mozo** or **camarero** (**mesero,** Mex.).

3.   To use **equivocarse**: **me he equivocado de piso,** *I'm on
the wrong floor*; **me equivoqué** (§ 63, 1) **de número,** *I had the wrong
number,* etc.

4.   **saber el camino,** *to know (which is) the (right) way,*
contrasts with **conocer el camino,** *to know (be familiar with) the road.*

La inmigración

The Immigration Bureau

— (Oficial de inmigración) ¿Me hace usted el favor de su tarjeta de turista?
>   (*Immigration officer*) *May I trouble you for your tourist card?*

— Aquí la tiene usted en este sobre.
>   *Here it is in this envelope.*

— ¿Cómo se llama[1] usted? ¿Y dónde nació?
>   *Your name? And where were you born?*

— (Me llamo) Roberto Blanco (para servirle). Nací en Nueva York.
>   (*My name is*) *Robert White. I was born in New York.*

— ¿Cuántos años tiene usted?
>   *How old are you?*

— Tengo veinticinco años. De hoy en ocho días cumpliré veintiséis.
>   *I am twenty-five. I'll be (or will reach the age of) twenty-six a week from today.*

— ¿Es usted ciudadano (–a) norteamericano (–a)?
>   *Are you an American citizen?*

— Sí, señor. Aquí traigo mi pasaporte, mi certificado médico, de vacuna y de policía, y mi partida de nacimiento.[2]
>   *Yes, sir. I have my passport (here), my health, vaccination, and police certificates, and my birth certificate.*

---

[1] se llama (lit. "you call yourself").   [2] **la partida de nacimiento (de matrimonio)** = **el acta (§ 2) de nacimiento (de matrimonio**,) *birth* (*wedding*) *certificate.*

— ¿De modo que está usted vacunado (–a)?
So you're vaccinated?

— Me vacuné hace quince días.
I was vaccinated two weeks ago.

— Siendo norteamericano (–a), no necesita usted estos documentos para ir a México ahora.
Being an American, you won't need these documents to go to Mexico now.

— Pero voy a visitar otros países, si me alcanza el dinero.
But I'm going to visit other countries, if my money lasts (or holds out).

— Se necesitan[3] estos documentos aquí sólo cuando ha habido[4] una epidemia.
These documents are needed here only when there has been an epidemic.

— O alguna enfermedad contagiosa ¿verdad?
Or some contagious disease, I suppose?

— Así es. Pero va[5] usted bien prevenido (–a).
Just so. But you are well prepared.

— Hombre prevenido nunca fue vencido.
"Forewarned is forearmed" (lit. *"a prepared man was never defeated"*).

— Tiene usted razón.
Right.

NOTAS

1. American citizens who plan to visit Mexico may obtain tourist cards from a Mexican consul or through their travel agent.

---

[3] **necesitar: se necesitan,** *are needed.* § 53a. [4] **haber,** *to have*; **ha habido,** *there has (have) been.* § 56a. [5] **va**=**está.** § 51b.

2.   A Spaniard or Spanish American, when mentioning his name, profession, or nationality, often adds **para servirle (a usted)** or **a sus órdenes**.

3.   **ocho días**, *eight days* = *a week*; **quince días**, *fifteen days* = **dos semanas**, *two weeks*.

4.   **me vacuné** = **fui vacunado (-a)**, *I was vaccinated*. Cf. **me corté el pelo**, *I had my hair cut*; **me retraté**, *I had my picture taken*.

En la frontera—la aduana

At the Border—Customs

— ¿Cuándo llegamos a la frontera?
>*When do we get to the border?*

— Ahora mismo[1] llegamos. Aquí paramos una hora.
>*We're getting there right now. We stop here for an hour.*

— ¿Tenemos que bajar(nos)?
>*Do we have to get off?*

— No, señor. Los aduaneros registran (or revisan) el equipaje aquí mismo.
>*No, sir. The customs officers examine (or search) the baggage right here.*

— (Aduanero) ¿Tiene usted algo que declarar?
>(*Customs officer*) *Have you anything to declare?*

— Que yo sepa,[2] no. Aquí tiene usted mi declaración.
>*Not that I know of. Here is my declaration.*

— ¿Tiene usted tabaco, cigarros,[3] cigarrillos, licores?
>*Have you any tobacco, cigars, cigarettes, liquor?*

— No, señor. Tengo un resfriado y acabo de beberme lo poco que tenía.
>*No. I have a cold and I have just finished drinking the little I had.*

---

[1] **ahora mismo = ahorita** (Mex.).   [2] Subjunctive of **saber**, *to know.* § 67, 16.
[3] **cigarro, puro, tabaco,** *cigar.*

— Haga el favor de abrir estas dos maletas grandes.
Please open these two large suitcases.

— Ya está. ¿Abro[4] esta pequeña?
There you are. Shall I open this small one?

— No hace falta. ¿Esta ropa es de su uso personal?
It's not necessary. Are these clothes for your own use?

— Sí, señor. Todo esto es ropa usada. No tengo nada nuevo sino lo que está aquí.
Yes, sir. All this is used clothing. I have nothing new except what's here.

— ¿Son para la venta?
Are these for sale?

— No, señor. Son regalos para mis amigos.
No. Those are gifts for my friends.

— ¡Cuántos amigos tendrá[5] usted!
What a lot of friends you must have!

— Muchas gracias. Es favor que me hace.
Thank you. That's a real compliment.

— No tiene usted nada que pague[6] derechos.
You have nothing dutiable (lit. "that pays duty").

— ¿Cuándo puedo romper estos sellos?
When may I break these seals?

— Después de pasar la próxima estación.
After passing the next station.

NOTAS

1. **cigarrillo, pitillo** (Spain) = **cigarro** (Span. Am.), *cigarette*; **petaca** *f.*, *cigarette case*; **boquilla** *f.*, *holder*; **cajetilla** *f.*,

---

[4] **abrir**, *to open*. [5] Future of **tener** expressing conjecture. § 40*d*, § 67, 19.
[6] Subjunctive of **pagar**. § 46.

package. **Contrabandista** *m.* and *f.*, *smuggler*; **hacer contrabando,** *to smuggle.*

2.   **acabar,** *to end, finish*: **acabo de comer,** *I have just eaten*; **acababa de comer,** *I had just eaten.* In Argentina (especially). Chile and Bolivia the use of **recién** is common: **recién comí** = **acabo de comer; recién casado** = *newlywed.*

3.   **beber,** *to drink*: **beberse,** *to drink down*; **comer,** *to eat*: **comerse,** *to eat up.* Applied to persons, **beber** is less common in Spanish America than **tomar.**

4.   An alternative to ¿**abro?** is ¿**quiere usted que abra?** *do you want me to open?* §§40a, 43a.

Objetos perdidos

Lost (and Found) Articles

— He dejado olvidada en el tren una maleta.
  I forgot (lit. "left forgotten") a suitcase on the train.

— ¿Cómo era? ¿De qué color era?
  What was it like? What color was it?

— Era (de color) café. Llevaba[1] una etiqueta roja.
  It was brown. It had a red label.

— ¿Cómo era[1] de grande? ¿Qué tamaño tenía?[1]
  How large was it. What size was it?

— Era así de larga, y así de ancha.
  It was so long and so wide.

— ¿Dónde la tenía usted?
  Where did you have it?

— Estaba[1] debajo del asiento en el tren y tenía una cartera con cheques para viajeros.
  It was under the seat on the train and had a billfold with traveler's checks in it.

— Bueno pues, aquí está su maleta.
  Well, here's your case.

— Esa es. A ver. ¡Dios mío, la cerradura está rota!
  That's it. Let's see. Good Lord, the lock's broken!

---

[1] **llevaba (llevar), era (ser), tenía (tener), estaba (estar)**, imperfects. § 59, § 40*b*.

— Regístrela usted bien a ver si falta algo.
Go through it carefully to see if anything's missing.

— Pues falta la cartera precisamente.
Well, it's (precisely) the billfold that's missing.

— Tranquilícese,[2] señora. No se aflija.[3]
Don't get excited, lady. Don't get upset.

— ¿Qué hago, señor? No tengo más que unos pocos dólares encima.[4]
What'll I do? I only have a few dollars with me.

— Vamos a telefonear al jefe de estación.
Let's telephone the stationmaster.

— ¿Tardará mucho? Tengo que irme.
Will it take long? I have to go.

— Vuelva usted dentro de media hora.
Come back in half an hour.

— Si la encuentran, ¿me avisa usted? Aquí tiene el número de mi teléfono.
If they find it, will you let me know? Here's my telephone number.

— Con mucho gusto, señora. ¡Que le vaya bien!
Sure. Good luck!

NOTAS

1. **¿cómo es?** *what is it like?* To ask for the dimensions of objects: **¿qué tamaño tiene?** *how big is it* (lit. "what size has it")? **¿cómo es de grande (pequeño, largo, corto, ancho, estrecho,** etc.)? *how big (small, long, short, wide, narrow,* etc.) *is it?* or **¿es muy grande?** *is it very large?* etc. The answers may be: **tiene** (or **es de**) **un metro de largo (de ancho)**, *it is a meter long (wide)*; **tiene** (or **es de) una altura (una profundidad) de quinientos pies**, *it is 500 feet high*

---

[2] **tranquilizarse=calmarse**, *to be calm, calm down.* [3] **afligirse**, *to be upset.* § 63, 5. [4] **encima**, *above, over.*

(*deep*). In Mexico however, a special formula is used in asking dimensions: **¿qué tan grande (pequeño, largo,** etc.) **es?** *how big* (*small, long*, etc.) *is it?*

2.   A useful expression might be: **no se altere usted** or **no se exalte usted**, *don't get excited.* §§ 41; 63, 4.

3.   **tener encima,** *to have on one's person, about one.*

3
El viaje en automóvil

The Trip by Car

La partida

The Departure

— ¿Hay estación (or puesto) de gasolina por aquí?
    Is there a gasoline station around here?

— Aquí a la vuelta de la esquina, señor.
    Right around the corner, sir.

— Muchas gracias. Dice que a la vuelta de la esquina. . . .
Aquí es.
    *Thank you. He says around the corner. . . . Here it is (or
    this is it).*

— Buenas tardes. ¿Necesita usted gasolina?
    Good afternoon. Do you need gas?

— Sí, señor. Llene usted el tanque (or depósito).
    Yes. Fill up the tank.

— Bien. Caben[1] veinte litros.[2]
    O.K. It holds twenty liters.

— Y déme[3] también aceite, y agua para el radiador. Y haga
el favor de limpiar el parabrisas.
    *And give me oil too, and water for the radiator. And clean
    the windshield please.*

— ¿Qué marca y qué número de aceite quiere usted?
    What kind and number of oil do you want?

---

[1] **caber,** *to fit.*   [2] **litro,** *liter* = 1.05 *quarts.* § 69.   [3] **dar,** *to give.*

— Lo mismo da,[4] con tal que no sea muy pesado.[5]
It makes no difference, provided it's not very heavy.

— ¿Ponemos aire?
Should we put in some air?

— Si me hace el favor. Pero no sé qué presión tienen.
Please. But I don't know what the pressure is.

— A ver. Treinta y dos libras.
Let's see. Thirty-two pounds.

— Ponga usted aire también en las llantas de repuesto. ¿Dónde está el lavabo?
Put air in the spare tires also. Where is the rest room?

— La segunda puerta a la derecha.
Second door to the right.

— (Volviendo) Vámonos. ¿Es ésta la carretera de Laredo?
(Returning) Let's go. Is this the highway to Laredo?

— Sí, señor. Siga usted todo derecho y luego doble[6] a la izquierda.
Yes, sir. Go straight ahead and then turn to the left.

— Gracias. ¿Qué distancia hay[7] de aquí a Laredo?
Thank you. How far is it from here to Laredo?

— Unas veinte millas.[8]
About twenty miles.

NOTAS

1. **estación de gasolina** = **gasolinera** = **expendio de gasolina** = **surtidor de gasolina** *m.* (Spain); **gasolina** = **nafta** (Arg.).

---

[4] **lo mismo da** = **no importa** = **es igual**, *it makes no difference, it's all the same* = **no le hace** (Span. Am.). [5] **pesado, espeso,** *heavy.* [6] **doble (doblar)** = **tuerza (torcer)** = **tome (tomar)**, *turn, take.* [7] **¿qué distancia hay?** = **¿cuánto hay?** [8] **unas,** *about, some.* § 5; **veinte millas** (20 *miles*) = **treinta y dos kilómetros** (32 *kilometers*); 1 kilometer = $\frac{5}{8}$ of a mile. § 69.

2.   An idiom with **caber**: **no cabemos aquí**, *there is no room for us here* (lit. "we don't fit here"). **caber** is irregular: (present) **quepo, cabes**, etc.; (future) **cabré, cabrás**, etc.; (preterite) **cupe, cupiste**, etc.; (present subjunctive) **quepa, quepas**, etc.

3.   A useful expression: **revisar el nivel del aceite**, *to check the oil.*

4.   Other ways to describe the oil: **mediano**, *medium*; **ligero, fino**, *light.*

5.   **inflar las llantas** (or **los neumáticos**), *to inflate the tires*; **llanta** (originally *rim*, now *tire*, particularly in Span. Am.), also **un neumático**; **llanta de repuesto = de recambio = de refacción** (Mex.), *spare tire*; **goma** *f.*, *tire* (lit. "rubber") is heard in Span. Am.; **limpiaparabrisas** *m.*, *windshield wiper.*

6.   Other words for *rest room*: **retrete** *m.* = **servicio** *m.* (**para señoras**, *for ladies*) or (**para caballeros**, *for men*).

7.   Another expression in giving directions: **conserve su derecha**, *keep to the right.*

De camino

On the Road

— ¿Es éste el camino más corto para Laredo?
> *Is this the shortest way to Laredo?*

— No, señor. Regrese usted dos o tres cuadras¹ y siga usted a lo largo del ferrocarril.
> *No, sir. Go back two or three blocks and follow the railroad tracks.*

— ¿Está en buen estado aquel camino?
> *Is the road in good condition?*

— No está en buen estado pero es transitable.
> *It's not in good condition but it's passable.*

— ¿Está pavimentado (or asfaltado) o es de tierra?
> *Is it paved or is it a dirt road?*

— El primer trozo² está bien pavimentado; luego sigue un trozo de grava y otro de tierra.
> *The first part is well paved; then there's a stretch of gravel and another stretch of dirt road.*

— Y dígame, ¿hay desviaciones?³
> *And tell me, are there any detours?*

— Solamente una. Por eso el camino resulta más largo que antes.
> *Only one. That's why the road is longer than before.*

---

¹ **cuadra**=**manzana** (Spain), *block*.   ² **trozo**=**tramo**.   ³ **desviación** *f.*=**desvío** *m.*

— Espero que no haya curvas peligrosas (cerradas) en la desviación.

I hope there are no dangerous (sharp) curves on the detour.

— Si funcionan bien sus frenos, no hay nada que temer.

If your brakes are working well, there's nothing to worry about (lit. "fear").

— Pues ayer me apretaron[4] y ajustaron[4] los frenos.

Well, yesterday they tightened and adjusted my brakes.

— ¿Garantizaron[4] el trabajo?

Did they guarantee the job?

— Lo garantizaron por seis meses.

They guaranteed it for six months.

— En ese caso no hay cuidado, porque llegará a Laredo dentro de una hora.

In that case you won't have any problem, because you'll get to Laredo within an hour.

— En las curvas tocaré el claxón[5] para no chocar con nadie.

On the curves I'll blow the horn so as not to crash into anyone.

— ¡Que le vaya bien!

Good luck to you!

NOTAS

1. A bigger road (*a highway*) would be **una carretera**.

2. Besides meaning *to collide*, **chocar** means *to surprise, astonish*; **han chocado dos autos**, *two cars collided*; **hubo un choque**, *there was a collision*; **me choca**, *it surprises* or *astonishes me. to shock* = **escandalizar**: **me escandalizó**, *it shocked me*; *it was a shock to her* = **la dejó fría** (lit. "it left her cold").

---

[4] **apretaron (apretar), ajustaron (ajustar), garantizaron (garantizar)**, preterites. § 59, § 40*c*.   [5] **tocar el claxón** = **tocar la bocina**.

3.   A few road signs (**señales**): **Adelante** or **Siga**, *Go*; **Alto**, *Stop*; **Angosto**, *Narrow*; **Bajada**, *Down grade*; **Cuidado**, *Caution*; **Curva inversa**, *"S" curve*; **Derecha**, *Right*; **Despacio**, *Slow*; **Empalme**, *Junction*; **Escuela**, *School*; **F. C. (ferrocarril)**, *R. R.(railroad)*; **Frene con el motor**, *Use low gear*; **Izquierda**, *Left*; **Modere su velocidad**, *Reduce speed*; **Peligro**, *Danger*; **Población**, *Town*; **Poblado proximo**, *Town ahead*; **Prohibido el estacionamiento**, *No parking*; **Prohibido dar vuelta a la izquierda**, *No left turn*; **Vado**, *Dip*; **Velocidad máxima**, *Speed limit*; **Paso a nivel**, *Railroad crossing*; **Playa** (Arg.), *Parking place*; **Aparcamiento** (Spain), *Parking place*.

En la frontera

At the Border

Hágame usted el favor de sus documentos.
Your documents, please.

— Aquí los tiene usted: la tarjeta de turista, el pasaporte, la licencia para manejar.
Here they are: tourist card, passport, driver's license.

— Muy bien. A ver el número de la placa.[1] Todo está en regla.
Fine. Let's see the license plate number. Everything is in order.

— Ayer fuimos al departamento de tránsito para arreglar todo.
Yesterday we went to the traffic department to have everything attended to.

— ¿Cuánto tiempo piensan ustedes quedarse en México? ¿Más de un mes?
How long do you intend to stay in Mexico? More than a month?

— Unas tres semanas. Nada más.
About three weeks. Not longer.

— Entonces les doy un permiso para el coche por un mes. ¿Quién es el dueño del coche?
Then I'll give you a permit for the car for one month. Who's the owner of the car?

---

[1] **placa** = **chapa** = **patente**.

— Soy yo (or un servidor). ¿Tenemos que regresar por esta población?

> *I am. Do we have to come back through this town?*

— Sí, señor. Si no, tendrán que pedir permiso especial.

> *Yes, sir. Otherwise you'll have to get a special permit.*

— ¿En dónde lo puedo conseguir?

> *Where can I get it?*

— En la aduana o en la oficina de turismo. Allí le dirán[2] si necesita usted una fianza.

> *At customs or the tourist office. They'll tell you there whether you need a bond.*

— Muchas gracias.

> *Thank you.*

— No hay de qué. ¡Ah! si al regresar por aquí faltan algunos de estos accesorios, tendrán que pagar derechos sobre ellos.

> *You're welcome. Oh, if on your return here any of these accessories are missing, you'll have to pay duty on them.*

— Gracias por la advertencia. Adiós.

> *Thanks for the tip. Good-bye.*

— Que les vaya bien.

> *Good-bye.*

— ¡Ah, se me olvidaba! ¿Cuánto hay de aquí al primer[3] pueblo?

> *Oh, I nearly forgot. How far is it from here to the next town?*

— Unos dieciséis kilómetros, o sea unas diez millas.

> *About sixteen kilometers, or about ten miles.*

— Gracias ¿eh?

> *Thank you.*

---

[2] Future of **decir**. § 67, 5.   [3] § 22a.

NOTAS

1. Other ways of saying *driver's license*: **permiso para conducir** (Spain); **tarjeta de circulación**; **carnet de conductor** (Arg.); **cartera dactilar** (Caribbean).

2. **soy yo = yo soy**, *I am*; **es él**, *it's he*; **son ellos**, *it's they*; **eres tú**, *it's you* (*familiar*); **soy yo**, *it's me*. Note agreement of subject and verb.

3. **no hay de qué (dar las gracias)**, *don't mention it* (lit. "there is no reason to give thanks") = **no las merece** (lit. "it does not deserve thanks") = **de nada**.

4. Other car accessories and parts: **acumulador**, *m.*, *battery*; **bomba de agua** *f.*, *water pump*; **bujía** *f.*, *spark plug*; **cámara** *f.*, *inner tube*; **capó** *m.*, *hood*; **cajuela** *f.*, *trunk* (Mex.); **contador** *m.*, *speedometer*; **defensa (parachoques** *m.***)** *f.*, *bumper*; **destornillador** *m.* (**desarmador**, Mex.), *screwdriver*; **eje** *m.*, *axle*; **faro trasero** or **de piloto (calavera** *f.*, Mex.) *m.*, *taillight*; **faro delantero** *m.*, *headlight*; **gato** *m.*, *jack*; **guardabarro** *m.*, *fender*; **herramientas** *f. pl.*, *tools*; **lámpara** *f.*, *bulb, light*; **lámpara eléctrica** *f.*, *flashlight*; **muelle** *m.* (*f.* in Mex.), *spring*; **perno** *m.*, *bolt*; **tapa del agua** *f.*, *radiator cap*; **tuerca** *f.*, *nut*; **válvula** *f.*, *valve*; **ventilador** *m.*, *fan*; **volante** *m.* or **dirección** *f.*, *steering wheel*.

En el garage (taller)

In the Garage (Repair Shop)

— ¿Cuál es el mejor taller de reparaciones por aquí?
> *Which is the best repair shop around here?*

— El de en frente. Es garage y taller.
> *The one across the way (or directly opposite). It's a garage and repair shop.*

— Muchas gracias. . . .
> *Thank you. . . .*

— Buenos días. ¿Está descompuesto el coche?
> *Good morning. Is your car out of order?*

— Sí, señor. Revíselo todo con cuidado.
> *Yes. Give it a careful check-up.*

— ¿Qué desperfectos ha notado usted?
> *What have you noticed that's wrong?*

— Parece que falla una de las bujías.
> *One of the spark plugs seems to miss (doesn't fire).*

— ¿Nada más?
> *Nothing else?*

— El radiator gotea, y el motor golpea en las subidas y se calienta mucho.
> *The radiator leaks, and the engine knocks and heats up too much going uphill.*

—Pues vamos a ver. Creo que el acumulador no carga. Tendré que revisarlo.

> *Well, we'll see. I think the battery isn't charging. I'll have to check it.*

—Haga el favor de hacerlo todo cuanto antes.[1]

> *Could you do it all as soon as possible, please.*

— Haré lo posible.

> *I'll do my best.*

— ¿Cuánto tiempo tarda todo eso?

> *How long does all that take?*

— Unas dos horas. Cuando termine[2] le llamaré por teléfono (or le daré un telefonazo).

> *About two hours. When I finish, I'll call you (or give you a call).*

— Muy bien. Estaré en el hotel. ¿Cierro el coche con llave?

> *All right. I'll be at the hotel. Should I lock the car?*

— No hace falta. Pero déjeme las llaves, por favor.

> *You don't need to. But leave the keys with me, please.*

— Aquí las tiene. ¿Cuánto costarán las composturas?

> *Here they are. How much will the repairs cost?*

— Todavía no lo sé. Pero nuestros precios no son muy elevados.

> *I don't know yet. But our prices are not very high.*

NOTAS

1. Additional words or phrases: **aflojar**, *to loosen*; **apretar (ie)**, *to tighten*; **asentar (ie) las válvulas**, *to grind the valves*; **desinflar**, *to deflate*; **engrasar**, *to grease*; **fallar (el motor)**, *to stop, stall*; **inflar** (or **poner aire**), *to inflate*; **limpiar el carburador**, *to clean the car-*

---

[1] **cuanto antes=lo más pronto posible=tan pronto como sea posible.**   [2] Subjunctive of **terminar.** § 45*b*.

buretor; **pintar,** *to paint*; **silenciador** *m.*, *muffler*; **sistema de enfria-miento** *m.*, *cooling system*; **tener un corto circuito,** *to have a short circuit*; **está roto,** *is broken*; **no funciona,** *does not work*; **está torcido (chueco,** Mex.), *is crooked, bent*; **no se abre,** *doesn't open*; **no se cierra,** *doesn't close*.

2.   **cerrar con llave** = *to lock* (lit. "to close with a key"): **cierre usted la puerta pero no eche la llave,** *close the door but do not lock it*; **echar el cerrojo,** *to draw the bolt*.

3.   Another expression for prices: **los precios están por las nubes** (*clouds*), *prices are sky-high*.

Una avería

Car Trouble

— Dispense usted. He tenido un accidente. ¿Puede usted ayudarme?

Excuse me. I've had some trouble with my car (or I've had an accident). Can you help me?

— Vamos a ver. ¿Qué ha pasado?

Let's see. What's happened?

— No sé. El coche patinó y ahora está atascado en la arena (el barro). No quiere arrancar.

I don't know. The car skidded (lit. "skated") and now it's stuck in the sand (the mud). It won't start.

— Vamos a empujarlo a un lado del camino.

Let's push it to one side of the road.

— Muy bien. Aquí en medio es algo peligroso.

O.K. It's a bit dangerous here in the middle.

— Ya está. ¿Tiene usted una cadena para remolcarlo?

There you are. Do you have a chain to tow it with?

— No, cadena no tengo.

No, I don't have a chain.

— El pueblo más cercano está a tres kilómetros de aquí.

The nearest town is three kilometers from here.

— ¿Me hace usted el favor de mandar de allí un mecánico o un remolcador?

Could you send a mechanic or a tow truck from there?

— Con mucho gusto. ¡Pero mire! Se le[1] ha roto (or reventado) (or ponchado, Mex.) una llanta (or un neumático).

> *Sure. But look! You've had a blowout!*

— ¡Caramba! No lo había notado.

> *Good Lord! I hadn't noticed it!*

— ¿Quiere usted que le ayude a cambiarla?

> *Do you want me to help you change the tire?*

— Es usted muy amable. Menos mal que tengo una de repuesto que nunca ha tenido un pinchazo.

> *That's really good of you. Good thing I have a spare that has never had a puncture.*

— ¡Manos a la obra! ¿Dónde está el gato?

> *Let's get to work. Where's the "gato"?*

— ¿Qué gato? ¡Ah! la herramienta dice usted. Tome usted.

> *What cat? Oh, you mean the tool. Here.*

— Estas tuercas no quieren aflojarse. A ver la llave inglesa.

> *These nuts are hard to loosen. Give me the monkey wrench.*

— Mil gracias por su ayuda. Aquí espero al remolcador.

> *Thanks a million for your help. I'll wait here for the tow truck.*

— Muy bien. No tardará más que unos veinte minutos.

> *O.K. It'll only take about twenty minutes.*

NOTAS

1. **tener una llanta picada** or **ponchada, tronada**, or **volada** (Mex.), *to have a puncture, flat tire.*

2. **de repuesto = de recambio = de refacción** (Mex.), *spare.*

3. **gato** *m.*, *cat*, also means *jack* and therefore may be misinterpreted as here; in Chile **gata** *f.* is used for *jack.*

[1] **le** is dative of interest.

Infracciones

Violations

— Me está siguiendo un policía de tránsito.
  A traffic officer is following me.

— (Policía) ¡Alto! Arrime usted el coche a la acera[1] y pare el motor.
  (Officer) Stop! Pull up to the curb and stop your motor.

— ¿Qué he hecho ahora? Soy forastero[2] y no conozco[3] los reglamentos.
  What have I done now? I'm a stranger and I don't know the regulations.

— Pues ¿no es usted quien iba zigzagueando y por poco choca con otro coche?
  Well, aren't you the one who was zigzagging and nearly collided with another car?

— No, señor. No fui yo. Yo iba muy despacio. No he excedido de[4] 32 (treinta y dos) kilómetros por hora, que es la velocidad máxima aquí.
  No. It wasn't me. I was going very slowly. I haven't exceeded (or gone over) thirty-two kilometers an hour, which is the speed limit here.

---

[1] **acera** = **banqueta** (Mex.) = **vereda** (Arg., Chile, Peru, etc.). [2] **forastero**, *stranger* = **fuereño** (Mex.); **extranjero**, *foreigner*. [3] **conocer**, *to know, be acquainted with*, § 63. 9: **saber**. *to know* [4] **exceder de**, *to exceed, go faster than*.

— ¿No es usted quien por poco atropella a[5] una vieja? ¿No interrumpió usted el tránsito?

> *Aren't you the one who nearly ran over an old lady? Didn't you block the traffic?*

— No, señor. No fui yo. Lo único que atropellé fue una gallina. Fue sin querer.

> *No. It wasn't me. The only thing I ran over was a chicken. It was unintentional (or I didn't mean to).*

— ¿Qué tienen ustedes en el asiento de atrás?[6]

> *What have you got in the back seat?*

— Las maletas de los que van en el asiento delantero.

> *The suitcases belonging to the people in the front seat.*

— ¿Por qué no paró[7] usted en seguida?

> *Why didn't you stop right away?*

— Dispense usted. No oí[8] su señal.

> *I'm sorry. I didn't hear your signal.*

— Pues, maneje[9] usted con más cuidado en el futuro. Y no se estacione[10] en las calles de dirección única.

> *Well, drive more carefully in future. And don't park in one-way streets.*

— No volveré a hacerlo.

> *I won't do it again.*

— Bueno, pues, esta vez no le voy a multar.

> *All right, then, I'll not fine you this time.*

— Muchas gracias. Es usted muy amable. (¡Qué susto me he llevado!)

> *Thank you very much. That's very kind of you. (What a scare I had!)*

---

[5] personal a, § 11; **atropellar,** *to run over* = **llevar por delante** (Arg., Chile). [6] **asiento de atrás** = **asiento trasero.** [7] **parar(se),** *to stop* = **detenerse.** [8] **oír,** *to hear.* § 67, 11. [9] **manejar,** *to drive* = **conducir** (Spain). [10] **estacionarse** = also **aparcar** (Spain), *to park.*

NOTAS

1. **policía (agente) de tránsito (tráfico)**, *traffic officer* = **agente de circulación** or **guardia de la porra** (colloq. in Spain); **guardia** *m.*, *policeman* = **gendarme (cuico, mordelón**, colloq. in Mexico); **¡circule!** *keep moving!*

2. **por poco**, *nearly*, is generally followed by the present tense with a past meaning: **por poco me caigo**, *I nearly fell.*

3. **pararse** in Spanish America means also *to get up, stand up*: **ponerse de (en) pie.**

4. **calle de un sentido, de una corrida** (Mex.) = **de una sola mano** (Arg.), etc., *one-way street*; **tener preferencia (en el cruce)**, *to have the right of way.*

5. **volver a** + infinitive = *to do again* the act of the infinitive: **volvió a hablar**, *he spoke again.*

6. **multa** *f.*, *fine*; **poner multa**, *to fine*: **me impuso** (or **puso**) **una multa de diez dólares** = **me multó con diez dólares**, *he fined me ten dollars*; **sus antecedentes son buenos (malos)**, *your past record is good (bad).*

4

En la ciudad de México

In Mexico City

El taxi en México

Taxis in Mexico City

— (Al cargador[1]) ¿Me hace el favor de llamar un coche?
  (To the porter) Would you call a taxi?

— (Cargador) ¡Libre! ¡Libre! Ya viene, señor.
  (Porter) Taxi, taxi! It's coming, sir.

— ¿Cinco pesos al Hotel Victoria?
  Five pesos to the Hotel Victoria?

— Veinticinco pesos.
  Twenty-five pesos.

— Pero ¿no cobran ustedes cinco pesos por dejada?
  But don't you charge five a trip (or a run)?

— Hace muchísimos años de eso. Ya no se acuerda nadie de esos precios.
  That was many many years ago. Nobody remembers those prices any more.

— Hace muchos años que no vengo a México. Me parece que el hotel está a la vuelta.
  I've been out of Mexico for many years. I think the hotel is around the corner.

— Veinte pesos y no gano nada. Suba usted.
  Twenty pesos and I'm not making a penny. Get in.

— Bueno. Vámonos. No vaya tan de prisa.
  All right. Let's go. Don't drive so fast.

---

[1] **cargador** (Mex.) = **mozo (de cuerda)**.

— ¿No quiere usted llegar cuanto antes?
Don't you want to get there as soon as possible?

— Quiero llegar pero sano (–a) y salvo (–a). No corra tanto
I want to get there, but safe and sound. Just don't speed.

— Muy bien. Aquí hay un atajo.
O.K. There's a short cut here.

— Pero ha pasado usted el hotel.
But you've passed the hotel.

— Es verdad. Daré la vuelta a la cuadra.
Right. I'll go around the block.

— Pare usted. Aquí estamos.
Stop. Here we are.

— Ya llegamos,[2] señor.
We're here (lit. "we have already arrived").

— (Bajando del taxi) Tome usted. Quédese con el vuelto.
(Getting out of the taxi) Here you are. Keep the change.

— Muchas gracias.
Thank you.

NOTAS

1.   **taxi (taxímetro) = coche de alquiler = libre** in Mexico because when unoccupied it carries the sign **Libre** (*Free*). Elsewhere one sees occasionally the sign **Se alquila** (*For hire*)

2.   **dejada** (Mex.) = **carrera**, *trip, run*; **¿cuánto cobra usted por hora?** *how much do you charge by the hour?*

3.   **el vuelto** (Span. Am.), *change* = **la vuelta** (Spain); **no tengo suelto**, *I haven't got any change* = **no tengo cambio.**

[2] **ya llegamos** (preterite) = **ya hemos llegado.** § 40c.

El hotel

The Hotel

— Buenos días, señor. ¿En qué puedo servirle?
> *Good morning, sir. What can I do for you?*

— ¿Tiene usted cuarto para una persona?
> *Do you have a single room?*

— ¿En qué piso lo quiere usted?
> *On what floor would you like it?*

— Cuanto más alto, mejor.[1] Y lo quiero exterior, es decir con vista a la calle.
> *The higher up, the better. And I want an outside room; that is, with a view of the street.*

— Aquí no hay ningún[2] cuarto interior. Todos dan a la calle. Están bien ventilados y son tranquilos.
> *We have no inside rooms. They all face the street. They are all well ventilated and are quiet.*

— ¿Puede usted enseñarme uno?
> *Can you show me one?*

— Con todo gusto. Vamos a subir en el elevador (or ascensor). Por aquí.
> *With pleasure. Let's go up in the elevator. This way.*

— ¿Cuál es el precio del cuarto que me va a enseñar?
> *What is the price of the room you are going to show me?*

---

[1] § 21.   [2] **ningún** = **ninguno**, *no one, none.* § 22a.

— ¿Cuánto tiempo piensa usted permanecer aquí?
How long do you plan to stay here?

— Pienso quedarme dos o tres semanas.
I expect to stay two or three weeks.

— Entonces doscientos cincuenta pesos diarios sin pensión (or sin comida).[3]
Then (it'll be) two hundred fifty pesos a day without meals.

— Me parece algo caro. Pero vamos a verlo.
That seems a little high. But let's see it.

— Éste es. ¿Qué le parece a usted?
This is it. How do you like it?

— Me parece muy pequeño. ¿Tiene agua corriente?
It seems very small. Does it have running water?

— Tiene agua corriente caliente y fría, calefacción central, luz eléctrica y teléfono.
It has hot and cold running water, steam heat(ing), electricity, and telephone.

— (El agua estará caliente en verano y fría en invierno.) A ver cómo está la cama. Muy blanda (dura).
(The water is probably hot in summer and cold in winter.) Let's see how the bed is. Very soft (hard).

— El baño está al lado. Muy limpio. Aquí no hay bichos: ni moscas, ni mosquitos, ni pulgas.
The bath is next door. Very clean. There are no bugs here: no flies, mosquitoes, or fleas.

— Muy bien. Me quedo con este cuarto.
Very well. I'll take this room.

---

[3] **asistencia** *f.*, board (Mex.).

— Aquí tiene la llave. Cuando baje[4] usted, ¿me hace el favor de firmar el libro de registro?

> *Here's the key. When you come down, would you please sign the register?*

— Perfectamente.

> *Certainly.*

— Con permiso.

> *Excuse me, please.*

— Usted lo tiene.

> *Surely.*

— (Telefoneando) ¡Bueno!

> *(On the telephone) Hello!*

— ¡Bueno! ¿Desea algo?

> *Hello! Can I help you (lit. "do you want something")?*

— ¿Me hace el favor de subir jabón y toallas?

> *Would you please send up some soap and towels?*

— En seguida, señor.

> *Right away, sir.*

— (Camarera)[5] ¿Se puede?

> *(Chambermaid) May I come in?*

— Adelante. Pase usted.

> *Come in. Come right in.*

— Aquí tiene usted las toallas y el jabón. También le traigo agua fresca (agua helada).

> *Here are the towels and the soap. I've also brought (lit "I bring") some fresh water (ice water).*

— ¿Está filtrada el agua?[6]

> *Is the water filtered?*

---

[4] Subjunctive of **bajar**, § 45b.   [5] **camarera**=**recamarera** (Mex., where **alcoba**, *bedroom*=**recámara**)=**mucama** (Arg.).   [6] **el agua**, § 2.

— Sí, señor. Está filtrada y hervida. Puede usted beberla con toda confianza.

> *Yes, sir. It's filtered and boiled. You can drink it without being in the least afraid (lit. "with all trust").*

— ¿Puede usted cambiarme la almohada? Ésta está muy dura.

> *Can you change the pillow? This one is very hard.*

— Bien. ¿Quiere usted más cobertores? En estos días ha hecho mucho frío.

> *All right. Would you like more covers? It's been very cold the last few days.*

— No, gracias. Pero le agradecería unos cuantos ganchos (unas cuantas perchas, Spain). Tengo mucha ropa y pienso comprar más.

> *No, thanks. But I'd appreciate a few hangers. I have a lot of clothes and I expect to buy more.*

— Muy bien. Si necesita otra cosa, haga el favor de tocar el timbre.

> *Very well. If you need anything else, please ring the bell.*

— Por ahora no necesito nada. No quiero que me molesten porque voy a descansar un poco.

> *For the time being I don't need anything. I don't want to be disturbed because I am going to rest a while.*

— Perfectamente, señor. Puede usted descansar bien porque este cuarto es muy tranquilo. Aquí no se oye ningún ruido.

> *Yes, sir. You can rest well because this room is very quiet. You don't get any noise at all here.*

— Que me llamen[7] a las siete.

> *I'd like to be called (lit. "let them call me") at seven.*

[7] § 42.

— Muy bien, señor. Se lo diré[8] al botones para que se lo diga[9] a la telefonista.
>*Very well, sir. I'll tell the bellboy so that he can tell the telephone operator.*

— Es más fácil llamarla desde aquí mismo.
>*It's easier to call her from right here.*

NOTAS

1.   **cuarto** (or **habitación** or **recámara**) **para una persona** = **sencillo** (Mex.), *a single room*; **cuarto** (**habitación**) **para dos personas** = **doble** (Mex.), *a double room*; **cuarto amueblado**, *furnished room*; **sin amueblar**, *unfurnished*; **un cuarto soleado** (**asoleado** is more frequent in Mexico), *a sunny room*.

2.   **con vista a la calle** = **da a la calle** = **tiene vista a la calle**, *faces the street.*

3.   If the telephone is not in the hotel room, one may hear: **el teléfono está en el pasillo**, *the telephone is in the hall.*

4.   Other vocabulary concerning the bathroom: (**cuarto de**) **baño**, *bath(room)*; **bañera**, *bathtub* = **tina** = **bañadera** (Arg.); **ducha** *f.*, *shower* = **regadera** (Mex.) **baño de China** (Arg.).

5.   Some bugs: **mosquito** = **zancudo**, *mosquito* (long-legged American variety); **cucaracha** (**voladora**) *f.*, (*flying*) *cockroach*; **chinche** *f.*, *bedbug* (**chinche** also means *thumbtack*); **hormiga** *f.*, *ant*; **polilla** *f.*, *moth.*

6.   Note the use of the subjunctive in the following sentences: **cuando salga** (subjunctive of **salir**) **usted, cierre la puerta con llave**, *when you leave, lock the door*; **cuando se vaya** (from **irse**) **usted mañana, no deje la llave puesta**, *when you go away tomorrow, don't leave the key in the lock.*

7.   On the telephone, *hello* is: **Bueno** in Mexico, **Diga** in Spain, **Hola** in Argentina and Uruguay, **A ver** in Colombia, and **Aló** nearly everywhere else. *Message* is **recado** or **mensaje** *m.*

---

[8] § 34*b*.   [9] Subjunctive of **decir**. § 45*a*. § 67, 5.

8. Other useful vocabulary: **toalla limpia (sucia)**, *clean (dirty) towel*; **toalla afelpada**, *Turkish towel*; **cepillo de baño** *m.*, *bath brush*; **estropajo** *m.*, a bundle of maguey or esparto fibres used as a scrubbing brush; **funda (de almohada)** *f.*, *pillowcase*; **sábana**, *sheet*; **cobertores** *m. pl.*, *covers* = **cobijas** *f. pl.* (Mex. and elsewhere); **manta, frazada** *f.*, *blanket*; **colcha** *f.*, *quilt*; **colchón** *m.*, *mattress*; **colchón de muelles** *m.*, *spring mattress*; **catre** *m.*, *cot*; **hamaca** *f.*, *hammock*; **camita (de niño)** *f.*, *crib*; **vela** *f.*, *candle*; **candelero** *m.*, *candlestick*; **espejo** *m.*, *mirror*.

El teléfono

The Telephone

— Descuelgo[1] el receptor,[2] espero un momento, meto una ficha en la ranura. ¿ Está el señor Gómez?
> *I take down the receiver, I wait a minute, I put a token in the slot. Is Mr. Gómez in?*

— Con él habla.
> *Speaking (lit. "you are speaking with him").*

— Habla el señor López.
> *This is Mr. López.*

— Ah, ¿cómo le va? Esperaba su llamada de un momento a otro.
> *Oh, how are you? I was expecting your call any minute.*

— ¿Cómo? No oigo. ¿Quién habla? ¿Con quién hablo?
> *What? I can't hear. Who's speaking? Who is this? (lit. with whom am I speaking?")*

— Esperaba su llamada de un momento . . .
> *I was expecting your call any . . .*

— Haga el favor de hablar más alto (or más recio).
> *Please speak louder.*

— Esperaba su llamada de . . .
> *I was expecting your . . .*

---

[1] **descolgar (ue)**, *to take down* (the receiver).   [2] **receptor** = **audífono** or merely **fono** = **aparato**, or **teléfono**.

— Acérquese más al receptor.

Please speak into (or come nearer to) the receiver.

— Esperaba su . . .

I was . . .

— ¿Cómo dice? Estoy en una cabina[3] y hay mucho ruido. No oigo nada.

What do you say? I'm in a booth and it's very noisy here. I can't hear anything.

— Voy a pasar a su hotel.

I'll come over to your hotel.

— Haga el favor de no gritar. ¿Viene a mi hotel?

Please don't shout. You're coming to my hotel?

— Sí, porque no entiendo nada.

Yes, because I can't hear (or understand) a thing.

— Ni yo tempoco. Estamos en paz.[4] Le espero aquí.

I can't either. We're even. I'll wait for you here.

— Muy bien. Estaré allí dentro de diez minutos.

All right. I'll be there within ten minutes.

— ¿Cómo? No oigo. ¡Nos han cortado! ¡Qué malo es este servicio!

What? I can't hear. They've cut us off! What terrible service!

NOTAS

1. The opposite of **descolgar (ue)** is **colgar (ue)**.

2. Some useful expressions: **conferencia de larga distancia** = **conferencia interurbana** (Spain) = **comunicación a larga distancia**

---

[3] **cabina** or **caseta telefónica** *f.*, *telephone booth* = **gabinete del teléfono** *m.*
[4] **estamos en paz**, *we're quits* = **estamos a mano** (Span. Am.).

(Arg.); **guía telefónica** or **de teléfonos**, *telephone directory*; **comuníqueme usted con el número**———— = **sírvase ponerme en comunicación con el número**———, *kindly connect me with number*———; **la línea está ocupada**, *the line is busy*; **tomar un recado** (or **mensaje**), *to take a message.*

La lavandera

The Laundress

— Buenas tardes, señor.
   Good afternoon, sir.

— Buenas tardes. Usted es la lavandera ¿verdad?
   Good afternoon. You're the laundress, aren't you?

— Para servir a usted. Me dijeron abajo que usted me había llamado.
   Yes, sir (lit. "at your service"). They told me downstairs that you had called me.

— Sí. Tengo mucha ropa (sucia) que lavar.
   Yes. I have a lot of (soiled, dirty) clothes to be washed.

— ¿Ha hecho usted la lista?
   Have you made out the list?

— Todavía no. En seguida cuento la ropa y hago la lista. He tenido que hacer una infinidad de cosas.
   Not yet. I'll count the clothes right away and make out the list. I've had to do a great many things.

— No se apure[1] usted. ¡No corre prisa!
   Don't worry, sir. There's no hurry at all.

— Dicho y hecho. Aquí la tiene usted.
   No sooner said than done. Here it is.

---

[1] no se apure (usted)=no se preocupe=no tenga cuidado.

— Los cuellos y los puños de las camisas ¿los quiere un poco almidonados?

Do you want the collars and cuffs of your shirts starched a little?

— Sí, pero no almidone usted los calzoncillos.

Yes, but don't starch the shorts.

— ¡Qué chistoso[2] es el señor!

Oh, you're a real joker, sir.

— Estos calcetines de lana deben lavarse a mano con agua tibia.

These woolen socks should be washed by hand in lukewarm water.

— Sí, señor. Con agua hirviendo se encogen y se destiñen.[3]

Yes, sir. In boiling water they'd shrink and fade.

— ¿Cuándo puede usted traer la ropa?

When can you bring the clothes?

— ¿Para cuándo la necesita usted?

When do you need them?

— Para pasado mañana a más tardar. Sin falta.

By the day after tomorrow at the latest. Without fail.

— No se preocupe usted. Puede contar conmigo. Adiós, señor.

Don't worry. You can depend on me. Good-bye, sir.

— ¡Que le vaya bien!

Good-bye.

— Aquí le traigo la ropa, señor, y la cuenta.

I've brought (lit. "I bring") your laundry, sir, and the bill.

— Muchas gracias. La trae usted muy tarde.

Thank you. You're bringing it very late.

---

[2] **chistoso = bromista = guasón**, *joker, wag.*   [3] § 64, III.

— Sí, señor. Ha llovido[4] mucho y la ropa tarda[5] mucho en secarse.

> *Yes, sir. It's rained a good deal and the clothes take a long time to dry.*

— Bueno. A ver si está toda.

> *Well, let's see if it's all here.*

— Sí está. Nunca se me pierde nada.

> *Of course it is. I never lose anything.*

— ¡Cómo se ha desteñido esta camisa!

> *This shirt has really faded!*

— Es posible, señor. El sol de aquí es muy fuerte. Pica mucho.

> *That's possible, sir. The sun here is very strong. It's scorching.*

— La próxima vez me hace el favor de no colgar estas camisas al sol.

> *Next time, please don't hang these shirts in the sun.*

— Como usted guste. Pero sin sol no quedan blancas.

> *O.K. But without sun they won't come out white.*

— Me parece que esta camisa no es mía.

> *I don't believe this shirt is mine.*

— Perdone usted, pero aquí tiene sus iniciales.

> *Excuse me, but here are your initials.*

— Ah, sí. Voy a contar los calcetines. Uno, dos, tres, cuatro, cinco, seis, siete, ocho . . . Está bien. Ocho pares.

> *Oh, yes. I'll count the socks: one, two, three, four, five, six, seven, eight. . . . That's right. Eight pairs.*

— ¿No le dije[6] que no se me ha perdido nada?

> *Didn't I tell you I haven't lost a thing?*

---

[4] **llover,** *to rain*; **llueve,** *it is raining.*   [5] **tardar = demorar(se) = dilatar(se)** in Span. Am.   [6] Preterite of **decir.** § 67, 5.

— Es verdad. ¡Qué bien ha remendado usted el pijama! ¡Qué bien sabe usted planchar!

> *That's right. You've mended the pajamas really well! You iron so nicely.*

— Es favor que me hace usted, señor.

> *Thank you for the compliment, sir.*

— No es favor. Es la verdad. (Pagándole) Tome. Y esto para usted.

> *It's not a compliment. It's the truth. (Paying her) Here you are. And this is for you.*

— Muchas gracias, señor. Hasta el lunes.

> *Thank you, sir. I'll see you Monday.*

NOTAS

1. Some words on the list might be: **blusa** *f.*, *blouse*; **calzones** *m. pl.*, *panties*; **combinación** *f.* or **camisa (de señora)**, **refajo** *m.*, *slip*; **camiseta** *f.*, *undershirt*; **corbata** *f.*, *necktie*; **falda**, *skirt* = **pollera** (Arg., Chile); **faja** *f.*, *girdle* or *sash*; **cinturón** *m.*, *belt*; **media** *f.*, *stocking* (also *sock*, Arg.); **pantalón** or **pantalones** *m.*, *trousers*; **pantimedia** *f.*, *pantyhose*; **pañuelo** *m.*, *handkerchief*; **pijama** *m.* and *f.*, *pajamas*; **ropa interior** *f.*, *underwear*; **saco** *m.*, *coat* = **americana** *f.* (Spain); **traje** *m.*, *suit;* **vestido** *m.*, *dress*.

2. A word to go with **chistoso**: **ocurrente**, *witty*.

3. An additional useful word: **remojar**, *to soak*.

4. Concerning "late" and "early": **tarde**, *late*; **tarde** *f.*, *afternoon*; **a última hora de la tarde**, *late in the afternoon*; **a primera hora de la mañana**, *early in the morning*.

5. Some idioms with the idea of "rain": **llueve a cántaros**, it is pouring; **llueva o no**, *rain or shine*; **ha escampado**, *it has stopped raining* = **ha parado de llover** (Mex.).

6. **se me pierde** (lit. "it loses itself to me") is used to indicate unintentional loss: **se me perdió el boleto**, *I lost the ticket*; **se me etxravió la carta**, *I mislaid the letter. Cf.* **dejé caer el reloj**,

I dropped my watch; **se me cayó el reloj**, *I dropped my watch* (unintentionally).

7.   **saber** denotes mental ability, **poder** physical ability: **¿sabe usted nadar?** *can you swim?* **¿sabe usted cantar?** *can you sing?* **sé cantar, pero hoy no puedo porque tengo un resfriado**, *I know how to sing, but I can't today because I have a cold.*

8.   The days of the week are: **lunes** (*Monday*), **martes** (*Tuesday*), **miércoles** (*Wednesday*), **jueves** (*Thursday*), **viernes** (*Friday*), **sábado** (*Saturday*), **domingo** (*Sunday*).

En la tintorería

At the (Dry) Cleaner's

— Buenas tardes. ¿Qué se le ofrece a usted?
   Good afternoon. What can I do for you?

— Deseo que me limpien[1] este traje y este vestido.
   I'd like to have this suit and dress cleaned.

— El vestido está desteñido. ¿Quiere usted que se lo[2] tiña?[3]
   The dress is faded. Do you want me to dye it?

— ¿Qué color se lleva (or se estila) más ahora?
   What color is being worn most now?

— Hemos teñido muchos trajes de café y de azul.
   We've dyed a great many suits brown, and blue.

— ¿Cuánto cobra usted por teñirlo?
   How much do you charge for dyeing it?

— Doscientos pesos, pero queda como nuevo.
   Two hundred pesos, but it'll look like new.

— Bien. ¿Cuánto tardará[4] usted en teñirlo?
   All right. How long will it take to dye it?

— A ver. ¿A cuántos estamos hoy?
   Let me see. What day is today?

— Hoy estamos a doce.
   Today's the twelfth.

---

[1] **limpiar (en seco),** *to (dry-)clean.* §43*a*.   [2] **se lo,** §34*b*.   [3] **teñir,** *to dye.* §64, III.
[4] **tardar,** also **dilatar** (Span. Am.).

— Bueno, pues, para pasado mañana a las seis de la tarde lo tiene usted.

> *Well then, you'll have it the day after tomorrow at six o'clock (in the afternoon).*

— Muy bien. Y lo plancha también ¿no?

> *Fine. And you press it too, don't you?*

— No se preocupe. Hasta pegamos (or cosemos) los botones que faltan.

> *Don't worry. We even sew on buttons that are missing.*

— Y si necesita compostura ¿lo remiendan también?

> *And if it needs repairing, do you mend it too?*

— Lo remendamos también. Ya verá usted.

> *We mend it too. You'll see.*

— Entonces hasta el miércoles.

> *I'll see you Wednesday, then.*

— Hasta pasado mañana.

> *(Right); the day after tomorrow.*

NOTAS

1.   **usar**, *to use* = **llevar**, *to wear, to use*; **estar de moda**, *to be in fashion.*

2.   Other colors: **amarillo**, *yellow*; **blanco**, *white*; **café** (*coffee, coffee-color*), *brown*; **castaño**, *chestnut, maroon*; **claro**, *light*; **gris**, *gray*; **morado**, *purple*; **negro**, *black*; **oscuro**, *dark*; **pardo**, *dark gray*; **rojo, encarnado**, *red* = also **lacre** (Chile); **rosado**, *pink*; **verde**, *green*; **vivo**, *bright*.

3.   Ways of asking the date: ¿a **cuántos estamos hoy?** ¿**qué día del mes tenemos hoy?** ¿**qué día es hoy?** ¿**cuál es la fecha?** *what is the date?* The respective replies are: **estamos a doce** = **tenemos el doce** = **hoy es el doce**, etc. The cardinal numerals are used except for the first, which is **primero** and not **uno**. § 68.

4.   **ya** +future implies something like *in due time, when the time comes, surely,* etc. **ya** may mean *now* (with present): **ya viene,** *he's coming now*; *already* (with preterite): **ya vino,** *he's already come,* § 40*c*; *later,* etc. (with future): **ya vendrá** *he'll come later*; **ya no**=*no longer*: **ya no lo tengo,** I don't have it anymore; **ya que,** *since*: **ya que lo tengo, se lo doy,** *since I have it, I'll give it to you*; emphatic **ya**= *to be sure, of course.*

Cosiendo (remendando) el vestido

Sewing (Patching) the Dress

— Se me ha roto[1] el vestido y no tengo con qué remendarlo.
   I've torn my dress and I have nothing to mend it with.

— ¿Quiere que se lo remiende, señora?
   Would you like me to mend it for you?

— No, gracias. Haga el favor de traerme aguja, seda (hilo), un dedal y unas[2] tijeras.
   No, thank you. Would you bring me a needle and thread, a thimble, and a pair of scissors.

— En seguida vuelvo.
   I'll be right back.

— ¡Qué siete más grande me he hecho!
   What a big rip I've made!

— (Volviendo) Aquí le traigo toda la cestita de labor.
   (Returning) I've brought you (lit. "I bring you here") the whole sewing basket.

— Mil gracias. ¡Ay! Esta aguja es algo gruesa y no tiene punta.
   Thank you so much. Oh, this needle is very thick and it's dull (lit. "it has no point").

— Señora, aquí hay más finas. Mire ésta.
   There are some finer ones here. See this one.

[1] **romper**, *to break, tear.*   [2] **unos, unas**, *some, a pair of.*

— A ver. Pero el ojo es tan pequeño que no puedo enhebrarla.
> *Let's see. But the eye is so small I can't thread it.*

— Permítame, señora. Ya está. Tome usted.
> *Allow me (madame). There. Here you are.*

— Gracias. ¡Ay! Me he pinchado. Yo no sirvo para esto.
> *Thanks. Ow! I pricked myself. I'm no good at this.*

— Déjeme a mí. Lo hago en un abrir y cerrar de ojos.[3]
> *Let me do it. I can do it in less than no time (lit. "in an opening and closing of the eyes").*

— Si me hace el favor.
> *I'd be grateful.*

— Pues, la costura está descosida.
> *Well, the seam is ripped.*

— Ya que es usted tan amable, aprovecho la ocasión para que me cosa[4] estos botones . . . No son más que cinco.
> *Since you're so kind, I'll take advantage of the opportunity to have you sew on these buttons. . . . There are only five of them.*

— Con mucho gusto, señora. Estamos aquí para servirla.
> *It will be a pleasure (madame). We're here to serve you.*

— ¿Y podría usted componer esta media de nylon? Se me enganchó en un clavo.
> *And could you fix this nylon stocking? I caught it on a nail.*

— ¡Qué carrera! (Aparte) ¡Y qué mujer más exigente!
> *What a run! (Aside) And what a demanding woman!*

NOTAS

1. Some additional vocabulary: **rasgar**, *to tear*; **un rasgón** (**una rasgadura**), *a rent or tear*; **un siete** (lit. "a seven") is so called from its shape.

---

[3] **en un abrir y cerrar de ojos = en un instante.**   [4] Subjunctive of **coser.** § 45a.

2. **pellizcar**, *to pinch.*

3. **pegar** (*to fasten on*, *sew on*) **un botón; ensartar**, *to thread, string* (beads, etc.).

4. **tengo una carrera en la media**, *I have a run in my stocking* = **se me corrió un punto** (lit. "a stitch has run").

El tranvía y el ómnibus

The Streetcar and the Bus

— ¿Para aquí el tranvía que va al parque?
> *Does the streetcar that goes to the park stop here?*

— Sí, señor. Aquí mismo para.
> *Yes. It stops right here.*

— ¿Me dejará en la entrada del parque?
> *Will it take me to the entrance of the park?*

— Sí, en la misma ·entrada. Hace diez minutos que lo estoy esperando.[1]
> *Yes, right to the entrance. I've been waiting for it for ten minutes.*

— ¿Cada cuánto tiempo pasa?
> *How often does it come by?*

— Pasa cada diez minutos. Ahora no debe de tardar.
> *It comes by every ten minutes. It shouldn't be long (in coming) now.*

— Ahí viene. Pero viene lleno;[2] no hay sitio.
> *There it comes. But it's full; there's no room.*

— No podemos subir. Pero creo que por aquí para también el ómnibus.
> *We can't get on. But I believe the bus stops here too.*

---

[1] §57*b*.   [2] **viene lleno**=**está lleno**. § 51*b*.

— Menos mal. Vamos a preguntar.

That's good. Let's ask.

— Dispense usted, ¿para aquí el ómnibus que va al parque?

Excuse me. Does the bus that goes to the park stop here?

— Sí, señores. Aquí mismo para. Los dejará a una cuadra del parque.

Yes, right here. It'll drop you off one block from the park.

— ¿Pasa a menudo?

Does it run often?

— Cada diez minutos. Ahora debe venir de un momento a otro. Hace quince minutos que lo espero.[1]

Every ten minutes. It ought to be coming along any minute now. I've been waiting for fifteen minutes.

— Miren ustedes. Ahí viene. Pero completo. (El ómnibus no para; pasa de largo.)

Look. There it comes. But it's full. (The bus does not stop; it goes right by.)

— ¡Qué servicio a estas horas de aglomeración!

It's terrible service during these rush hours!

— Lo malo es que el metro[3] no llega hasta aquí. ¿Qué hacemos?

And the bad part of it is that the subway doesn't come this far. What shall we do?

— Podríamos los tres tomar un taxi, ya que vamos en la misma dirección.

The three of us could take a taxi, since we're going in the same direction.

— ¡Taxi! . . . Subamos antes de que se nos vaya[4] también.

Taxi! . . . Let's get in before it gets away from us too.

---

[3] **el metro(politano)**, *the subway* = **el subte(rráneo)** in Buenos Aires.   [4] Subjunctive of **irse**. § 45*b*; § 67, 9.

NOTAS

1.   **tranvía** = also **tren** in Mexico. **ómnibus**, *bus*, assumes a variety of names according to locality: **camión** (*truck*) *m.* in Mexico, **chiva** (*kid, female goat*) *f.* in Panama,; **guagua** (*baby* in S.A.) in Cuba; **góndola** *f.* in Chile; **micro** *f.* (a larger express bus) in Chile; **colectivo** *m.* in Argentina, etc. In Mexico a small car carrying passengers is **turismo**. Private cars plying along certain avenues charge a fixed sum per person for any distance on theroute. *Commutation tickets* = **abonos**; *transfer*, **transferencia** *f.* or **transbordo** *m.*; **¡favor de parar!** *please stop* = **¡esquina!** (Mex., lit. "corner").

2.   **mismo**, *same, self, very*; **aquí mismo**, *right here* = **aquí mero** (pop. Mex.); **ayer mismo**, *only yesterday*; **hoy mismo**, *this very day*; **mañana mismo**, *tomorrow for sure*; **yo mismo (-a)**, *I myself*, etc.; **en la misma capital**, *right in the capital* = **en la mera capital** (Mex. and Cent. Am.).

3.   **lo malo (del caso)**, *the bad part of it*; **lo peor (del caso)**, *the worst of it.* § 3.

En un café mexicano

In a Mexican Coffeehouse

— Tengo mucha sed.[1] Entremos en este café.
> *I'm very thirsty. Let's go into this coffeehouse.*

— Como quieras (or Como usted quiera).
> *O.K.*

— Ya estamos. (Llamando a la mesera) ¡Señorita! (Llamando al mesero) ¡Joven!
> *Here we are. (Calling the waitress) Waitress (lit."Miss ")! (Calling the waiter) Waiter!*

— Ya voy. ¿Qué les traigo, señores (señoras)?
> *I'm coming. What shall I bring you, gentlemen (ladies)?*

— Tráigame una cocacola.
> *Bring me a Coca-Cola.*

— ¿Helada o al tiempo (or natural)?
> *Iced (or chilled, cold) or at room temperature?*

— Fría, pero sin hielo.
> *Cold but without ice.*

— Y a mí trae usted té caliente con limón (con leche). Me gusta el té muy claro. Y un sandwich de pollo (jamón, queso).
> *And bring me hot tea with lemon (cream, lit. "milk"). I like my tea very weak. And a chicken (ham, cheese) sandwich.*

[1] § 55b.

— Ya volvió la muchacha.
>   *The girl's back already (lit. "has already come back").*

— No ha tardado nada.[2]
>   *It didn't take her long at all.*

— ¿Cuánto es, señorita?
>   *How much is it?*

— Veinticinco pesos.
>   *Twenty-five pesos.*

— Tome usted, señorita.
>   *Here you are.*

— Mire usted, señor. Este peso no vale.
>   *Look, sir. This peso's no good.*

— ¿Por qué no? Acaban de dármelo a mí.
>   *Why not? It was just given to me (lit. "they have just given it to me").*

— ¿No ve usted que no es de plata?
>   *But it's not silver, see?*

— Es verdad. Parece ser de plomo.
>   *That's right. It looks like lead.*

— No reciba usted nunca las monedas de a peso que no sean[3] de plata.
>   *You should never take peso coins that aren't silver.*

— Muchas gracias por la advertencia.
>   *Thank you for the advice (or warning, tip).*

— De nada. Hay que estar sobre aviso.
>   *You're welcome. You have to be on your guard.*

---

[2] no (se) ha tardado=no (se) ha demorado=no (se) ha dilatado (Span. Am.).
[3] Subjunctive of ser. § 46.

NOTAS

1.   **como (tu) quieras** is the familiar form, used with members of one's family and very intimate friends.

2.   **camarera**, *waitress* = **mesera** (Mex.); **camarero** = **mesero**; **camarera**, *maid* = **recamarera** (Mex.) = **mucama** (Arg.).

3.   *weak* (for tea and coffee) = **débil, simple, claro, suave, ralo**; *strong* = **fuerte, cargado**.

4.   **acabo de hacerlo**, *I have just done it*; **acababa de hacerlo cuando usted entró**, *I had just done it when you came in*. Note the tenses and meanings.

5.   Other ways to express **estar sobre aviso**: **estar en guardia, tener mucho ojo**; **estar de guardia**, *to be on duty*.

El desayuno

Breakfast

— ¿Sirven ustedes el desayuno aquí?
> *Do you serve breakfast here?*

— Sí, señor. Siéntese. ¿Le traigo café con leche y pan dulce?
> *Yes, sir. Just take a seat. Shall I bring you coffee and sweet rolls?*

— No, señorita. Quiero desayunarme a la norteamericana. ¿Qué frutas hay?
> *No. I want an American breakfast. What kind of fruit do you have (lit. "is there")?*

— Hay jugo de tomate, de naranja, de piña, de toronja . . . melón, papaya, mangos . . .
> *We have tomato, orange, pineapple, and grapefruit juice . . . melon, papaya, mangos . . .*

— Jugo de naranja. Y después huevos . . .
> *Orange juice. And then eggs. . . .*

— ¿Cómo los quiere: tibios, revueltos, o fritos?
> *How do you like them: soft-boiled, scrambled, or fried?*

— Fritos, pero tiernos — es decir, no muy cocidos, — con jamón.
> *Fried, but soft — that is, not well done, — and ham.*

— Se nos ha acabado el jamón, señor.
> *We've run out of ham, sir.*

— Entonces con tocino. Pan tostado con mantequilla . . .
> *Then bacon. Buttered toast.*

— ¿Qué desea beber: café con leche, té con limón, chocolate?
> *What would you like to drink: coffee (with cream, lit. "milk"), tea with lemon, chocolate?*

— Chocolate a la francesa.
> *French chocolate.*

— Muy bien. Permítame ponerle el cubierto: el cuchillo, el tenedor, la cucharita, la servilleta y el vaso. Ya está.
> *All right. Let me set your place: knife, fork, teaspoon, napkin, and glass. There you are.*

— Gracias. ¡Ah! Estos huevos están muy tiernos (crudos). ¿Los podría freír un poquito más?
> *Thanks. Oh! These eggs are too soft (raw). Could you cook (fry) them a little more?*

— ¡Cómo no! ¿Le doy un poco más de chocolate caliente?
> *Sure. Do you want me to give you a little more hot chocolate?*

— Si me hace el favor. Muchas gracias.
> *Please. Thank you.*

— ¡Cuidado con quemarse!
> *Be careful not to burn yourself.*

— ¡Ay! Por poco me quemo la lengua.
> *Ow! I nearly burned my tongue.*

— Tome un poco de agua fría.
> *Drink a little cold water.*

— Gracias. (Más tarde) La cuenta, por favor.
> *Thank you. (Later) Check, please.*

— Aquí la tiene. Gracias, señor.
> *Here you are. Thank you, sir.*

NOTAS

1. **desayunar(se)**, *to have breakfast*. A Spanish breakfast generally consists of coffee (a mixture of milk and coffee) or chocolate, and rolls (**panecillos, bollos; bolillos,** Mex.) or sweet rolls (**pan dulce,** Mex.).

2. **a la norteamericana,** *American style*: **avena** *f., oatmeal;* **con crema o leche caliente,** *with cream or hot milk;* **cereales** *m. pl., cereals;* **queques** (Mex.) *m. pl., hot cakes, waffles,* **con jarabe o miel,** *with syrup or honey.*

3. **tomate** = **jitomate** in Mexico, where **tomate** means a small green *tomato*.

4. **papaya** should be carefully avoided in Cuba, where it has acquired another meaning; the Cubans say **fruta bomba**.

5. **huevos** are sometimes referred to as **blanquillos** in Mexico.

6. **se acabó,** *it's all over;* **se me ha acabado,** *I've run out of it* (lit. "it has ended on me").

7. **tostar,** *to toast:* **pan tostado,** *toast* = **tostadas** (Spain), that is, **rebanadas** (*slices*) **de pan tostadas**.

8. **mantequilla,** *butter* = **manteca** (**de vaca**) in Spain.

9. **chocolate a la española,** *Spanish* (*style*) *chocolate,* an exceedingly thick preparation served in a **jícara** (*small cup*) into which **bizcochos** (*lady fingers*) are dipped; **chocolate a la francesa** is more like our hot chocolate in consistency; **chocolatera** *f., chocolate pot;* **cafetera** *f., coffee pot;* **tetera** *f., teapot.*

La comida

Dinner

— Vamos a entrar en este restaurante francés. Dicen que aquí se come muy bien.

> *Let's go into this French restaurant. They say the food is good (lit. "one eats well") here.*

— Entremos. Me encanta la cocina francesa. (Entrando) Pero aquí hay mucho lujo.

> *Let's go in. I really like French cooking. (Entering) But this is a pretty elegant place (lit. "there is much luxury here")*

— Nos van a cobrar un ojo de la cara, pero ya no podemos salir.

> *They'll charge us a fortune, but we can't leave now.*

— Sentémonos en este reservado. Camarero, a ver el menú (la carta, la minuta, la lista).

> *Let's sit in this booth. Waiter, may we see the menu?*

— Tome usted. El plato del día es pollo asado.

> *Here you are. Today's specialty is roast chicken.*

— Tráiganos primero una docena de ostras en su concha.

> *Bring us a dozen oysters on the half shell first.*

— Y que sean bien frescas y bien grandes.

> *And we want them (lit. "let them be") really fresh and big.*

— ¡Y que tengan mucho jugo y que no tengan la concha muy gruesa!

> *And we want a lot of juice, and we don't want the shells too thick.*

— Tráiganos después un poco de pollo. Pero que sea tierno. Y que esté bien cocido.

> *Bring us a little chicken later. But we want it tender. And we want it well done.*

— Y muy sabroso. Tráiganos la pechuga y un ala.

> *And very tasty (or delicious). Bring us the breast and a wing.*

— (Camarero) ¿Quieren ustedes el ala[1] derecha o el ala izquierda?

> *(Waiter) Do you want the right wing or the left wing?*

— (Nos está tomando el pelo.)

> *He's kidding us.*

— Un vaso de cerveza clara (or blanca) y un tarro de (la) negra. Y de postre, frutas frescas y queso importado.

> *One glass of light beer and a stein of dark (beer). And for dessert, fresh fruit and imported cheese.*

— (Al poco rato) ¡Pero estas cerezas están picadas!

> *(After a while) But these cherries are beginning to spoil (or are speckled)!*

— Vamos a comerlas antes de que se pasen del todo.

> *Let's eat them up before they spoil completely.*

— Nadie diría que este queso es importado, sino más bien «deportado».

> *Nobody would (ever) say that this cheese is imported, but rather "deported."*

NOTAS

1. **comida** is *meal* in general and specifically *dinner*. In many Spanish-speaking countries the heavy meal is served at noon (about 1:00 to 3:00 P.M.) and is called **la comida**; the lighter evening meal is then **la cena** (7:00 to 9:00 P.M.). Elsewhere the noon meal

[1] §2.

may be called **el almuerzo** (*lunch*) and the evening meal is **la comida** (*dinner*).

2.   **me encanta** = **me gusta mucho**.

3.   **un ojo de la cara** = **mucho dinero** = **un dineral**; **dinero** = generally **plata** (lit. "silver") in Span. Am. = **pisto** in Cent. Am.; **adinerado**, *rich*, is **platudo, pistudo** respectively.

4.   **camarero** = **mesero** (Mex.).

5.   **ostras** *f. pl.* = **ostiones** *m. pl.* in Mex.

6.   **nos está tomando el pelo** = **se está burlando de nosotros**.

7.   **cerveza de barril**, *beer on draught*; **cerveza embotellada, en botella**, *bottled beer*.

8.   **pasarse**, *to become tainted* (as meat) or *spoiled* (as fruit): **la carne está pasada**, *the meat is tainted* (*or spoiled*).

Una comida mexicana

A Mexican Meal

— Primero pedimos un coctel de ostiones u ostiones en concha.

> *First we'll order an oyster cocktail or oysters on the half shell.*

— Los ostiones de Guaymas son ricos (or deliciosos).

> *The Guaymas oysters are delicious.*

— Después, unos huevos rancheros.

> *Then some eggs ranchero style.*

— ¡Ah!´ Ya los probé. Son huevos fritos con salsa de chile. Muy buenos.

> *Oh, I've already tasted them. They're fried eggs served with a chile sauce. . . . They're good.*

— Algo picantes. Los comeremos con tortillas — esas tortas de harina de maíz.

> *A bit hot. We'll eat them with tortillas — those round, flat pancakes made of cornmeal.*

— Ya se me hace agua la boca.

> *It makes my mouth water (lit. "my mouth is watering already").*

— Después, chiles rellenos. Ya los conoces. Son chiles llenos de carne de ternera o de puerco y . . .

> *After that, stuffed peppers. You must know what they are. They're peppers stuffed with veal or pork and . . .*

— Ya sé. Y unos tacos — esas tortillas tostadas con tomate, carne, lechuga y frijoles.
> *Yes, I know. And some tacos — those toasted tortillas filled with tomato, meat, lettuce, and beans.*

— Pero que sean tacos de pollo.
> *But we want (lit. "let them be") chicken tacos.*

— Sí. Y por fin mole de guajolote.
> *Yes. And finally, turkey mole.*

— ¿Y nada de enchiladas, ni de tamales?
> *And no enchiladas or tamales?*

— Pero hombre, no podemos comer todos los antojitos de México de una vez. Mañana será otro día.
> *Hey, we can't eat all the popular Mexican dishes at once. Tomorrow is another day.*

— Es decir, si hoy no morimos de una indigestión.
> *That is, if we don't die of indigestion today.*

— Para evitar eso, tomemos un trago de tequila.
> *To avoid that we'll take a drink of tequila.*

— Ya está. ¡Salud, pesetas y amor!
> *Here it is. Here's looking at you (lit. "health, wealth, and love")!*

— ¡Qué vida ésta!
> *What a life!*

NOTAS

1. **o**, *or*, becomes **u** before words beginning with **o** or **ho**.

2. **Guaymas** is a Mexican port on the Gulf of California, noted as a fishing resort and famous for its large, tasty oysters.

3. **guajolote** (Mex.) *m.*, *turkey* = **pavo**; **mole de guajolote** *m.*, turkey served with a heavy dark sauce made of different kinds of chiles, spices, etc.

4.   Other **antojitos** or popular Mexican dishes are: **quesadillas**, maize dough with beans or cheese fried like a turnover; **peneques**, rolls of maize dough filled with cheese; **pozole**, a stew of pork, corn, chile, etc.; **frijoles refritos con queso**, (twice) fried Mexican beans with cheese; **guacamole** *m.*, salad of avocado (**aguacate** *m.*) mashed with tomato, onion, chile, olive oil, etc.

5.   **peseta**, Spanish monetary unit. Though the coin does not exist in Span. Am., the expression ¡**salud y pesetas!** is common, meaning *health and wealth!*

Comida y bebidas

Food and Drinks

■ **Condimentos**   *Seasonings*

aceite *m.* oil
ají *or* **chile** *m.* chile
ajo *m.* garlic
azúcar *m.* sugar
mantequilla *f.* butter
mayonesa *f.* mayonnaise
mole (Mex.) *m.* red-pepper sauce
mostaza *f.* mustard

pimienta *f.* (black) pepper
pimiento *m.* (red) pepper
rábano picante *m.* horse-radish
sal *f.* salt
salsa de tomate *f.* catsup
salsa inglesa *f.* Worcestershire sauce
setas *f. pl..* mushrooms
vinagre *m.* vinegar

■ **Pan**   *Bread*

bollo, panecillo *m.* roll
pan blanco *m.* white bread
pan casero *m.* home-made bread
pan de centeno *m.* rye bread
pan de maíz *m.* corn bread
pan del día *or* **tierno** *m.* fresh bread

pan duro *or* **sentado** *m.* stale bread
pan francés *m.* French bread
pan negro *or* **moreno** *m.* dark bread
corteza *f.* crust; **miga** *f.* soft part
galletas *f. pl.* crackers, cookies
rebanada *f.* slice

■ **Entremeses**   *Hors D'Œuvres*

aceituna *f.* olive
alcachofa *f.* artichoke

anchoa *f.* anchovy
apio *m.* celery

cebolla *f.* onion
chorizo *m.* pork sausage
encurtido *m.* pickle
pepinillo *m.* pickled cucumber

rábano or rabanito *m.* radish
salchicha *f.* sausage
salchichón *m.* Bologna (sausage)

■ **Sopas**   *Soups*

caldo *m.* broth
consomé *m.* consommé
gazpacho *m.* cold soup
sopa de arroz *f.* rice soup
sopa de cebada *f.* barley soup

sopa de cebolla *f.* onion soup
sopa de fideos *f.* noodle soup
sopa de lentejas *f.* lentil soup
sopa de pollo *f.* chicken soup

■ **Huevos al gusto**   *Eggs Any Style*

blanquillos (Mex.) *m. pl.* eggs
huevos duros *m. pl.* hard-boiled eggs
huevos fritos or estrellados *m. pl.* fried eggs
huevos rancheros (Mex.) *m. pl.* fried eggs with chile sauce

huevos revueltos *m. pl.* scrambled eggs
huevos tibios or pasados por agua *m. pl.* soft-boiled eggs
tortilla a la española *f. pl.* omelet with potatoes
tortilla a la francesa *f.* omelet

■ **Pescados y mariscos**   *Seafood*

almeja *f.* clam
anguila *f.* eel
arenque (ahumado) *m.* (smoked) herring
bacalao *m.* cod
camarón *m.* shrimp
cangrejo *m.* or jaiba (Span. Am.) *f.* crab
escabeche *m.* pickled fish

huachinango (Mex.) or pargo (Cuba) *m.* red snapper
hueva *f.* roe
langosta *f.* lobster
langostino *m.* prawn
lenguado *m.* sole, flounder
merluza *f.* hake, (kind of) bass
mero *m.* bass
ostra *f.* or ostión *m.* oyster

ostiones en concha *m. pl.* oysters on the half shell
pejerrey *m.* a variety of mackerel

robalo *m.* haddock
salmón *m.* salmon
sardina *f.* sardine
trucha *f.* trout

■ **Carne** *Meat*

ajiaco *m.* meat stew and **ají**
albóndigas *f. pl.* meatballs
bistec or **biftec** *m.* beefsteak
cabrito *m.* kid
carne de vaca or **de res** *f.* beef
carnero *m.* mutton
cerdo or **puerco (asado)** = **chancho** *m.* (Span. Am.) (roast) pork
cordero *m.* lamb
chuleta or **costilla** *f.* chop, cutlet
chuleta a la parrilla *f.* grilled chop
empanada *f.* meat pie
estofado or **guisado** *m.* stew
fiambres *m. pl.* cold cuts
filete *m.* tenderloin
hamburguesa *f.* hamburger

hígado *m.* liver
jamón *m.* ham
lechón or **lechoncillo** *m.* young pig
lengua *f.* tongue
menudillo *m.* giblets
milanesa *f.* breaded veal cutlet
mondongo *m.* or **callos** *m. pl.* tripe
mollejas *f. pl.* sweetbreads
morcilla *f.* blood sausage
picadillo *m.* chopped meat, hash
pierna de carnero *f.* leg of mutton
pozole (Mex.) *m.* stew of pork, corn, and chile
riñones *m. pl.* kidneys
sesos *m. pl.* brains
solomillo *m.* sirloin

■ **Aves** *Fowl*

capón *m.* capon
gallina *f.* hen
ganso *m.* goose
guajolote (Mex.) *m.* turkey
pato *m.* duck

pavo (asado) *m.* (roast) turkey
pavo relleno *m.* stuffed turkey
pechuga de pollo *f.* breast of chicken

pollo (asado) *m.* (roast) chicken

pollo a la parrilla *m.* broiled chicken

pollo cocido *m.* boiled chicken

vol au vent de pollo *m.* chicken vol-au-vents

■ **Caza**   *Game*

conejo *m.* rabbit
faisán *m.* pheasant
liebre *f.* hare

pato silvestre *m.* wild duck
perdiz *f.* partridge
venado *m.* venison

■ **Legumbres y verduras**   *Vegetables*

alverjas (Span. Am.) *f. pl.* peas
arroz con pollo *m.* chicken rice
berenjena *f.* egg plant
berro *m.* water cress
betabel *m.* beet
camote (Mex.) or **batata** or **boniato** sweet potato
col *m.* cabbage
coles de Bruselas *m.* Brussels sprouts
coliflor *f.* cauliflower
chauchas (Arg.) *f. pl.* string beans
chícharos (Mex.) green peas
choclo (Span. Am.) *m.* sweet corn
ejotes (Mex.) *m. pl.* string beans
elote (Mex.) *m.* sweet corn
escarola *f.* chicory
espárragos *m. pl.* asparagus

espinacas *f. pl.* spinach
frijoles *m. pl.* (kidney) beans
garbanzos *m. pl.* chick-peas
guisantes or **chícharos** *m. pl.* green peas
habas *f. pl.* (Lima) beans
habichuelas (or **judías**) **verdes** *f. pl.* string beans
lechuga *f.* lettuce
maíz tierno *m.* green corn
nabo *m.* turnip
patata or **papa** (Span. Am.) *f.* potato
puré de patata mashed potatoes
pepino *m.* cucumber
perejil *m.* parsley
remolacha *f.* beet
tomate or **jitomate** (Mex.) tomato
zanahoria *f.* carrot

■ **Postres, dulces**   *Desserts, Sweets*

almendra *f.* almond
almíbar *m.* syrup
arroz con leche *m.* rice pudding
budín *m.* pudding
compota *f.* stewed fruit
confitura or **conserva** *f.* pre-
serves
flan *m.* or **natillas** *f.* custard
helado or **mantecado** *m.* ice
cream
sabores *m. pl.* flavors

vainilla *f.* vanilla
chocolate *m.* chocolate
fresa *f.* strawberry
jalea *f.* jelly
merengue *m.* meringue
mermelada *f.* marmalade
miel *f.* honey
nuez *f.* walnut
pastel *m.* pie, pastry
queso *m.* cheese

■ **Frutas**   *Fruit*

aguacate (Mex. and Cent. Am.)
palta (Span. Am.) alligator
pear, avocado
albaricoque or **chabacano** *m.*
apricot
anona or **guanábana** *f.* custard
apple
cereza *f.* cherry
ciruela *f.* plum
ciruela pasa *f.* prune
chirimoya *f.* cherimoyer
dátil *m.* date
frambuesa *f.* raspberry
fresa (**frutilla,** Arg.) strawberry
granada *f.* pomegranate
grosella *f.* currant
guayaba *f.* guava
higo (paso) *m.* (dry) fig
hueso *m.* stone, pit

lima *f.* lime
limón *m.* lemon
mandarina *f.* tangerine
mango *m.* mango
manzana *f.* apple
melocotón or **durazno** *m.* peach
melón *m.* melon
membrillo *m.* quince
naranja *f.* orange
pepita *f.* seed
pera *f.* pear
piña *f.* or **ananá(s)** *m.* or *f.*
pineapple
plátano *m.* or **banana** *f.* banana
sandía *f.* watermelon
toronja *f.* grapefruit
tuna *f.* prickly pear
uva *f.* grape

■ Bebidas   *Drinks*

agua (potable) *f.* (drinking) water
agua de Seltz *f.* Seltzer water
agua de soda *f.* soda water
agua gaseosa *f.* charged water
agua mineral *f.* mineral water
aguardiente or **coñac** *m.* brandy, cognac
alcohol *m.* alcohol
aperitivo *m.* apéritif, appetizer
cacao *m.* cocoa
café *m.* coffee
cerveza *f.* beer
cerveza clara (or **blanca**) *f.* light beer
cerveza de barril *f.* draught beer
cerveza embotellada *f.* bottled beer
cerveza inglesa *f.* ale
cerveza negra *f.* dark beer
cóctel *m.* cocktail
champaña *f.* chanpagne
chica (Span. Am.) fermented corn
gaseosa *f.* pop, soft drink
ginebra *f.* gin
guarapo *m.* cane cider
licor *m.* liqueur
leche (de vaca) *f.* (cow's) milk
leche condensada *f.* condensed milk

leche descremada *f.* skim milk
leche malteada *f.* malted milk
leche pasteurizada *f.* pasteurized milk
limonada *f.* lemonade, soft drink
mezcal (Mex.) *m.* maguey brandy
naranjada *f.* orangeade
ponche *m.* punch
pulque (Mex.) *m.* maguey wine
refresco *m.* refreshment
ron *m.* rum
sidra *f.* cider
té *m.* tea
tequila (Mex.) *f.* cactus brandy
vino *m.* wine
vino blanco *m.* white wine
vino de Borgoña *m.* Burgundy wine
vino de Burdeos *m.* Bordeaux wine
vino de Jerez *m.* sherry wine
vino de Oporto *m.* port wine
vino espumoso *m.* sparkling wine
vino tinto *m.* red, claret wine
yerba mate (Span. Am.) *f.* Paraguay tea

Visitando un museo

Visiting a Museum

— Dispense usted, ¿éste es el museo que tiene la colección de obras de Rivera, Orozco, Tamayo, y Velázquez?

Pardon me, is this the museum that has the collection of works by Rivera, Orozco, Tamayo, and Velasquez?

— Sí, tiene cuadros de estos tres artistas mexicanos. Pero a lo mejor usted quería decir Velasco, pintor mexicano del siglo pasado, y no Velázquez, el gran pintor español. Para ver cuadros de éste, tiene usted que ir al Prado.

Yes, it has paintings by the three Mexicans, but perhaps you meant to say Velasco, the Mexican painter of the last century and not Velazquez, the great Spanish painter. To see the latter, you have to go to the Prado.

— Sí, me he equivocado. ¿Hasta qué hora está abierto el museo?

Yes, I made a mistake. What time is the museum open until?

— Ya está cerrado. Las horas de visita son de una a cuatro.

It's already closed. Visiting hours are from one to four.

— ¿Cuesta algo la entrada o se entra gratis?

Is there an admission charge or is it free?

— Los domingos y días festivos es gratis, pero los demás días se paga la entrada.

Sundays and holidays it's free, but on the other days there's an entrance fee.

— Es decir, solamente los lunes, martes, miércoles, jueves, viernes y sábados.

> *That is, only on Mondays, Tuesdays, Wednesdays, Thursdays, Fridays, and Saturdays.*

— Eso es. No debe usted perderlo. Es digno de verse.

> *That's right. You shouldn't miss it. It's worth seeing.*

— ¿Y hay costumbre de dar propinas?

> *Is it usual to give tips?*

— Hay costumbre de dar algo al guía.

> *It's usual to give something to the guide.*

— ¿Está en venta algún catálogo del museo?

> *Is there a museum catalogue for sale?*

— Sí. Dentro del museo se venden catálogos, como también tarjetas con vistas de todas las obras de arte más interesantes.

> *Yes. Catalogues are sold inside the museum, as well as (post) cards with views of all the most interesting works of art.*

— Muchas gracias por los informes.

> *Thank you for the information.*

— No hay de qué. Venga usted temprano porque necesitará usted dos horas para verlo todo.

> *You're welcome. Come early because you'll need two hours to see everything.*

NOTAS

1. **día festivo** or **día de fiesta** *m.*, *holiday*; **día de entre semana**, *week day* = **día de semana** = **día de trabajo**; **día de descanso**, *day off*.

2. **el guía**, *the guide*; **la guía**, *the guidebook*.

3. **temprano**, *early*; *to get up early*, **madrugar**; *early in the morning* (*in the afternoon*), **a primera hora de la mañana (de la tarde)**; *early riser*, **madrugador, -ora**; *night owl*, **trasnochador, -ora**.

En el banco

At the Bank

— ¿Es este banco sucursal del Banco Nacional?
Is this bank a branch of the National Bank?

— Sí, señor. A sus órdenes.
Yes, sir. What can I do for you? (lit. "at your service").

— Aquí traigo[1] una carta de crédito.
I have a letter of credit here.

— ¿Qué cantidad quiere usted retirar?
What amount do you wish to withdraw?

— Quiero retirar cien[2] dólares. ¿Cuál es el tipo de cambio?
I'd like to withdraw a hundred dollars. What is the rate of exchange?

— Hoy el cambio no es favorable para usted.
The exchange is not favorable to you today.

— ¿Qué le vamos a hacer? Aunque no me conviene cambiarlo hoy, me hace falta el dinero.
We can't do anything about that. Even though it's not good for me to change it today, I need the money.

— Ya sabe usted que el cambio sube y baja según las últimas noticias políticas y financieras.
Of course you know that the rate rises and falls according to the latest political and financial news.

---

[1] **traigo,** *I bring* = **tengo.**   [2] **ciento,** *a hundred.* § 22d.

— La noticia de la guerra habrá producido[3] la baja de hoy.

> *The war news must have made it go down today.*

— Eso es. (Contando) Diez, veinte, treinta, cuarenta, cincuenta, sesenta, setenta, ochenta, noventa, ciento.

> *That's right. (Counting) Ten, twenty, thirty, forty, fifty, sixty, seventy; eighty, ninety, one hundred.*

— Quisiera también cobrar (or cambiar) este cheque.

> *I should also like to cash this check.*

— Haga usted el favor de endosarlo.

> *Would you endorse it, please?*

— Ya está.

> *There.*

— Tome usted esta contraseña. En seguida le llamarán por ese número en la ventanilla de Pagos, donde recibirá usted su dinero.

> *Take this number. You'll be called immediately by that number at the window marked "Payments," where you will get your money.*

— Gracias. Mañana viene un amigo mío a abrir una cuenta. Quiere depositar unos doscientos dólares.

> *Thanks. A friend of mine is coming here tomorrow to open an account. He wants to deposit two hundred dollars.*

— Muy bien. Aquí se paga el cinco por ciento.

> *Fine. We pay five percent here.*

— No es mucho que digamos.

> *That's not (what you'd call) a great deal.*

— No, pero «más vale pájaro en mano que ciento volando».

> *No, but "a bird in the hand is worth two in the bush" (lit. "a bird in the hand is worth more than a hundred flying").*

---

[3] **habrá producido,** future perfect of conjecture = **probablemente ha producido.** § 40*d.*

NOTAS

1. **firmar un cheque,** *to sign a check*; **girar en falso (falsi-ficar),** *to write a check without due security (forge)*; **talonario (de cheques)** *m., checkbook*.

2. **depositar** = **imponer** (Spain); **hacer un depósito** = **hacer una imposición** (Spain), *to make a deposit*; **depositante** *m., depositor* = **imponente** (Spain); **caja de ahorros** *f., savings bank*; **libreta (de banco)** *f., bankbook, passbook*.

El limpiabotas

The Bootblack

— ¿Hay limpiabotas por aquí?
> *Is there a bootblack around here?*

— En esta misma cuadra (or manzana) encontrará usted dos.
> *You'll find two right in this block.*

— Gracias. Ya los veo.
> *Thank you. I see them now.*

— Siéntese, señor. Aquí tiene usted el periódico (or diario) que acaba de salir.
> *Have a seat, sir. Here's the newspaper that's just come out*

— Gracias. Quiero que me limpien los zapatos.
> *Thanks. I'd like to have my shoes shined.*

— ¿Qué color de betún quiere usted?
> *What color polish would you like?*

— El color más oscuro que tenga.[1] Estos zapatos eran amarillos en un principio.
> *The darkest color you have. These shoes were tan once (lit. "in the beginning").*

— Se han oscurecido bastante. Más vale este color café.
> *They've become very dark. I'd better use this brown.*

— Lo que a usted le parezca.[2]
> *Whatever you think best.*

---

[1] Subjunctive. § 46.   [2] Subjunctive of **parecer**, *to seem, appear.* §§ 46; 63, 9.

— Primero les quitaré las manchas con una esponja húmeda.

First I'll remove the spots (or stains) with a wet sponge.

— ¡Cuidado con mojarme los calcetines!

Just don't get my socks wet.

— No se preocupe, señor. Ya tendré cuidado.

You needn't worry, sir. I'll be careful.

— He traído éstos para que me los tiña de negro y les ponga cordones nuevos.

I've brought these to be dyed black and to have new laces put in.

— Perfectamente, señor. Estarán listos para mañana.

Very well, sir. They'll be ready by tomorrow.

— Muy bien. Por la tarde vendré por ellos.

All right. I'll come for them in the afternoon.

— Listo (or Servido), señor.

(It will be) ready, sir.

— Han quedado muy bien. Tome. Quédese con el vuelto.

They've come out nicely. Here you are. Keep the change·

— Muy agradecido.

Thank you.

NOTAS

1.   *bootblack* also = **lustrador** = **bolero** (Mex.).

2.   **limpiar** (*to clean*) **los zapatos,** *to shine shoes* = **sacarles lustre** or **brillo** = **lustrar** = **dar una lustrada** = **dar grasa** (Mex.) = **dar una boleada** (Mex.) = **embolar** = **dar bola.**

3.   *shoe polish* = **lustre** *m.* = **grasa** *f.* (Mex.) = **bola** *f.* (Mex.).

4.   **amarillo,** *yellow, tan* (of shoes).

5.   *at the beginning, once* also = **al principio** = **primero.**

6.   *shoelaces* also = **agujetas** or **cintas** *f. pl.*

7.   **el vuelto** (Span Am.) = **la vuelta** (Spain).

Tienda de curiosidades mexicanas

Mexican Curio Shop

— Quisiera comprar un sarape.
> *I'd like to buy a sarape.*

— Mire usted nuestro surtido. Los tenemos de todas las regiones de México.
> *Look at our supply (or stock). We have them from every region in Mexico.*

— ¿Y los colores y dibujos son distintos en cada región?
> *Are the colors and designs different in each region?*

— Sí, señor. ¿Le agrada este gris y negro?
> *Yes, sir. Do you like this gray and black one?*

— ¿Cuánto vale ése?
> *How much is that one worth?*

— Trescientos cincuenta pesos. Pero fíjese en la calidad de la lana.
> *Three hundred fifty pesos. But just look at the quality of the wool.*

— Es muy caro. Le doy doscientos por él.
> *It's very expensive. I'll give you two hundred for it.*

— No puedo, señor. Me cuesta más que eso. Trescientos veinte.
> *I can't (do that). It costs me more than that. Three hundred twenty.*

— Imposible. Doscientos treinta, y me lo llevo.

> *Impossible. Two hundred thirty and I'll take it with me.*

— No, señor. Usted no se da cuenta de la calidad . . .

> *No, sir. You don't realize (how fine) the quality (is).*

— Bueno. No puedo pagar más. Adiós.

> *All right. I can't pay more. Good-bye.*

— Venga acá, señor. Se lo dejo en trescientos y se lo lleva usted de una vez.

> *Come here, sir. I'll let you have it for three hundred and you (can) take it away without further ado (lit. "once and for all").*

— Bueno, le doy doscientos sesenta, porque no me gusta regatear.

> *Well, I'll give you two hundred sixty, because I don't like to haggle.*

— Tómelo en doscientos sesenta pero no se lo diga a nadie.

> *Take it for two hundred sixty, but don't tell anyone about it*

— Me gusta también aquella batea de laca.

> *I also like that lacquer tray over there.*

— Acabamos de recibirla. También tenemos novedades de cuero hechas a mano, huaraches, cestas, cerámica, alfarería.

> *We've just received it. We also have handmade leather novelties, sandals, baskets, ceramics, pottery.*

— Volveré otro día cuando tenga más tiempo.

> *I'll come back some other day when I have more time.*

— Cuando usted quiera.

> *Whenever you wish.*

■ **Joyas**   *Jewelry*

— ¿Tiene usted joyas antiguas?

> *Do you have antique jewelry?*

— Tenemos anillos, aretes, pulseras, collares de plata antigua . . .

> *We have rings, earrings, bracelets, necklaces of antique silver . . .*

— A ver esos aretes de filigrana. ¿Son para orejas perforadas?

> *Let me see those filigree earrings. Are they for pierced ears?*

— No, señorita; tienen tornillos. Son preciosos y no son caros. Se los dejo en doscientos pesos el par.

> *No (Miss); they have screws. They're beautiful and they're not expensive. I'll let you have them for two hundred pesos a pair.*

— Hacen juego con este anillo ¿verdad?

> *They match this ring, don't they?*

— Sí, señorita. El mismo dibujo. ¿Quiere probárselo?

> *Yes. The same design. Would you like to try it on?*

— Por favor. Me queda grande. ¡Qué lástima! Es el único que me gusta.

> *Please. It's too big for me. What a pity! It's the only one I like.*

— Pero se lo arreglamos para que le quede bien. Ya verá usted.

> *But we'll adjust it for you so it will fit. You'll see.*

— Bueno. También me gustaría un prendedor que haga juego con los aretes y la sortija.

> *All right. I'd also like a brooch (or pin) that will match the earrings and the ring.*

— Mire usted éstos. Están de moda ahora. ¿Qué le parecen?

> *Look at these. They're in style now. What do you think of them?*

— ¡Qué turquesa más linda! ¡Me encanta este jade!

> *What a pretty turquoise! I love this jade!*

— ¿No le gustan los ópalos mexicanos? Éstos son muy bonitos. Tienen mucho fuego.

> *You probably like Mexican opals. These are very pretty. They have a lot of fire.*

— Me gustan, pero dicen que los ópalos traen mala suerte.

> *I do like them, but they say that opals bring bad luck.*

— No hay que hacer caso de esa superstición. Nuestros ópalos siempre traen buena suerte.

> *You mustn't pay any attention to that superstition. Our opals always bring good luck.*

— ¿De veras? ¿A quién?

> *Really? Who to?*

— A nosotros cuando vendemos muchos.

> *To us when we sell a lot of them.*

NOTAS

1. **doy** (*I give*) = **daré** (*I shall give*). § 40*a*.
2. **llevar**, *to take, carry*; **llevarse**, *to take away* (with one).
3. **darse cuenta de**, *to realize*; **realizar**, *to fulfill, carry out*.
4. **se lo dejo** = **se lo pongo** = **se lo doy**. § 34*b*, § 40*a*.
5. Other articles: **botellón** *m.*, *water bottle*; **candelero** *m.*, *candlestick*; **cartera** *f.*, *billfold*; **caja de madera tallada** *f.*, *carved wooden box*; **cuadro de madera incrustada** *m.*, *inlaid wooden picture*; **cuero labrado** *m.*, *carved leather*; **deshilado(s)** *m.*, *drawn work*; **florero** *m.*, *vase*; **jarra** *f.*, *pitcher* or *jar* (**resquebrajado, -a**, *cracked*); **juego de bridge** *m.*, *bridge set*; **juego de té** *m.*, *tea set*; **loza** *f.*, *pottery*; **maceta** *f.*, *flowerpot*; **marco de lata** *m.*, *tin picture frame*; **mantel** *m.*, *tablecloth*; **ónice** *m.*, *onyx*,; **pisapapeles** *m.*, *paperweight*; **plata cincelada** *f.*, *hand-hammered silver*; **servilleta hecha a mano** *f.*, *handmade napkin*; **vidrio soplado** *m.*, *blown glass*.
6. **anillo** *m.*, *ring* = **sortija** *f.*; **anillo** (or **sortija**) **de matrimonio** or **de boda** or **de casamiento**, *wedding ring*; **anillo de prometida**

m., *engagement ring* = **anillo de compromiso** (Mex.); **anillo** = **argolla** in some countries of Spanish America.

    7. **arete** *m.*, *earring* = **arracada** (*earring with pendant*) *f.* = **zarcillo** (*drop earring*) *m.* = **pendiente** *m.*

    8. **pulsera** *f.*, *bracelet* = **brazalete** *m.*; **reloj de pulsera** *m.*, *wrist watch.*

    9. **hacer juego con** = **ir bien con.**

    10. *brooch* = **broche** or **prendedor**; **montadura** *f.*, *setting* = **engaste** *m.*; **gemelos** (spain) *m. pl.*, *cuff links* = **mancuernas** or **mancuernillas** (Span Am..) *f. pl.* = **colleras** (Chile) *f. pl.* Popular stones are: **ámbar** *m.*, *amber*; **amatista** *f.*, *amethyst*; **diamante** *m.*, *diamond*; **esmeralda** *f.*, *emerald*; **rubí** *m.*, *ruby*; **zafiro** *m.*, *sapphire.* Popular metals are: **oro** *m.*, *gold*; **plata** *f.*, *silver*; **peltre** *m.*, *pewter*; **plata chapada** *silver plate*; **acero inoxidable** *m.*, *stainless steel*; **¿ qué es esa piedra?** *what is that stone?* **¿de qué está hecho?** *what is it made of?*

Aparatos y materiales fotográficos

Cameras and Photographic Supplies

— ¿Aquí revelan películas?
> *Do you develop films here?*

— Sí, señor. Si las deja usted ahora, las tendrá mañana a las seis de la tarde.
> *Yes, sir. If you leave them now, you'll have them tomorrow afternoon at six o'clock.*

— Bueno. Dejo estos tres rollos. Quiero dos copias de cada una.
> *Fine. I'll leave these three rolls. I want two prints of each.*

— ¿Brillante o mate?
> *Glossy or dull (finish)?*

— Brillante, por favor. ¿Me da usted dos rollos de películas?
> *Glossy, please. Will you give me two rolls of film?*

— ¿De qué número?
> *What number?*

— Ciento veinte. ¿Puede decirme por qué han salido tan mal estas fotografías (or fotos) que saqué la semana pasada?
> *A hundred twenty. Can you tell me why these pictures that I took last week have come out so badly?*

— A ver. Ésta no tiene suficiente exposición y está mal enfocada.
> *Let's see. This one is underexposed and is badly focused.*

— ¿Y estas exposiciones de tiempo?
And these time exposures?

— Pues parece que ha entrado mucha luz. Debe de estar[1] descompuesta su cámara (or kodak).
They seem to be overexposed. There must be something wrong with your camera.

— ¿La puede usted componer?
Can you fix it?

— Sí, pero tiene usted que dejarla por ocho días, porque estamos ocupadísimos en este momento.
Yes, but you'll have to leave it here for a week, because we're very busy just now.

— Entretanto ¿me puede usted prestar alguna cámara de segunda mano?
Can you let me have (lit. "can you lend me") a secondhand camera meanwhile?

— Vamos a ver. Puede usted llevarse ésta. Le dará buenos resultados.
Let's see. You can take this one. You'll get good pictures with it (lit. it will give you good results).

— Muchas gracias. Hasta mañana.
Thank you. I'll be back tomorrow.

— Hasta mañana.
Good-bye (lit. "until tomorrow").

NOTAS

1. **aparato fotográfico** *m.*: **cámara** *f.* = **kodak** *m. and f.*; **cámara de cine** *f.*, *movie camera*; **cámara oscura** *f.*, *dark room*; **fotógrafo** *m.*, *photographer*; **aficionado, -a**, *amateur*.

[1] **debe de estar** = **estar**á. § 40*d*.

2.   **materiales** *m. pl. materials supplies* = **útiles**: **disparador** *m. trigger, release*; **fijativo** or **fijador** *m., fixative*; **filtro** *m.,* **filtra-rayos** *m., ray filter*; **lente (telescópico)** *m., (telescopic) lens*; **medidor** *m., meter*; **obturador** *m., shutter*; **papel sensible** *m., sensitized paper*; **placa** *f., plate*; **revelador** or **baño** *m., developer*; **trípode** *m., tripod.*

3.   **película pancromática** *f., panchromatic film*; **películas cortadas,** *cut films*; **películas en paquetes,** *film packs*; **película de dieciséis milìmetros,** *sixteen-millimeter film.*

4.   **instantánea** *f., snapshot*; **exposición de tiempo** or **a voluntad** *f., time exposure*; **prueba** *f., proof*; **(prueba) positiva, negativa,** *positive, negative*; **ampliación** *f., enlargement* = **amplificación**; **a medio cuerpo,** *half length*; **imprimir,** *to print.*

5.   **sacar** *or* **tomar una foto(grafía),** *to take a picture*; **retratarse,** *to have one's picture taken*; **montar,** *to mount*; **retocar,** *to retouch*; **me retraté ayer,** *I had my picture taken yesterday.*

6.   **no tiene suficiente exposición** = **está poco expuesta,** *it is under-exposed*; **tiene mucha exposición,** *it is over-exposed*; **nítido, -a,** *clear(-cut).*

7.   **enfocar,** *to focus*; **foco** *m., focus*, **lente (pantalla) para enfocar** *m., focusing glass (screen).*

En la peluquería (barbería)

At the Barber's

— ¿Sigo yo, o tengo que esperar?
> *Am I next (lit. "do I follow") or do I have to wait?*

— Usted sigue ahora mismo. ¿Qué deseaba usted?
> *It's your turn right now. What would you like?*

— Que me corten el pelo y que me afeiten.
> *A haircut and shave.*

— (Enjabonándole la cara) ¿Lo quiere muy corto?
> *(Lathering his face) Do you want it (cut) very short?*

— Corto por detrás, pero largo por delante.
> *Short in back but long in front.*

— Muy bien. No usaré la máquina por los lados (or costados).
> *O.K. I won't use the clippers on the sides.*

— Puede usted cortar un poquito de arriba, pero muy poco.
> *You can cut off a little from the top, but very little.*

— Ya está. ¿Le afeito el cuello? ¿Le lavo la cabeza? ¿Le doy masaje?
> *There you are. Do you want me to shave your neck, give you a shampoo, a massage?*

— Nada de eso. ¡Uf! Me ha metido usted la brocha en la boca.
> *No (lit. "none of that"). Ugh! You stuck the brush right into my mouth!*

— Es que usted habló cuando yo no lo esperaba.

That's because you spoke when I wasn't expecting it.

— Con razón dicen «en boca cerrada no entran moscas».

They're right when they say "Flies can't get into a closed mouth."

— ¿Le mojo el pelo?

Do you want me to wet your hair?

— No, señor. Cepíllelo en seco.

No. Brush it dry.

— ¿Dónde se hace usted la raya: a la izquierda, a la derecha o en medio?

Where do you part your hair: on the left, on the right, or in the middle?

— Péineme el pelo para atrás. ¡Ay! me lastimó ese peine.

Comb it (straight) back. Ow! That comb hurt me.

— (Ya está usted) servido, señor. Tenga la bondad de mirarse al espejo.

There you are, sir. Just look in the mirror.

— Recorte un poco las puntas de este lado. Bien. Tome usted. Quédese con el vuelto.

Trim the edges a little on this side. Fine. Here you are. Keep the change.

— Gracias por la propina.

Thank you for the tip.

NOTAS

1. **¿quién sigue?** *who's next?* **ahora le toca a usted,** *it's your turn* (to do something) *now.*

2. Another way to ask for a haircut is: **quiero que me corten el pelo** = **quiero cortarme el pelo** = **quiero un corte de pelo**; **cabello** (for **pelo**) is much more frequently used in Spanish America

than in Spain, where it is generally reserved for poetic usage; **emparejar**, *to even up, make even*; **cortar al rape**, *to clip short, shave*.

3.   **afeitar**, *to shave* = **rasurar**; **me afeito (me rasuro) todos los días**, *I shave (myself) every day*.

4.   *to lather the face* = **dar jabón** (*soap*) **en la cara**.

5.   Other possible questions: **¿le doy shampoo** or **champu? ¿le recorto los bigotes (las patillas, la barba)**? *do you want me to trim your mustache (sideburns, beard)?* § 40*a*, § 4*g*; **afilar (repasar, suavizar) la navaja**, *to sharpen the razor*; **correa** *f.* or **asentador** *m., strap*; **máquina de afeitar** *f., safety razor*; **hoja (de repuesto)** *f.,* (*spare*) *blade*.

6.   *it hurt me* can also be **me hizo daño**.

En el salón de belleza

At the Beauty Parlor

— ¿Puede usted darme un lavado y peinado esta tarde o hay que fijarme hora?

> *Can you give me a wash and set this afternoon or must I make an appointment?*

— Ahora mismo puede usted pasar, señora. En este gabinete por favor.

> *You can come in right now, madam. In this booth, please.*

— Por casualidad ¿tendría usted tiempo para darme también un retoque del mismo color? Ya se ven las raíces oscuras.

> *You wouldn't also have time to give me a touch up of the same color would you? My (dark) roots are already showing.*

— Sí, habrá tiempo y también para un corte de pelo si usted quiere, incluso para una permanente. Da la casualidad de que me han cancelado varias citas y tengo bastante tiempo disponible.

> *Yes, there will be time. For a hair cut too if you want one Even for a permanent. It's just that several appointments happen to have been canceled and I have enough time free.*

— ¡Qué suerte! A ver si he traído bastante dinero. ¿Cuánto cobra por un enjuague de color, un corte y un masaje facial?

> *That's lucky! Let's see if I've brought along enough money. How much do you charge for a color rinse, a hair cut and a facial massage?*

— No hay cuidado, señora. Usted puede pagar después. ¿Cómo quiere que le corte el pelo, con flequillo, con patillas, o quiere que sólo iguale[1] las puntas? Están muy maltratadas por los tintes.

> *Don't worry. You can pay later. How do you want me to cut your hair, with bangs or sidecuts, or do you want me to just even up the ends. They look in bad shape from the dye.*

— Hágalo como le parezca mejor a usted. Pero acuérdese que me hago la raya en medio y que también quisiera peinarme para atrás. No me gustan las ondas o los rizos.

> *Do what seems best to you. But remember that I part my hair in the middle and also that I would like to comb it back. I don't like waves or tight curls.*

— Entonces usted va a querer los tubos grandes y nada de laca o de enredar.

> *Then you are going to want big rollers and no lacquer or teasing.*

— Veo que usted me entiende perfectamente. Ahora, ¿quiere usted enseñarme su muestrario? Tengo que señalarle mi color.

> *I see that you understand me perfectly. Now, would you show me your color chart? I have to point out my color to you.*

— Un rubio claro, ¿verdad? Favorece sus ojos. A propósito, ¿no quiere usted también una depilación de las cejas?

> *A light blond, right? It goes with your eyes. By the way, wouldn't you like me to tweeze your eyebrows too?*

— No, pero mientras que el pelo se está secando, usted puede darme un manicure. Tengo las uñas peor que el pelo.

> *No, but while my hair's drying, you could give me a manicure. My nails are worse than my hair.*

[1] § 43a.

— ¿De qué color va usted a querer que las pinte?[2] Tengo un gran surtido pero sugiero rosa pálido o colorado.

> *What color do you want me to paint them? I have quite a range, but I suggest pale rose or red.*

— Prefiero un color natural. ¿Cuánto tiempo voy a tardar en el secador? ¿Tiene usted algunas revistas?

> *I prefer a natural looking color. How long will my hair have to dry? Do you have some magazines?*

— Las últimas, señora. Allí están cerca de la caja.

> *The latest ones. There they are, near the cashier's desk.*

— Necesito un lápiz para los labios.

> *I need a lipstick.*

— Mire usted éste. Acabamos de recibirlo. Le va a gustar.

> *Look at this one. We've just received it. You'll like it.*

— Bueno. ¿Tiene usted una crema o un aceite que quite las pecas, las arrugas, las patas de gallo, los lunares y la caspa?

> *Fine. Have you some kind of cream or oil that will remove freckles, wrinkles, crow's feet, moles, and dandruff?*

— Sí tengo. Ésta es muy buena para un cutis delicado y suave como el suyo.

> *Yes I have. This is very good for a skin that's delicate and tender like yours.*

— ¿Cómo se usa? ¿Se puede usar como base de polvos?

> *How is it used? Can it be used as a powder base?*

— Sí. Se aplica todos los días antes de poner el maquillaje.

> *Yes. You apply it every day before putting on your make-up.*

— Perfectamente. Me la llevo. Ah, se me olvidaba. Necesito también esmalte (or barniz).

> *All right. I'll take it. Oh, I nearly forgot. I need some nail polish too.*

---

[2] §43a.

— Mire usted los colores que tenemos. ¿Cuál prefiere usted?

> *These are (lit. "Look at") the colors we have. Which do you prefer?*

— Vamos a ver. Me encanta éste, pero no hace juego con el colorete que uso.

> *Let me see. I love this one, but it doesn't match the rouge I use.*

— Éste le va mejor. Queda muy bien con los polvos que usa.

> *This is a better match. It goes very well with the powder you use.*

— Me quedo con éste. ¿Tiene usted tintura (or tinte) para las canas?

> *I'll take this one. Have you any dye for gray hair?*

— ¡Pero usted no tiene canas, señorita!

> *But you have no gray hair (Miss)!*

— Dos o tres nada más — aquí en las sienes.

> *Only two or three, here at the temples.*

— Eso se arregla fácilmente con este frasco. Le quitará diez años de la cara.

> *That can easily be fixed with this bottle. It will make you look ten years younger.*

— Déme usted la mitad. Estaré contenta si me quita cinco años.

> *I'll take half of it. I shall be satisfied if it makes me look five years younger (lit. "if it removes five years").*

NOTAS

1. **Fijar hora** (or **día**), to make an appointment (lit. "to fix an hour or a day); **pedir** (or **dar**) **un turno**, *to ask for* (or *make*) *an appointment*. This expression is commonly used when referring to doctors, dentists, hairdressers, or most kinds of appointments

where people have to wait their turn, either as patients or customers. For example:

Enfermera, deseo pedir un turno para ver al doctor la semana que viene, *Nurse, I'd like to make an appointment to see the doctor next week.*

Señorita, necesito un lavado de cabeza y un peinado, ¿puede darme un turno para mañana? *I need a wash and a set, can you give an appointment for tomorrow?*

Cita means *appointment* or *date.* For example:

Tengo una cita con mi novio esta noche. *I have a date with my boyfriend tonight.*

José tiene una cita con su abogado el jueves. *Joe has an appointment with his lawyer on Thursday.*

2.   **un corte con tijeras,** *a scissors cut.* **Cortar el pelo (cabello** instead of **pelo** is sometimes used in Spanish America).

3.   **teñido,** *dyed;* **con mechones dorados,** *with blond streaks.*

4.   **pelo rizo o crespo,** *(naturally) curly hair;* **pelo chino** (Mex.), **colocho** (Guatemala), **ondeado** *m., wavy hair;* **pelo rizado, encrespado,** *curly hair;* **con un moño,** *in a bun;* **con bucles,** *in curls;* **alisar,** *to straighten;* **acondicionador** *m., conditioner;* **fijador** *m., hair spray.*

5.   **rubia = güera** or **huera** (Mex.); **morena,** *brunette, dark* (in Cuba, *black woman*); **pelirroja,** *red-haired* = **colorina** (Chile).

6.   **depilar las cejas,** *to pluck the brows.*

7.   **manicurista** *f., manicurist;* **pedicurista** or **callista,** *chiropodist;* **lima para las uñas,** *nail file;* **esmalte** *m., nail polish.*

8.   **cutis aceitoso** or **graso,** *oily skin;* **cutis (re)seco,** *(very) dry skin;* **granos** or **barros** *m. pl., pimples;* **espinillas** *f. pl., blackheads.*

9.   **polvos (de arroz)** *m. pl., face powder;* **polvo** *m.* or **tierra** *f., dust;* **pólvora** *f., gunpowder;* **polvera** *f., powder box, compact;* **borla** or **bellota)** *f., powder puff;* **ponerse polvos,** *to powder one's face;* **embellecerse,** *to beautify oneself.*

10.   **hacer juego con,** *to match, harmonize with, go well with* = **ir** or **quedar) bien con** = **pegar con; desentonar con,** *to clash with.*

Presentando una carta de recomendación

Presenting a Letter of Recommendation

— ¿Está (en casa) el señor López?
> *Is Mr. López in?*

— ¿A quién debo anunciar?
> *Whom shall I say is calling?*

— Aquí tiene usted mi tarjeta.
> *Here is my card.*

— Pase usted y espere un momento. Tenga la bondad de sentarse.
> *Come in and wait a minute. Please be seated.*

— Buenos días. Dispense usted que le haya hecho esperar.[1] Permítame su sombrero.
> *How do you do? I'm sorry to have kept you waiting. Let me take your hat.*

— Gracias. Permítame entregarle esta carta del señor García.
> *Thank you. I should like to give you this letter from Mr. García.*

— Ah, mi buen amigo. ¿Cómo está él, y su familia?
> *Oh, he's a (lit. "my") good friend! How is he, and his family?*

— Muy bien, gracias. Le manda (a usted) mil saludos.
> *Very well, thank you. He sends you greetings.*

---

[1] **que le haya hecho esperar = por haberle hecho esperar.** § 43*a*.

— Permítame. (Leyendo): «Te estimaré las atenciones que prestes[2] a mi amigo (–a) ——, portador (–a) de la presente.» Pues tengo mucho gusto en conocer a usted.

> *Excuse me. (Reading): "I shall be grateful to you for any kindnesses you may show my friend ——, the bearer of this letter." Well, I am very happy to know you.*

— El gusto es mío, se lo aseguro.

> *The pleasure is mine, I assure you.*

— Ha tomado usted posesión de su casa.

> *You are very welcome here (lit. "you have taken possession of your house").*

— No sabe usted cuánto le agradezco su amable recibimiento.

> *I am very grateful (lit. "you don't know how grateful I am") for your kind reception.*

— Venga usted a comer con nosotros un día de éstos. ¿Cuánto tiempo piensa usted estar aquí?

> *Come and have dinner with us one of these days. How long do you expect to stay here?*

— Unos tres días, nada más. Pero si el clima me sienta bien, estaré cuatro.

> *About three days, not longer. But if the climate agrees with me, I'll stay four.*

— ¡Ah, vamos! ¿Que día está usted libre?

> *Oh, I see. What day are you free?*

— A ver. Mañana voy al teatro, y pasado mañana al cine con unos amigos. ¿El martes, si le parece a usted?

> *Let's see. Tomorrow I'm going to the theater, and the day after tomorrow to the movies with some friends. Tuesday, if that's agreeable with you?*

---

[2] **prestar**, *to lend, give, show*, etc. § 46.

— Convenido. Quedamos en el martes. Conocerá usted a mi familia.

> *Agreed. We'll make it Tuesday (lit. "we agree on Tuesday").*
> *You can meet my family.*

— Mil gracias. Ahora con su permiso, me retiro.

> *Many thanks. With your permission, I'll go (lit. "withdraw")*
> *now.*

— Le acompaño a la puerta.

> *I'll see (or accompany) you to the door.*

— No se moleste.

> *Please don't bother.*

— No es molestia. Es un verdadero placer.

> *It's no bother. It's a real pleasure.*

NOTAS

1. When a Spaniard or Spanish American mentions his house, he politely refers to it as yours. Such reference, unless made very definite, is not to be considered an invitation to call: **¿dónde vive usted ahora?** *where do you live now?* **en la calle Mayor, número 12, donde tiene usted su casa,** *on Main Street, number 12, where you have your house,* etc.

2. **conocer** means *to meet* as well as *to know, be acquainted with,* but note the past tenses: **le conocí (ayer),** *I met him (yesterday)*; **le conocía,** *I knew him, used to know him.*

3. On leaving a room, or a table, or a person with whom one is speaking, or when passing in front of a person, one asks permission: **con (su) permiso,** *with (your) permission.* The answer is usually: **usted lo tiene,** *you have it,* or one may merely nod assent.

4. On taking leave of a person after a visit one may say: **ya no molesto más,** *I'll not bother you any longer*; **si no manda usted otra cosa** (or **nada**), **me retiro** (or **me despido**), (*unless you have some-*

thing else to ask (or *order*), *I'll withdraw* (or *take leave*). And then, as the host rises to accompany the visitor to the door: **no se moleste usted (en acompañarme)**, *don't bother* (*to accompany me*). **no es molestia (ninguna)**, *its no bother* (*at all*), etc.

El tenis

Tennis

— ¿Sabe usted jugar al tenis?
   Do you play tennis?

— Muy poco, aunque soy aficionado a ese juego.
   Not very well, although I like the game.

— ¿Quiere usted jugar un partido conmigo[1] mañana por la mañana?
   Will you play a game with me tomorrow morning?

— Encantado (–a). Pero le advierto que juego muy mal.
   (I'd be) glad to. But I warn you, I play very badly.

— Eso lo veremos mañana. No olvide las raquetas y las pelotas.
   We'll see about that tomorrow. Don't forget the rackets and the balls.

— ¡Qué buena cancha es ésta!
   This court is really good!

— ¿Verdad? Está marcada con líneas blancas para juego sencillo o doble.
   Right. It's marked with white lines for singles or doubles.

— Usted saca (or sale).
   You serve (or begin).

---

[1] **con + mí = conmigo**. § 31, note.

— ¡Ahí va!
> *There it goes!*

— ¡Qué saque tan magnífico!
> *What a terrific serve!*

— Es favor que me hace.
> *You're just flattering me (lit. "it's a favor you're doing me").*

— No es favor. Es la verdad. Es usted un(–a) jugador(–a) de primera.
> *It's not flattery. It's the truth. You're an excellent player.*

— Usted juega mucho mejor que yo. Un reportero diría que mi «actuación» es bastante torpe.
> *You play much better than I do. A reporter would say that my "performance" is pretty awkward.*

— ¿No ve que usted me ha ganado?
> *Don't you see you've beaten me?*

— Pero mañana se desquita usted.
> *But tomorrow you'll get even.*

— ¡Quién sabe! A lo mejor empatamos.[2]
> *Who knows? We'll probably tie.*

— Entonces será al día siguiente.
> *Then it'll be the day after.*

— Quizás. El ejercicio hace al maestro
> *Maybe. "Practice makes perfect" (lit. "exercise makes the master").*

NOTAS

1. **jugar a**, *to play* (a game); **tocar**, *to play* (a musical instrument): **no sé tocar el violín**, *I can't play the violin.*

2. **aficionado, -a**, *m.* and *f.*, *fan, amateur.*

---

[2] **empatamos = tendremos un empate.**

3.   **mañana por la tarde**, *tomorrow afternoon*; **mañana por la noche**, *tomorrow night*; **ayer por la mañana**, *yesterday morning*.

4.   A useful phrase: **estoy desentrenado, -a**, *I'm out of practice*.

5.   Some additional vocabulary: **la raqueta tiene las cuerdas flojas (gastadas)**, *the racket has loose (worn) strings*; **colocar la pelota**, *to place the ball*; **la madera está resquebrajada**, *the wood is cracked*.
court = **campo** (Spain) *m.* = **mesa de tenis** (Mex.).

7.   Additional words connected with **saque**: **sacar**, *to serve*; **sacador** *m.*, *server*; **(golpe de) revés** *m.*, *backhand (stroke)*.

8.   Words suggested by **ganado**: **tanteo** *m.*, *score* = **anotación** *f.*, **resultado** *m.*, *final score*, **tanto** *m.*, *point*.

9.   An alternative for **desquitarse** is **tomar revancha**.

El fútbol

Soccer

■ **Primer tiempo**   *First Half*

— Va a empezar el partido.
> *The game's going to begin.*

— Apuesto a que gana el equipo del Club Deportivo.
> *I bet the Athletic Club team will win.*

— Y yo a que gana el equipo del Club Vasco.
> *And I (bet) that the Basque Club team will win.*

— ¿Cuánto va?
> *What do you bet (lit. "how much goes")?*

— Cincuenta pesos.
> *Fifty pesos.*

— Apostados.
> *It's a bet (lit. "they — the pesos — have been bet").*

— Ya se están alineando los jugadores.
> *The players are already lining up.*

— Van a patear (salir).
> *They're going to kick off (to begin).*

— ¡Caramba! ¡Con qué fuerza sale la pelota!
> *Wow! What a powerful kick (lit. "with what force the ball goes")!*

— ¡Qué patada más estupenda!
> *What a wonderful kick!*

— ¡Pocas he visto como ésa!

> *I've seen (very) few like that.*

— Mire cómo aquel jugador abre brecha en la línea defensiva de los adversarios.

> *Look at that player breaching the opponents' (line of) defense.*

— Pues ése va a marcar el primer tanto (gol).

> *Well, he's going to make the first goal (point).*

— Los otros actúan como si estuvieran[1] entrenándose.

> *The others are playing as if they were (only) practicing.*

— Es verdad. Ponen poco interés en el partido. Algunos parecen desentrenados.

> *Right. They're not showing much interest in the game. Some of them seem out of practice.*

— Ya sonó el pito (or silbato) y acabó el primer tiempo.

> *There went the whistle, and the first half's over (lit. "has ended").*

— ¿Cuál es la anotación?

> *What's the score?*

— Un empate. Dos a dos.

> *A tie. Two to two.*

■ **Segundo tiempo**   *Second Half*

— El arbitraje no me convence.

> *The refereeing isn't what it ought to be (lit. "doesn't convince me").*

— A mí tampoco. El árbitro (or referí) no sabe lo que hace (no cumple con su cometido).

> *I'm with you (lit. "nor me either"). The referee doesn't know what he's doing (isn't doing his job).*

---

[1] Imperfect subjunctive of **estar**. §§ 45d; 67, 6.

— Permite que los jugadores hagan lo que les dé la gana.[2]
  He lets the players do just as they please.

— Mire. Van a hacer un pase.
  Look. They're going to pass.

— ¡Caray! Cómo le derribaron a ése!
  Oh! They really knocked that guy down!

— ¡Cómo corre aquél! Es una flecha.
  Look at that guy over there run! Like lightning (lit. "he's an arrow").

— Si no le detienen podrá anotar (or marcar) un tanto.
  If they don't stop him, he'll be able to score.

— ¡Vaya un choque! Parece que se ha desmayado.
  What a crash! It looks as if he's fainted.

— Estará[3] lastimado.
  He's probably hurt.

— No será grave la cosa. Ya verá usted cómo se repone en seguida.
  It can't be very serious. You'll see how quickly he'll get over it.

— Ya corre otro jugador a ocupar su sitio.
  Now another player is running out to take his place.

— Pero de nada ha servido, pues ya terminó el partido.
  But it's no use, because the game's over.

— El resultado es quatro a dos, a favor del Club Deportivo.
  The (final) score is four to two for the Athletic Club.

— Pues yo he ganado el partido, digo la apuesta.
  Well, I've won the game, I mean the bet.

---

[2] **hagan**, subjunctive of **hacer**; **dé**, subjunctive of **dar**. §§ 43a, 46.   [3] Future of conjecture. § 40d.

— Aquí tiene usted los cincuenta pesos.

Here are your fifty pesos.

— Gracias. ¿Son falsos? (Mirándolos) No. ¡Honor a quien honor merece!

Thanks. Are they counterfeit? (Looking at them) No. Honor to whom honor is due (lit. "Honor to him who deserves honor").

NOTAS

1. Some positions: **centro** *m.*, *center*; **defensa** *m.*, *fullback*; **medio** *m.*, *halfback*; **futbolista** *m,. football player*; **ala** *f.*, *wing*.

2. Additional vocabulary: **un juego brusco**, *a rough game*; **ugar a las bochas**, *to bowl*; **cancha de bochas**, *bowling alley*.

El jai alai

Jai Alai

— En esta gradería están nuestros asientos.
   Our seats are in this tier.

— ¡Cuántos aficionados hay aquí esta noche!
   There are really a lot of fans here tonight!

— Parece que ya empezó el partido.
   It looks as if the game's already begun.

— ¡Qué va! Los jugadores (or pelotaris) están entrenándose.
   No! The players are just practicing.

— Mire. Son cuatro. Dos de ellos llevan camisa blanca y los otros dos camisa azul.
   Look. There are four of them. Two are wearing white shirts and the other two (are wearing) blue shirts.

— Son los dos equipos. Cada equipo consta de un delantero y de un zaguero.
   They're the two teams. Each team consists of a forward and a back.

— ¡Qué cesta más curiosa lleva cada jugador atada a la mano derecha!
   That's a really interesting basket each player wears tied to his right hand.

— Es de mimbre. Sirve para coger y arrojar la pelota.
   It's (made) of wicker. It's used to catch and throw the ball.

— Mire. Van a echar una moneda a cara o cruz.
> *Look. They're going to toss a coin.*

— Para ver quién saca. Ya está.
> *To see who serves. Now!*

— ¡Qué bien lanzó (or tiró) la pelota contra la pared!
> *Look at the way he hurled the ball against the wall!*

— Ahora la recoge el delantero del otro equipo sin dejarla tocar el suelo más de una vez.
> *Now the other team's forward picks it up (or catches it) without letting it touch the floor more than once.*

— Y vuelve a tirarla contra la pared.
> *And he throws it against the wall again.*

— ¡Qué rebote! Pero el jugador se cayó al suelo.
> *What a rebound! But the player fell to the floor.*

— No comprendo cuándo se gana un tanto.
> *I don't understand when they make points.*

— Se gana un tanto cuando el adversario comete una falta. El equipo que tenga[1] primero treinta tantos, gana el partido.
> *A point is scored when the opponent makes an error. The team that has thirty points first, wins the game.*

— ¿Pero cuáles son las faltas que puedan[1] cometer?
> *But what errors can they make?*

— Si un jugador deja botar la pelota más de una vez, si la tiene mucho tiempo en la cesta o si la pelota cae fuera de aquellas líneas.
> *If a player lets the ball bounce more than once, if he keeps it in the basket too long, or if the ball falls outside of those lines (down there).*

— ¡Qué juego más vigoroso (or recio)!
> *It's a really vigorous (or strenuous) game!*

---

[1] Subjunctive of **tener**; Subjunctive of **poder**. § 46.

NOTAS

1.   **el juego de jai alai** or **de pelota**=**el frontón** (Mex.); **frontón** or **frontis** *m*. is the name of the front wall against which the ball is thrown; **frontón** *m*., *building* or *court* (**cancha** *f*.) for **jai alai**.

2.   Because of another meaning **coger**, *to catch, pick*, has acquired, this verb is taboo in some Spanish American countries (particularly in Argentina and Chile). It is there replaced by **agarrar** (*to seize*), **tomar** (*to take*), **recoger** (*to pick up*), and the like. Elsewhere (Colombia, etc.) **tirar** (*to throw, throw away*) has acquired a similar meaning, and is replaced by **arrojar** (*to hurl*), for *to throw*, and by **botar** (*to pitch, cast away*) for *to throw away*; **tirarse**, *to jump* =**botarse**.

3.   **echar una moneda a cara** (*heads*, lit. "face") **o cruz** (*tails*, lit. "cross"), *to toss a coin*=**echar un volado** (in Mexico) for **águila** (*eagle*) or **sol** (*sun*), symbols which figure respectively on the face and reverse of Mexican coins=**cara o sello** (Argentina, Chile, Colombia, etc.).

4.   The **rebote** is the difficult play of recovering the ball from the back wall (**la pared de rebote**) so swiftly that the player is often thrown to the floor; **al rebote**, *on the rebound*.

La corrida de toros

The Bullfight

— ¡Cuánta gente! ¡La plaza está de bote en bote!
> *What a lot of people! The (bull) ring is packed (or crowded).*

— ¡Todos se empujan! ¡Ay, me pisaron el pie (or me han dado un pisotón)!
> *They're all pushing each other. Ow! Somebody stepped on my foot!*

— Venga por acá. Aquí están nuestros sitios. Estamos a la sombra.
> *Come over here. Our seats are here. We're in the shade.*

— Gracias a Dios. Sería insoportable estar al sol con el calor que hace.
> *Thank heaven! It would be unbearable to be in the sun in this heat.*

— Sentémonos.[1] Ya está tocando la banda.
> *Let's sit down. The band's already playing.*

— ¡El desfile de la cuadrilla! ¡Qué caballos tan briosos! ¡Y qué trajes! ¡Todo de oro y de plata!
> *The parade of the bullfighters! What spirited horses! And the costumes! All made of gold and silver!*

---

[1] **sentémonos (sentemos + nos) = vamos a sentarnos.** §§ 42, 61*a*.

— Allí vienen los matadores, los banderilleros, los picadores, los capeadores, y por último los monosabios. Ya se retiran.

> *There come the matadors, the banderilleros, the picadors, the capeadors, and finally the assistants. Now they're going off.*

— El redondel está despejado. ¡Mire, ya sale el toro!

> *The arena is clear. Look, there (lit. "now") comes the bull!*

— ¡Qué animal tan bravo! ¡Cómo embiste!

> *A really fierce animal! Look at the way he attacks!*

— Los capeadores ondean (or agitan) sus capas en la cara del toro.

> *The capeadors are waving their capes in the bull's face.*

— ¡Pero aquél sí tuvo que correr como una flecha!

> *But that fellow had to run like lightning (lit. "like an arrow").*

— ¡Y saltó la barrera! ¡Qué emoción!

> *And he's jumped over the barrier! This is really exciting!*

— ¡Qué bien trabaja aquel picador! ¡Caramba! ¡Se cayó del caballo!

> *That picador (over there) is giving a fine performance. Wow! He fell off his horse!*

— Pero no se hizo daño.[2] Ya volvió a montar.

> *But he didn't hurt himself. He's back on his horse (lit. "he has mounted again").*

— Tiene las piernas bien protegidas.[3]

> *His legs are well protected.*

— El pobre caballo sí parece que está herido. Recibió dos cornadas.

> *The poor horse really seems to be wounded. He was gored twice (lit. "he received two gorings").*

---

[2] **hacerse daño** (or **lastimarse**), *to hurt oneself.* § 67, 8.   [3] § 55c.

—Ahora llega el banderillero. ¡Qué bien sabe clavar las banderillas!

> *Now comes the banderillero. He sure knows how to handle (lit. "stick in") the banderillas!*

—Ya metieron dos pares de banderillas en el morrillo del toro.

> *They've already stuck two pairs of banderillas into the bull's neck.*

—¡Mire al matador! ¡Ése de la muleta y la espada!

> *Look at the matador! The guy with the red flag and the sword.*

—Ah, ya. ¡Qué tipo más alto y flexible!

> *Oh, yes. What a tall and wiry fellow he is!*

—Claro, el matador no puede ser gordo.

> *Of course, the matador can't be fat.*

—Ahora se pone frente al toro.

> *Now he's facing the bull.*

—No mueve los pies para nada. ¡Qué serenidad!

> *He doesn't move his feet at all. What poise!*

—¡Vaya faena! ¡Qué bien torea!

> *What a feat! Look how he "plays" the bull!*

—Dígame ¿es eso lo que llaman una verónica?

> *(Tell me), is that what they call a verónica?*

—No. La verónica es el lance de esperar al toro con la capa extendida con ambas manos.

> *No. The verónica is the play of waiting for the bull with the cape held out wide.*

—Ahora va a matar al toro.

> *Now he's going to kill the bull.*

— ¡Magnífico! ¡De una estocada lo mató! Mire los sombreros que le tiran al torero los espectadores entusiasmados.

Wonderful! He killed him with one thrust. Look at the hats that the crowd's throwing to the bullfighter; they're so enthusiastic!

— ¡Qué pronto salen los monosabios para llevarse al toro muerto!

Look how fast the assistants come out to drag off the dead bull!

— «A muertos y a idos no hay amigos» como dijo el filósofo.

"The dead and the departed have no friends," as the saying goes (lit. "as the philosopher said").

— A propósito, ¿cual es la diferencia entre un toro vivo y un toro muerto?

By the way, what's the difference between a live bull and a dead bull?

— El toro vivo embiste, y el muerto en bisté.

The live bull embiste (*attacks*) *and the dead one* en bisté (*in a beefsteak*).

— Lo ha acertado usted.

You've guessed it.

— Vámonos. Ya se acabó.

Let's go. It's over.

— Por fin he visto una corrida pero no pienso presenciar otra.

At last I've seen a bullfight, but I don't intend to go to another.

— Cuestión de gusto.

(*It's*) *a matter of taste.*

NOTAS

1. **corrida de toros** = **los toros**; **vamos a los toros**, *let's go to the bullfight.*

2.   Compare **me pisaron el pie** with **me puse el sombrero**, *I put on my hat*; **me guardé el boleto en el bolsillo**, *I put the ticket in my pocket*, etc. § 4g.

3.   **matador**, killer of the bull; **banderillero**, bullfighter who thrusts a pair of **banderillas** (long darts) into the bull's neck; **picador**, mounted bullfighter who wounds the bull with a pike and tries to hold him at a distance; **capeador**, bullfighter who "plays" the bull with a cape; **monosabio**, assistant who does various odd jobs in the ring.

4.   **trabajar**, *to work*; in reference to an artist, **trabajar bien** means *to give a good performance*: **aquel actor trabaja bien**, *that actor acts well, "is good"*; **aquella actriz trabaja mal**, *that actress can't act, is poor*.

5.   **gordo, -a**, *stout, fat*; **engordar**, *to get fat, put on weight*; **delgado, -a**, *thin, slim*; **adelgazar**, *to get thin, lose weight*; **flaco, -a** (said of animals, though not exclusively), *thin, skinny*; **enflaquecer**, *to become thin*.

6.   To understand the pun **embiste/en bisté** it must be remembered that an *n* immediately preceding a *b* is pronounced as *m*; therefore **embiste** (from **embestir**, § 64, III) is pronounced exactly like **en bisté** except for the stress, which in **embiste** (*he attacks*) falls on the second syllable and in **en bisté** (*in a beefsteak*) falls on the last. *Beefsteak* is **bisté or bistec** or **biftec**, but **bisté** is the most usual form today.

7.   **sobre gustos no hay disputas** or **sobre gustos no hay nada escrito** are equivalent to our *"every man to his own taste."* Some add: **pero gustos hay que merecen palos**, *but there are tastes that merit a beating*.

Algunos monumentos de México

A Few Mexican Monuments

— ¿Qué le parece Xochimilco?
> *How do you like Xochimilco?*

— «El lugar de las flores» y las chinampas, es decir, «los jardines flotantes». ¡Qué encanto! No he visto lugar más bonito.
> *"The flower spot," and the* chinampas, *that is, "the floating gardens"! Really charming! I haven't seen a prettier place.*

— ¿Le gustó Teotihuacán, «ciudad de los dioses»?
> *Did you like Teotihuacán, "city of the gods"?*

— ¡Qué cosa más interesante son las pirámides — la del Sol y la de la Luna!
> *The pyramids are extremely interesting — the pyramids of the Sun and the Moon.*

— ¿No le cansó subir tantas gradas?
> *Didn't it tire you to climb up all those steps?*

— Un poco. En cada descanso di la vuelta a la pirámide como antiguamente hacía la gente para no cansarse.
> *A bit. At each landing I walked around the pyramid as people used to do long ago so as not to get tired.*

— ¿Qué impresión le hizo el museo?
> *What impression did the museum make on you?*

— ¿El museo de Antropología, dice?   Pues, de lo más interesante.

You mean the Museum of Anthropology? Extremely interesting.

— Sobre todo el calendario azteca.

Especially the Aztec calendar.

— ¡Qué piedra más enorme con sus veinte toneladas! ¡Qné curiosas las figuras grabadas en ella!

What an enormous stone — twenty tons! And those really curious figures engraved on it!

— Impresionante.   Pero prefiero mirar los jardines, los antiguos conventos y las iglesias coloniales.

Impressive. But I prefer to look at the gardens, the old monasteries, and the colonial churches.

— Pues no debe usted dejar de ver Cuernavaca, residencia del conquistador Hernán Cortés — y Taxco y Acapulco.

Well, you shouldn't miss seeing Cuernavaca, where the conquistador Hernán Cortés lived, nor Taxco and Acapulco.

— Algo tengo que dejar para mi próximo viaje.

I must leave something for my next trip.

— En México tiene usted para diez viajes más.

You'll have enough for ten more trips to Mexico.

— ¡Ojalá pudiera[1] volver todos los años!

I wish I could come back every year.

NOTAS

1.   **¿qué le parece X?** (*how*) *do you like X?* = **¿le gusta X? ¿qué le ha parecido X?** or **¿qué le pareció X?** (*how*) *did you like X?* = **¿le gustó X?** The *x* of Xochimilco is pronounced like *s.*

[1] **¡ojalá pudiera!** = **¡quién pudiera!**

2. **chulo, -a** is very commonly used for **bonito, -a** (**simpático, -a, gracioso, -a**, etc.) in Mexico and Guatemala. In Spain and elsewhere **chulo** means *ruffian*, etc.

3. Slang expressions to indicate quality (**excelente, magnífico, -a**), equivalent to our *"swell"* or *"grand"*: **piocha, repiocha**, and **suave** in Mexico; **fenómeno** or **mundial** in Cuba; **macanudo** in South America, particularly Argentina; **cachos pa(ra) arriba** or **cachos pal cielo** (lit. "horns up," "horns in the sky") in Chile; **tres piedras** (Mex., Cent. Am.).

En una playa de Acapulco o de Viña del Mar

On a Beach at Acapulco or at
Viña del Mar

— ¿No sabe usted nadar?
  You know how to swim, don't you?

— Sí sé. Como un pez.
  I certainly do. Like a fish.

— Entonces vamos a la playa.
  Then let's go to the beach.

— No tengo inconveniente, pues hace mucho calor.
  I have no objection, because it's very hot.

— No sé nadar bien. Pero dicen que es fácil mantenerse a flote en el mar.
  I can't swim well. But they say that it's easy to keep afloat in the ocean.

— Mucho más fácil que en agua dulce.
  Much easier than in fresh (lit. "sweet") water.

— No me gusta nadar si no puedo tocar (el) fondo.[1]
  I don't like to swim if I can't touch bottom.

— (Entrando al agua) ¡Qué caliente está el agua hoy!
  (Going into the water) The water is really warm today!

— ¡Qué olas más gigantescas! No me atrevo a entrar. El mar está muy agitado (or bravo). Hay resaca.
  What huge waves! I don't dare go in. The ocean is very rough. There's an undertow.

---

[1] tocar (el fondo) = dar pie.

— Venga usted. No le pasa nada.
Come on. Nothing will happen to you.

— ¿No hay tiburones?
Aren't there sharks?

— Algunos chiquitos. Pero nunca comen turistas. Además si hay peligro, hay el salvador de vidas para sacarle (la). No más grite usted ¡socorro!
A few small ones. But they never eat tourists. Besides, if there is any danger there's the lifeguard to pull you out. Just yell "help!"

— Gracias, no quiero ahogarme. Prefiero asolearme[2] tendido (–a) aquí en la arena.
Thanks, I don't want to drown. I'd rather take a sunbath stretched out here on the sand.

— Ya está usted bastante bronceado (or tostado, –a). ¡Cuidado con quemarse!
You're tanned enough already. Watch you don't burn yourself.

— No echaré en saco roto su consejo. Con este sol tan fuerte puede que me dé una insolación.[3]
I'll remember what you say (lit. "I will not throw your advice into a torn sack"). With this strong sun I'm likely to get a sunstroke.

— Pues yo me voy a meter al agua.
Well, I'm going in.

— Vaya no más. Le (la) espero aquí.
Go ahead. I'll wait for you here.

— No se mueva de aquí hasta que yo vuelva.[4]
Don't move from this spot until I come back.

---

[2] (a)solearse = tomar un baño de sol.   [3] insolación = asoleada; puede que me dé = es posible que me dé, § 44.   [4] mueva (mover), vuelva(volver), subjunctives. §§ 64, I; 41; 45*b*

— Más tarde vamos a retratarnos juntos (–as).
Later we'll have our pictures taken together.

— (Paseante) ¡Qué día más hermoso! ¿Por qué no entra usted al agua?
(Stroller) What a beautiful day! Why don't you go in (to the water)?

— Es que no nado bien. Y usted ¿no nada nada?
Because I don't swim well. What about you? Don't you swim at all?

— No traje traje.
I didn't bring a suit.

NOTAS

1. **Acapulco** and **Viña del Mar** are two famous beach resorts on the Pacific, the first in Mexico, the second in Chile.

2. Some additional vocabulary connected with **nadar**: **la natación** *f.*,(the art of) *swimming*; **maestro de natación** *m.*, *swimming instructor*.

3. **pez**, *fish* (in the water); **pescado** *m.*, *fish* (on the table).

4. Vocabulary connected with **la playa**: **piscina** or **alberca** *f.*, *swimming pool* = **pileta de natación** (Arg.); **bañista** *m.* and *f.*, *bather*.

5. **mantenerse a flote** = **hacer el muerto** (*pretend to be dead*) = **hacer la plancha** = **flotar**, *to float*; **estilo pecho** *m.*, *breast stroke*; **estilo espalda** *m.*, *back stroke*; **estilo libre** *m.*, *free stroke*.

6. **le dió un ataque (cardíaco)**, *he (she) had an (heart) attack*; **me dió una insolación**, *I had a sunstroke*; **me dió un calambre**, *I had a cramp*.

7. **tirarse al agua**, *to jump into the water, dive* = **zambullirse** = **hacer un clavado** (Mex.).

8. **vaya no más** (Span. Am.) = **ándele pues** (Mex.) = **vaya usted** (Spain); **no más** in this case adds a note of assurance and consent.

9. **traje (de baño)** *m.*, (*bathing*) *suit* = **trusa** *f.* in Cuba = **bañador** *m.* in Spain; **bata (de baño)** *f.*, *bathrobe* = **salida** *f.* in Argentina.

El viajante

The Traveling Salesman

— ¿Puedo hablar con el gerente?
> *May I speak with the manager?*

— Servidor de usted.
> *I'm the manager.*

— (Dándole su tarjeta) Soy representante de la casa Gómez Hermanos de Buenos Aires. Quisiera enseñarle las muestras de nuestros artículos.
> *(Giving him his card) I'm the representative of Gómez Brothers of Buenos Aires. I should like to show you the samples of our merchandise.*

— Conozco la casa. Hemos quedado muy contentos de su último envío.
> *I know the firm. We were very much satisfied with your last shipment.*

— Muchas gracias. En ese caso estoy seguro de que encontrará usted algo que le convenga entre estas últimas novedades. Vea usted.
> *Thank you. In that case I'm sure you'll find something that will suit you among these latest novelties. Just look at them.*

— Me gustan estos dibujos y este género. ¿A cómo se vende este género?
> *I like these designs and this material. How much does this material sell for?*

— Para usted pondré un precio especial y se lo enviaremos franco (or con porte pagado).

I'll make a special price for you and we'll send it prepaid.

— ¿Cuáles son las condiciones de pago?

What are your terms?

— El pago a seis meses, fecha de la factura. Al contado con el cinco por ciento (de descuento).

Payment in six months from date of invoice. Five percent discount for cash.

— Me conviene el pago a seis meses. ¿Cuánto paga de derechos este artículo?

Payment in six months suits me. What is the duty on this article?

— El diez por ciento, nada más.

Only ten percent.

— Bien. Deseo tenerlo dentro de quince días.

Fine. I'd like to have it within two weeks.

— No se preocupe. Se hará como usted desea. Muchas gracias por su amable pedido.

Don't worry. We'll carry out your wishes. Thank you very much for your order.

— Que le vaya bien.

Good luck to you.

NOTAS

1. *traveling salesman* is also **comisionista** *m.*; other vocabulary: **agencia de publicidad** *f.*, *advertising agency*; **anunciar (hacer la propaganda de) un producto**, *to advertise (create publicity for) a product*.

2. Other ways of sending goods: **por gran velocidad** (Spain), *by express* = **express** = **por expreso** (Span. Am.); **por pequeña velocidad** (Spain), *by freight* = **ordinario** = **por carga** (Span. Am.).

La exposición de pinturas

The Painting Exhibition

— ¿Podría usted decirme dónde está la exposición de pinturas?
> *Could you tell me where the painting exhibition is?*

— Sí, señor. Yo también voy allá. Si usted quiere, iremos juntos.
> *Yes. I'm going too. If you like, we'll go together.*

— Con mucho gusto. Como soy extranjero (–a), no conozco estas calles.
> *With pleasure. I'm a foreigner, and I'm not familiar with these streets.*

— Pues ya llegamos. Ésta es la entrada.
> *Well, here we are (lit. "we have arrived already"). This is the entrance.*

— Mire usted este paisaje. Es una bellísima composición.
> *Look at this landscape. It's a very beautiful composition.*

— A mí me gusta más este cuadro impresionista.
> *I prefer this impressionistic painting.*

— ¿De veras? Pero le falta técnica. Está mal dibujado y peor pintado.
> *Really? But it lacks technique. The drawing is bad and the painting worse (lit. "it is badly drawn and worse painted").*

— Pero tiene emoción, calor, vida. El artista sabe ir al alma de las cosas sin poner detalles inútiles.
> *But it has emotion, warmth, life. The artist knows how to get at the soul of things without adding useless details.*

— Pero ha sacrificado el detalle a la impresión del conjunto.
   But he has sacrificed detail to the impression of the whole.

— ¡Mire los contrastes de luz y de sombra!
   Note the contrasts of light and shadow.

— Pero las figuras no son verosímiles. Están muy estilizadas (idealizadas).
   But the figures are not true to life. They are very much stylized (idealized).

— Claro que no es una obra maestra.
   Of course it's not a masterpiece.

— Ni mucho menos. De ningún modo (or ninguna manera).
   Far from it. By no means.

— Sin embargo, me entusiasma.
   Nevertheless, I admire it very much (lit. "it enthuses me").

— Veamos las otras salas.
   Let's see the other rooms.

— Mire usted este cuadro al óleo, señora. ¿Qué le parece?
   Look at this oil painting, madam. How do you like it?

— ¿Cuánto vale éste? ¿Qué precio tiene?
   How much is it worth? What's its price?

— Tres mil quinientos pesos. Y es una ganga.
   Three thousand five hundred pesos. And it's a bargain.

— Le doy a usted dos mil.
   I'll give you two thousand.

— Perdone usted; pero aquí no se regatea. Nuestros precios son fijos.
   Excuse me; but here one does not bargain. Our prices are firm.

— No lo sabía.
   I didn't know.

— ¡Claro! ¿Le agrada el cuadro que está en este caballete?

> *Well, that's the case. Do you like the painting that is on this easel?*

— Ya lo creo. ¡Qué cuadro más bello! ¡Se me hace agua la boca!

> *I really do. What a beautiful picture! It makes my mouth water.*

— ¿Qué dice? ¿Que se le hace agua la boca mirando una puesta de sol?

> *What did you say (lit. "what do you say")? (That) it makes your mouth water to look at a sunset?*

— ¿Eso es una puesta de sol?

> *Is that a sunset?*

— Claro.

> *It certainly is.*

— Pues yo creí que era un huevo frito.

> *Well, I thought it was a fried egg.*

— Se ve que tiene usted hambre.

> *Evidently (lit. "one sees that") you're hungry.*

— Pero éste sí me encanta. Es precioso. El colorido de esos buitres es magnífico. ¡Qué expresión tan feroz en los ojos! ¡Hombre, no debería usted pintar más que buitres!

> *But I do love this one. It's charming. The coloring of those vultures is magnificent. That's a really ferocious expression in their eyes! Hey, you should be painting nothing but vultures!*

— ¡Pero (si)[1] no son buitres! ¡Son ángeles!

> *But they're not vultures! They're angels!*

— (¡Hoy no hago más que meter la pata!)

> *(Today I can't do anything except put my foot in it.)*

---

[1] So-called unstressed expletive **si**, meaning *why, but,* etc.: **si ya lo sé**, *why, I know it already,* or *but I know it already.*

En (la casa de) correos

At the Post Office

— ¿Cuál es el porte[1] de una carta para los Estados Unidos?
What is the postage on a letter to the United States?

— Un peso sesenta para correo aéreo.
One peso sixty cents by air mail.

— Déme dos estampillas de a peso sesenta, por favor.
Give me two stamps for a peso sixty each, please.

— Son tres pesos veinte centavos.
That makes three pesos, twenty cents.

— Y quisiera certificar esta carta.
And I'd like to register this letter.

— A ver. También tengo que pesarla. Necesita usted otra estampilla de a dos pesos. Total, cinco pesos veinte centavos.
Let's see. I also have to weigh it. You need another stamp for two pesos. In all, five pesos and twenty cents.

— ¿Tengo que poner el nombre y la dirección del remitente al dorso[2] del sobre?
Do I have to put the sender's name and address on the back of the envelope?

— Sí, señor. Así le devuelven la carta si no hallan al destinatario. ¿Quiere usted acuse de recibo?
Yes. Then they'll return the letter if they can't find the addressee. Do you want a return receipt?

---

[1] *postage* = **franqueo.**   [2] **al dorso** = **en el reverso.**

— Si me hace el favor.

Please.

— Son cincuenta centavos más.

That's fifty centavos more.

— ¿Llegará esta carta mañana si la envío por correo aéreo?[3]

Will this letter get there tomorrow if I send it (by) airmail?

— Sí, señor. Sólo tarda cuatro horas en llegar.

Yes, sir. It only takes four hours to get there.

— ¿Pesa demasiado esta carta?

Does this letter weigh too much?

— No, señor. No tiene exceso.

No, sir. It's not overweight.

— ¿Dónde echo las cartas?

Where do I mail the letters?

— En el buzón de enfrente. Al lado hay buzón especial para la correspondencia aérea.

In the box opposite. There's a special letter drop for air mail, next to it.

— Buenos días. Hace tiempo mandé una carta certificada a Nueva York y no ha llegado a su destino.

Hello. Some time ago I sent a registered letter to New York and it hasn't arrived at its destination.

— ¿Tiene usted el recibo?

Do you have the receipt?

— Desgraciadamente se me ha extraviado.[4]

Unfortunately I've mislaid it.

— ¿Recuerda usted al empleado[5] que se lo dió?

Do you remember the clerk who gave it to you?

---

[3] **por correo aéreo**=**por avión.** [4] **se me ha extraviado**=**se me ha perdido,** *I have lost it.* [5] **¿recuerda usted al empleado?**=**¿se acuerda usted del empleado?**

— Sí, señor. Es aquel de los bigotes de foca.
> *Yes. It's the one with the walrus (lit. "seal") mustache.*

— Ya sé quién es. ¿A quién iba dirigida[6] la carta?
> *I know who it is. Who was the letter addressed to?*

— Al señor John Day y tenía mi nombre al dorso.
> *To Mr. John Day, and it had my name on the back.*

— Haga usted el favor de esperar un momento.
> *Would you wait just a minute, please?*

— Mientras espero voy a ver si hay (algunas) cartas para mí en la lista de correos (or en poste restante).
> *While I'm waiting I'll go and see if there are any letters for me at the General Dlelivery window.*

— ¿Me hace usted el favor de ver si hay (algunas) cartas para mí? Ésta es mi tarjeta.
> *Would you see if there are any letters for me, please? This is my card.*

— Hay dos cartas y estos impresos. ¿Me puede usted enseñar su pasaporte?
> *There are two letters and this printed matter. Can you show me your passport?*

— Aquí lo tiene usted.
> *Here it is.*

— Bien. Haga usted el favor de firmar este recibo.
> *O.K. Sign this receipt, please.*

— Con mucho gusto. ¿Podría usted remitir mis cartas a esta dirección?[7]
> *Sure. Could you forward my letters to this address?*

— Sí, señor; pero hay que llenar[8] este formulario.[9]
> *Yes, sir; but you'll have to fill out this form.*

---

[6] **iba dirigida**=estaba dirigida. § 51*b*.   [7] **la dirección**=las señas (Spain).   [8] **hay que llenar**=es necesario llenar. § 56*b*.   [9] **formulario**=hoja impresa.

— Muchas gracias.
Thank you.

NOTAS

1.   **el correo**, *the mail*; **administrador de correos** *m.*, *post-master*; **cartero** *m.*, *letter carrier, mailman*; **giro postal** *m.*, *money order*; **paquete postal** *m.*, *parcel post*; **valija** *f.*, *mailbag*; **apartado** *m.*, *post office box* = **casilla** *f.* (Arg., Chile); **reparto** *m.*, *delivery*; **recogida** *.*, *collection* = **recolecta** (Mex.); **recoger**, *to collect*; **hay dos repartos diarios**, *there are two deliveries a day.*

2.   **timbre** (Mex.), **estampilla** *f.* (Span. Am.) = **sello** *m.* (Spain), *stamp.*

3.   **recordar una cosa** = **acordarse de una cosa.**

4.   **el de (los) bigotes largos**, *the one with a long mustache*; **la de (los) ojos azules**, *the blue-eyed girl.*, etc

En telégrafos

At the Telegraph Office

— Deseo poner un telegrama.
　I want to send a telegram.

— En la tercera ventanilla a la derecha.
　The third window to the right.

— Muchas gracias. ¿Cuál es el número de la ventanilla?
　Thank you. What's the number of the window?

— El veinticinco.
　Number twenty-five.

— . . . Buenos días. Quisiera poner un telegrama.
　. . . Hello. I'd like to send a telegram.

— Haga usted el favor de redactarlo en este formulario.[1]
　Write (lit. "compose") it on this blank, please.

— Gracias. ¿Con lápiz o con tinta?
　Thanks. With a pencil or in ink?

— Es lo mismo,[2] con tal que se pueda leer.
　It makes no difference, provided it's legible (lit. "it can be read").

— Ya está. Quiero mandarlo diferido. ¿Cuál es la tarifa?
　Here it is. I want to send it as a night letter (lit. "deferred"). What is the rate?

---

[1] **formulario**＝**esqueleto** (Cent. Am., but mostly Mex.).　[2] **es lo mismo**＝ **da lo mismo**＝**es igual**＝ **no importa**＝**no le hace** (Span. Am.).

— Los diferidos se pagan a media tarifa. ¿Cuántas palabras son?

> *You pay for night letters at half rate. How many words are there?*

— A ver. Una, dos, tres, cuatro, cinco, seis, siete, ocho, nueve, diez. Son diez justas, sin contar la dirección.

> *Let's see. One, two, three, four, five, six, seven, eight, nine, ten. Exactly ten, without counting the address.*

— Sesenta pesos.

> *Sixty pesos.*

— Y deseo pagar la contestación.

> *And I want to pay for the answer.*

— Entonces son ciento veinte pesos. . . . Aquí tiene usted el recibo.

> *Then that's one hundred twenty pesos. Here's your receipt.*

— Gracias. ¿Hay servicio de cable a Europa?

> *Thanks. Is there cable service to Europe?*

— En el segundo piso. El elevador está al final del pasillo.

> *On the second floor. The elevator is at the end of the corridor.*

— ¿Hasta cuándo está abierto?

> *How late is it open?*

— Hasta media noche.

> *Until midnight.*

NOTAS

1. **escribir con** (or **a**) **lápiz**, *to write with pencil*; **escribir con** (or **a**) **pluma**, *to write in ink* (lit. "pen"); **escribir con tinta**, *to write in ink*.

2. **con tal que**, *provided that*, is followed by the subjunctive.

3.   **diferido**, *deferred*; **telegrama de madrugada** (*early morning telegram*) = **carta nocturna**, *night letter*; **telegrama por cobrar**, *wire collect*; **mensajero** *m.*, *messenger*; **sin hilos**, *wireless* = **inalámbrico**.

La visita

A Visit

— Me parece que han llamado. ¿Quién será?[1]

> *I think there was a knock at the door (or the doorbell has rung). Who can it be?*

— Soy yo, señor Blanco.

> *It's me, Mr. White.*

— Ah, buenos días. Pase usted y dispense que le haya hecho esperar.

> *Oh, hello. Come in. I'm sorry to have kept you waiting.*

— ¡Si acabo de llegar!

> *Why, I've just arrived!*

— Haga usted el favor de sentarse. Permítame su sombrero.

> *Do sit down. Let me take your hat.*

— Muchas gracias.

> *Thank you.*

— ¿A qué debemos el gusto de verle (verla)?

> *To what do we owe the pleasure of seeing you?*

— Vengo de parte de mamá que le (la) convida a cenar en casa mañana.

> *Mother sent me to invite you to have supper with us to-morrow (lit. "I come on behalf of Mother who invites you to sup at our house tomorrow").*

---

[1] Future of conjecture. § 40d.

— Pues diga a su mamá que acepto gustosísimo. Ah, ahora que me acuerdo, mañana tengo otro compromiso.

> *Tell your mother that it will be a great pleasure (lit. "that I accept with pleasure"). Oh, now that I remember, I have another engagement tomorrow.*

— ¡Qué lástima! Pero no se preocupe usted,[2] que ya le explicaré yo el caso a mamá.

> *That's too bad. But don't worry about it, (for) I'll explain the matter to Mother.*

— No sabe usted cuánto lo siento.

> *I'm very sorry (lit. "you don't know how sorry I am").*

— Pues nosotros lo lamentamos mucho.

> *Well, we're very sorry too.*

— Según parece, quedo mal con todos.

> *I seem to get into awkward situations with everyone.*

— Con mamá quedará usted bien. Eso corre de mi cuenta.

> *You won't offend Mother. I'll take care of that (lit. "that runs on my account").*

— No sabe usted cuánto se lo agradezco. Muchos recuerdos para su mamá.

> *I'm very grateful to you. Remember me to your mother (lit. "many remembrances for your mother").*

— Gracias de su parte.

> *Thank you (lit. "thanks on her behalf").*

— Que le vaya bien.

> *Good-bye (lit. "may it go well with you").*

— Que usted lo pase bien.

> *Good-bye (lit. "may you fare well").*

---

[2] Or **no tenga usted cuidado.**

NOTAS

1.   **voy a hacer una visita**, *I am going to make* (*pay*) *a call*; **devolver una visita**, *to return a visit*; **visita** *f.*, *visitor, caller*: **tengo visitas**, *I have visitors, I have company*; **visitar a un amigo**, *to visit a friend*.

2.   **llamar**, *to call*, *knock at the door, ring the doorbell*, etc.; **tocar (a) la puerta** (Span. Am.), *to knock at the door*.

3.   **convidar**, *to invite*, generally to a meal; **invitar**, *to invite*, is the more inclusive term.

4.   **no sabe usted cuánto lo siento** (or **lamento**) = **lo siento** (or **lamento**) **mucho** = **lo siento en el alma**, etc., *I am very sorry*. Note how the expression must be toned down in English in order to render the actual feeling and meaning of the Spanish.

5.   **quedar mal con**, *to offend*, *make a bad impression on* "*get in bad with*," etc.; **quedar bien con**, *to make a good impression on*; **desairar**, *to offend*, *slight*: **no quiero desairar a nadie**, *I don't want to slight anyone* = **no quiero hacer un desaire a nadie**.

La visita de despedida

The Farewell Visit

— ¡Ah! don Alberto. ¡Cuánto gusto me da verlo otra vez!
¡Qué sorpresa!

> *Ah, Mr. ——! I'm (really) glad to see you again. What a*
> *surprise!*

— ¡Querido don Carlos!

> *(Dear) Mr. ——!*

— Pase usted por aquí. Siéntese, siéntese.

> *Come right this way. Sit down.*

— Muchas gracias. Voy de prisa.

> *Thank you. I'm pressed for time.*

— Ya me dijeron que se va[1] usted mañana en el aeroplano.

> *I was told (lit. "they have already told me") you're leaving*
> *by plane tomorrow.*

— Es verdad. Y quería despedirme de usted antes de salir
para Guatemala.

> *That's right. And I wanted to say good-bye to you before*
> *leaving for Guatemala.*

— Muy agradecido, don Alberto.

> *I really appreciate that, Mr. ——.*

— No olvidaré las buenas atenciones que ha tenido usted
conmigo.

> *I won't forget the courtesies you have shown me.*

---

[1] **ir**, *to go*; **irse**, *to go away* = **marcharse**.

— Nada tiene que agradecer. Lo principal es que no se vaya usted descontento de nuestra tierra.

> *You have nothing to thank me for. The main thing is that you're not going away displeased with our country.*

— De ninguna manera (or de ningún modo).

> *By no means.*

— ¿Qué le ha parecido a usted?

> *What did you think of it?*

— Un encanto. He tomado cariño a México y a los mexicanos.

> *Delightful. I have learned to like Mexico and the Mexicans.*

— Muchas gracias, amigo Alberto.

> *Thank you, (my friend).*

— Ya no molesto más. Si no manda usted nada, me retiro. No se moleste en acompañarme.

> *I'll not trouble you any longer. If you have no objection (lit. "if you do not command anything else"), I'll take my leave. Don't bother to accompany me (to the door).*

— No es ninguna molestia. Cuando vuelva (or regrese) usted, aquí me encontrará para servirle.

> *It's no bother at all. When you come back, you'll find me right here ready to help you (lit. "at your service").*

— Muchas gracias, don Carlos.

> *Thank you, Mr. ——.*

— Ya sabe usted dónde tiene su casa.

> *You know you're very welcome here.*

— Muy agradecido. Adiós y un millón de gracias por todo.

> *I really appreciate that. Good-bye and thanks a million for everything.*

— ¡Adiós y feliz viaje!

> *Good-bye and bon voyage!*

NOTAS

1. **don (doña)** with the given name is a respectful form of address (often for older people) where in English we should use only *Mr.* or *Mrs.*, etc., with the family name. The given name alone implies sufficient intimacy for the use of the second person singular of the verb (the **tú** form).

2. **voy de prisa**=**estoy de prisa**=**tengo mucha prisa; no corre prisa**, *there's no hurry*; **dése (usted) prisa, apresúrese (usted), apúrese** (Span. Am.), *hurry up!*

3. **¿qué le parece (a usted)?** *how do you like it?*= **¿le gusta?** But in this sense **¿cómo le gusta?** is never used.

5

La América,
Central y del Sur

The Americas, Central and South

Viajando en avión

Traveling by Plane

■ **Sacando el boleto**   *Buying a Ticket*

— ¿Tienen ustedes servicio aéreo entre México y Guatemala?
   Do you have air service between Mexico and Guatemala?

— Sí, señor. Tenemos servicio diario.
   Yes, sir. We have daily service.

— ¿Cuánto vale el boleto de ida?
   How much is the one-way ticket?

— Ciento diez dólares; el de ida y vuelta vale doscientos dólares.
   One hundred ten dollars; the round-trip (ticket) costs two hundred.

— Los precios están por las nubes.
   The prices are sky-high.

— Igual que los aeroplanos.
   Just like the planes.

— Quisiera salir el día veinte de este mes.
   I'd like to leave the twentieth of this month.

— Es decir, pasado mañana. Tendré que poner un telegrama a ver si queda un asiento libre.
   That is, the day after tomorrow. I'll have to send a telegram to see whether there's a seat left.

— ¡Ojalá les quede por lo menos uno! El viaje es urgente.
   I hope you'll have at least one left. The trip is urgent.

— ¿Tiene usted el pasaporte en regla?
> *Is your passport in order?*

— Sí, señor. Ayer saqué la visa (or el visado) y tengo todos mis documentos. Aquí están.
> *Yes. I got the visa yesterday and I have all my documents. Here they are.*

— A ver, ¿cuánto pesa su equipaje, señor?
> *Let's see how much your luggage weighs, sir.*

— La báscula dice dieciocho kilos.[1]
> *The scale says eighteen kilos.*

— Es decir, casi cuarenta libras.
> *That is, almost forty pounds.*

— ¿Tienen servicio de transporte al aeropuerto?
> *Do you provide transportation to the airport?*

— Sí. Iremos a buscarle (la) a las ocho de la mañana.
> *We do. We'll call for you at eight in the morning.*

— Haré que me despierten a las seis.
> *I'll make them wake me at six.*

— En cuanto contesten al telegrama, le (la) llamaré por teléfono al hotel (a su domicilio).
> *As soon as they answer the telegram, I'll call (by phone) at your hotel (at your home).*

— Muchas gracias. Estaré allí toda la tarde.
> *Thank you. I'll be in all afternoon.*

NOTAS

1. *we'll call for you*=**pasaremos por usted**, *we'll pass by for you*=**le (la) recogeremos**, *we'll pick you up.*

[1] **un kilo(gramo)**=**2.2 libras.** § 69.

2. **haré que me llamen**, *I'll have them call me*; **haré que le manden (a usted) el dinero**, *I'll have them send you the money*, etc. § 43*a*, § 67, 8.

3. **llamar por teléfono** = **telefonear**; **dar un telefonazo**, *to give a call*: **le daré un telefonazo**, *I'll give you a call* = **le telefonearé**.

En el aeropuerto

At the Airport

— ¿Ha oído usted el aviso transmitido por el altoparlante? [1]
   Did you hear the notice broadcast over the loudspeaker?

— Sí, pero no lo entendí.
   Yes, but I didn't understand it.

— Dijo que el avión no tardará en aterrizar.
   It said that the plane is about to land.

— Eso es. Mírelo. ¡Qué bien ha aterrizado!
   That's right. Look at it. What a perfect landing!

— ¡Qué pocos pasajeros han llegado!
   That's really a small number of passengers to arrive!

— Ayer, en cambio, el aeroplano venía lleno.
   Yesterday, on the other hand, the plane was full.

— ¿Me da usted lumbre (or fuego)?
   Can you give me a light?

— Aquí está prohibido fumar.
   Smoking is not allowed here.

— Es verdad. Es peligroso. Soy un fumador empedernido.
¿Oyó usted otro anuncio?
   That's right. It's dangerous. I'm an inveterate smoker.
   Did you hear another announcement?

---

[1] **altoparlante = altavoz.**

— Es para que se embarque la tripulación.
> *That's for the crew to get on (lit. "embark").*

— Ya suben la escala: el capitán, el segundo piloto, el mecánico, la azafata. . . .[2]
> *Now they're going on board (lit. "going up the steps"): the captain, the second pilot, the mechanic, the stewardess. . . .*

— ¡Qué bien están con el uniforme!
> *They look really good in uniform!*

— Dicen que todas las muchachas quieren casarse con aviadores.
> *They say that all the girls want to marry aviators.*

— ¿Por qué será?[3]
> *Why do you suppose that is?*

— Porque los aviadores lo pasan todo por alto.
> *Because aviators overlook everything.*

— ¡Qué ocurrente es usted! ¡Otro aviso por el altavoz!
> *What funny things you think of! Another announcement over the loudspeaker!*

— Es para nosotros. Ya podemos ir a bordo.
> *That's for us. Now we can go aboard.*

NOTAS

1. **avión** = **aeroplano**; **hélice** *f.*, *propeller*; **ala** *f.*, *wing* (§ 2); **motor** *m.*, *motor*; **cabina** *f.*, *cockpit*; **timón de dirección** *m.*, *rudder*.

2. Words suggested by **aterrizar**: **acuatizar, amarar**, *to come down on water*.

3. **lumbre** *f.*, *light, fire* = **fuego** *m.*, *fire*; **encendedor** *m.*, (*cigarette*) *lighter*; **se acabó la mecha**, *the wick is used up*; **no arde**, *it doesn't burn*.

---

[2] **la sobrecargo** = **aeromoza** (Mex.) = **azafata** (Spain).   [3] Future of conjecture. § 40*d*.

4. **fumador empernido** suggests: **fumar con exceso**, *to smoke to excess*; **no puedo quitarme este vicio**, *I can't give up the habit*; **fumar en pipa**, *to smoke a pipe*.

5. **embarcarse** *to embark, go aboard* (used in Argentina in speaking of both trains and ships). §§63, 1; 45*a*.

6. **estar bien**, *to be well, look nice*: also **estoy bien**, *I am comfortable* = **estoy a gusto** = **estoy cómodo**.

7. **ocurrente**, *original, bright, witty*; **ocurrencia** *f.*, *witty remark*. Additional words: **avión de** (or **a**) **reacción** or **avión de propulsión a chorro** (or **reactor**, Spain) *m.*, *jet plane*; **cohete** *m.*, *rocket;* **colocar en órbita**, *to put into orbit;* **etapa** *f.*, *stage phase;* **helicóptero** *m.*, *helicopter*; **lanzar al espacio**, *to launch into space*; **satélite** *m.*, *satellite*.

El despegue

The Take-off

— Hagan el favor de abrocharse el cinturón de seguridad; vamos a despegar.

>   *Please fasten your safety belts; we're going to take off.*

— Ya está. ¡Qué despegue más suave! ¡Ya estamos volando!

>   *There. What a smooth take-off! We're flying (already)!*

— ¡Ay! ¿Qué fue eso? ¿Una bolsa de aire?

>   *Oh, what was that? An air pocket?*

— ¡Qué va! No hay las llamadas «bolsas de aire».

>   *No! There are no so-called "air pockets."*

— Entonces ¿qué lo que sucede?[1]

>   *Then what is it that's happening?*

— Son corrientes de aire. Se producen estos hundimientos cuando el avión pasa de una a otra corriente.

>   *Air currents. These dips are caused by the plane's passing from one current to another.*

— ¡Me asusté! Me siento mareado (–a).

>   *I was frightened. I feel sick (or nauseated).*

— Abra usted el ventilador (la toma) para que entre más aire fresco. Así. Échese atrás en el asiento, y aflójese el cuello.

>   *Open the ventilator (the air intake) so that more fresh air can come in. Like this. Just sit back in your seat and loosen your collar.*

---

[1] **¿qué sucede** (or **pasa, ocurre**)? *what's the matter?*

— Ya me siento mejor. Ya no necesito las bolsas (or los saquitos) de papel. ¿Me trae una revista?

> *I feel better now. I won't need the paper bags now. Will you bring me a magazine?*

— Me zumban los oídos.

> *My ears are ringing.*

— (Azafata) Tome usted este chicle, señor. Aquí todos lo mascan para evitar la molestia de los oídos.

> (*Stewardess*) *Take this gum, sir. Everyone chews it here to keep their ears from bothering them.*

— Entonces lo probaré porque me duelen un poco los tímpanos. ¿Bostezo y trago mucho?

> *Then I'll try it, because my eardrums are hurting a bit. Should I yawn and swallow a good deal?*

— Sí, y el sonarse (la nariz) ayuda también.

> *Yes, and blowing one's nose also helps.*

— Es verdad. Siento un alivio grande.

> *That's true. It's (lit. "I feel") a great relief.*

— Cuando me necesite, haga el favor de apretar este botón (de tocar este timbre).

> *When you need me, just press this button (ring this bell).*

— Muchas gracias. Veo que aquí están prohibidas las propinas.

> *Thank you. I see that tips are not allowed here.*

— Sí, señor; pero también la manzana estaba prohibida en el paraíso, y sin embargo . . .

> *Yes, sir; but in Paradise the apple was forbidden too, and yet . . .*

— Ya caigo.

> *I understand.*

NOTAS

1.   **sentir,** *to feel*; **me siento mal (cansado, triste, alegre),** *I feel ill (tired, sad, happy)*; **siento frío (calor),** *I feel cold (hot)*; **lo siento (mucho),** *I am (very) sorry*; **marearse,** *to get (sea) sick, nauseated, dizzy.*

2.   **se me tapan los oídos,** *my ears get stopped up*; **oído** *m., (inner) ear, sense of hearing*; **oreja** *f., (outer) ear.*

3.   **chaleco salvavidas** *m., life jacket*; **cenicero** *m., ashtray*; **aeropirata** *m., highjacker*; **secuestrar,** *to highjack*; **rehenes** *m. pl., hostages.*

El almuerzo en el avión

Lunch on the Plane

— Tengo (mucha) hambre. Voy a llamar a la azafata. (Oprimiendo[1] el botón.)

> *I'm (very) hungry. I'll call the stewardess (Pressing the button.)*

— A sus órdenes, señor.

> *Yes, sir.*

— ¿Puede usted decirme cuándo se sirve el almuerzo?

> *Can you tell me when lunch is served?*

— Muy pronto. Ya estamos subiendo las bandejas.[2] ¿Va usted a necesitar un menú especial (vegetariano o kosher)?

> *Very soon. We're already bringing up the trays. Are you going to require a special menu (vegetarian or kosher)?*

— Son ustedes muy amables. Yo como cualquier cosa.

> *You're very thoughtful. I eat anything.*

— Muy bien. En seguida vuelvo.

> *Very well. I'll be right back.*

— ¡Qué comodidad hay en estos viajes! No voy a viajar más que en aeroplano.

> *This is a really comfortable trip (lit. "what convenience there is on these trips")! I'm only going to travel by plane from now on.*

---

[1] **oprimir = apretar**. [2] **bandeja = charola** (also **charol**) in most of Spanish America.

— Ya está, señor. Aquí tiene usted la bandeja: la sopa, la ensalada, un sandwich de pollo, otro de jamón y queso, el café y la fruta.

> *Here you are, sir. Here is your tray: soup, salad, a chicken sandwich, a ham and cheese sandwich, coffee, and fruit.*

— (Comiendo) ¡Qué almuerzo más abundante y más rico!

> *(Eating) This lunch is really delicious — and generous, too.*

— ¡Buen provecho!

> *I hope you enjoy it!*

— Gracias. ¿Me trae usted un poco más de café?

> *Thank you. Will you bring me a little more coffee?*

— Con mucho gusto.

> *With pleasure.*

— Y un poco de agua caliente. El café está muy cargado.

> *And a little hot water. The coffee is very strong.*

— Voy a ver si hay.

> *I'll see if there is any.*

— (Media hora más tarde) Ya no queda nada. Puede usted llevarse la bandeja. He perdido el apetito.

> *(Half an hour later) There's nothing more left. You may remove the tray. I've lost my appetite.*

— (¡Qué raro!)

> *(How strange!)*

NOTAS

On sitting down at a table where others are dining, or on leaving the table, one says: **¡buen provecho!** or **¡que aproveche!** *I hope you will enjoy it* (lit. "may it benefit you"). On leaving a room or a person one says: **con (su) permiso**, *excuse me* (lit. "with your permission").

El viaje por barco

The Boat Trip

■ **Reservando el pasaje**   *Reserving Passage*

— ¿Cuándo sale el próximo barco para Buenos Aires?
When does the next boat leave for Buenos Aires?

— De hoy en ocho días sale el *Argentina*.
The Argentina *sails a week from today.*

— ¿Puede usted reservarme pasaje de segunda clase o de clase turista?
Can you reserve second-class or tourist passage for me?

— De clase turista me queda sólo la cama (or litera) alta del camarote quince, en la cubierta C.
In tourist the only thing I have left is the upper berth in stateroom fifteen, on C deck.

— Hace dos años tuve un camarote en la cubierta D, clase tercera. ¡Figúrese!
Two years ago I had a stateroom on D deck, third class. Imagine!

— Pero ¿por qué viajó usted en tercera?
But why did you travel in third?

— Porque no había cuarta.
Because there was no fourth.

— ¡Ah, vamos! Ya comprendo.
Oh, yes. I see.

— ¿Se puede ver el plano del vapor?
> *May I see the plan of the ship?*

— Sí, señor. Éste es. Todos estos camarotes están tomados desde hace un mes.[1]
> *Yes, sir. This is it. All these staterooms have been taken for a month now.*

— ¿Cuánto cuesta el pasaje?
> *How much is the fare?*

— Seiscientos dólares, más los impuestos.
> *Six hundred plus the taxes.*

— Está bien. Lo tomaré. ¿Va directo el vapor o hace escalas?
> *All right. I'll take it. Does the boat go directly or does it make stops?*

— Hace varias escalas. Toca en los puertos de Rio de Janeiro, Santos, y Montevideo.
> *It makes several stops. It touches at the ports of Rio de Janeiro, Santos, and Montevideo.*

— ¿Cuánto tiempo dura la travesía?
> *How long does the trip (lit. "crossing") take?*

— Unos veinte días si no hay tormenta.
> *About twenty days if there's no storm.*

— No me hable de tormenta, que en seguida me mareo.
> *Don't mention storms, because I get seasick in no time.*

— Si no le agrada la cama alta, puede hablar con el contador a ver si se la cambia.
> *If you don't like the upper berth, you can speak to the purser to see if he'll change it for you.*

— Muy bien. Mañana voy a hacer visar mi pasaporte.
> *Fine. Tomorrow I'm going to get a visa on my passport.*

---

[1] § 57*b*.

— Haga el favor de traerlo cuando venga a sacar el boleto.

Bring it when you come to get your ticket, please.

— A propósito ¿puede usted decirme dónde está el consulado de la Argentina?

By the way, can you tell me where the Argentine consulate is?

— Con mucho gusto. Le apuntaré la dirección en esta tarjeta. Las horas son de dos a cinco.

Certainly. I'll jot down the address for you on this card. The hours are from two to five.

— Iré ahora mismo. Muchísimas gracias.

I'll go right away. Thank you very much.

— No hay de qué.

Don't mention it.

NOTAS

1. Names of boats and rivers are masculine because **vapor** or **barco** *m.* and **río** *m.* are understood: **el Magdalena**, *the Magdalena* (*river*), etc.

2. **contador** *m.*, *purser* = **sobrecargo** = **comisario** (Arg.).

Sacando la visa

Getting a Visa

— Buenos días. ¿Está el cónsul?
How do you do? Is the consul in?

— Está ocupado en este momento. ¿Qué es lo que deseaba usted?
He's busy just now. What is it you wished?

— Vengo a que me vise el pasaporte.
I've come to have him give me a visa for my passport.

— Entonces yo le puedo atender. Siéntese.
In that case I can attend to you. Just sit down.

— Gracias. Creo que tengo todos los documentos.
Thank you. I believe I have all the documents.

— A ver: dos fotografías, certificados de vacuna, médico, de policía (or de buena conducta) . . .
Let's see: two photographs, certificates of vaccination, health, police . . .

— ¿Hace falta otra cosa?
Is anything else necessary?

— Nada. Está bien. Antes pedíamos también la partida de nacimiento, pero ahora no.
Nothing. This is fine. We used to require a birth certificate, but not now.

— Menos mal, porque no la tengo.
That's a good thing, because I don't have one.

— (Escribiendo a máquina) ¿Cómo se llama usted?
> (*Typing*) *What is your name?*

— Juan (–a) Moreno (para servirle).
> John (*Jean*) *Moreno.*

— ¿Cuándo nació usted?
> *When were you born?*

— Nací el 6 (seis) de julio de 1940 (mil novecientos cuarenta).
> *I was born July 6, 1940.*

— ¿Soltero (–a), casado (–a), viudo (–a), o divorciado (–a)?
> *Single, married, widowed, or divorced?*

— Soltero (–a).
> *Single.*

— ¿Cuánto tiempo piensa permanecer en nuestro país? ¿Viaje de negocios o de recreo?
> *How long do you plan to stay in our country? Business or pleasure trip?*

— Seis semanas o dos meses. Viaje de recreo.
> *Six weeks or two months. Pleasure trip.*

— Bien. Aquí tiene su pasaporte. Son cien pesos.
> *Fine. Here is your passport. It's one hundred pesos.*

— Tome usted. Muchas gracias.
> *Here you are. Thank you very much.*

— A usted. ¡Feliz viaje!
> *Thank you. Have a nice trip!*

NOTAS

The months of the year are: **enero** (*January*), **febrero** (*February*), **marzo** (*March*). **abril** (*April*), **mayo** (*May*), **junio** (*June*), **julio** (*July*), **agosto** (*August*), **septiembre** (*September*), **octubre** (*October*), **noviembre** (*November*), **diciembre** (*December*).

Sacando el pasaje

Buying a Ticket

— Buenos días. Aquí me tiene otra vez.
How do you do? Here I am again.

— ¿Ya consiguió todas las visas? Permítame . . .
Have you got all your visas? May I . . .

— Aquí está todo. Y aquí está el dinero.
Everything's here. And here's the money.

— Y éste es su boleto. Guárdelo en su cartera.
And here's your ticket. Keep it in your wallet.

— ¿Para qué sirven estas etiquetas?
What are these labels for?

— En ellas puede usted escribir su nombre y el número de su camarote.
You can write your name and the number of your stateroom on them.

— ¿Y después pegarlas en las maletas?
And then stick them on the suitcases?

— Eso es. ¿Cuánto equipaje tiene usted?
That's right. How much luggage do you have?

— Dos maletas y mi cartera. Nada más.
Two suitcases and my briefcase. Nothing else.

— Entonces no tendrá usted que pagar exceso.
Then you won't have to pay for overweight.

— ¿A qué hora puedo ir a bordo?
What time can I board the ship?

— Desde las tres de la tarde en adelante.
From three in the afternoon on.

— ¿A qué hora ha de salir[1] el barco?
What time is she sailing?

— A las cinco en punto, si no se retrasa.[2]
At five sharp, unless she's behind time.

— ¿Es fácil que se retrase?
Is she likely to be late?

— Es posible. Todo depende de la marea.
It's possible. It all depends on the tide.

— ¡Ah, se me olvidaba! Quería preguntarle qué tonelaje tiene el barco.
Oh, I nearly forgot. I wanted to ask what the boat's tonnage is.

— Treinta mil toneladas. Es un barco muy marinero.
Thirty thousand tons. She's very seaworthy.

— ¡Pues no faltaba más! Adiós.
Well, I should hope so (lit. "nothing else would be lacking")! Good-bye.

— Si no lo (la) veo en el muelle, ¡feliz viaje!
If I don't see you at the pier, bon voyage.

NOTAS

1.   **cartera** *f.*, *pocketbook, billfold, briefcase*; **portamonedas** *m.*, (*coin*) *purse*; **bolsa** *f.*, (*lady's*) *purse*; **bolsillo** *m.*, *pocket* = **bolsa** (Span. Am.)

2.   **marea alta**, *high tide*; **marea baja**, *low tide*.

[1] § 56c.   [2] **se retrasa** = **se atrasa**.

A bordo

On Board

— Hace tres días que navegamos[1] y cada vez me gusta más el mar.

> *We've been sailing for three days and I like the ocean more every day.*

— A mí también me encanta viajar por mar. ¡Pero mi pobre hermano (hermana)!

> *I love to travel by sea, too. But my poor brother (sister)!*

— ¿Qué le pasa? Hace dos días que no lo (la) veo.[1]

> *What's the matter with him (her)? I haven't seen him (her) for two days.*

— Es que está mareado (–a) y no sale de su camarote.

> *It's because he (she) is seasick and can't leave his (her) stateroom.*

— Pues el mejor remedio contra el mareo es quedarse sobre cubierta. El aire le haría bien.

> *Well, the best remedy for seasickness is to stay on deck. The air would do him (her) good.*

— Hace tiempo que se lo estoy diciendo[1] pero no me hace caso.

> *I've been telling him (her) that for some time but he (she) pays no attention to me.*

[1] 57b.

— ¡Pobrecito (–a)! ¿No va al comedor siquiera?

> *Poor fellow (girl)! Doesn't he (she) even go to the dining room?*

— Fue una vez. De vez en cuando pide un sandwich al camarero.

> *He (she) went once. Occasionally he (she) asks the steward to bring him (her) a sandwich.*

— Ya se aliviará. Todo es acostumbrarse.

> *He'll (she'll) recover, (don't worry). It's a matter of getting used to it.*

— ¡Ojalá! Porque si no, se le echa a perder el viaje.

> *I hope so. Because otherwise his (her) trip will be spoiled.*

— ¡Qué viento sopla aquí! ¡Y qué frío hace!

> *There's quite a wind blowing here! And it's really cold!*

— ¡Y cuando salimos hacía tanto calor!

> *And when we left, it was so hot.*

— Es que los meses de verano en los Estados Unidos son los de invierno en la América del Sur (al sur del ecuador).

> *It's because the summer months in the United States are the winter months in South America (south of the equator).*

— Pues espero que el invierno de Buenos Aires no sea tan riguroso como el de Nueva York.

> *I hope that the winter in Buenos Aires is not as bad as in New York.*

— Ni mucho menos. . . . Pero con este viento no se puede pasear.

> *It doesn't come near it. . . . But nobody can walk in this wind.*

— Vamos a entrar en el salón a jugar una partida de bridge.

> *Let's go into the lounge and play a game of bridge.*

— Con mucho gusto. Pero hace tiempo que no juego.[1]

> *I'd like to. But I haven't played for some time.*

— De todas maneras juega usted mejor que yo.
In any case you play better than I do.

NOTAS

silla de cubierta *f., deck chair*; **el ancla** *f., anchor*; **atracar,**
to draw alongside; **babor** *m., port (left) side*; **balancearse (moverse,**
bailar), *to rock, roll*; **bodega** *f., hold*; **cabecear,** *to pitch*; **carga** *f.,*
freight, cargo; **Cruz del Sur** *f., Southern Cross*; **hélice** *f., propeller*;
ir a tierra, *to go ashore*; **irse a pique (hundirse),** *to sink*; **pasamano** *m.*
or **plancha** *f., gangplank*; **popa** *f., stern*; **proa** *f., bow*; **salvavidas** *m.,*
life preserver; **muelle** *m., wharf, pier* = **malecón** *m.*; **dársena** *f., inner*
harbor, dock; **dique seco** *m., dry dock*; **astillero** *m., shipyard.*

Una partida de naipes (or cartas)

A Game of Cards

— ¿Echamos una partida de naipes?
  Shall we play a game of cards?

— Con mucho gusto, pero no somos más que tres.
  I'd be glad to, but there are only three of us.

— Podríamos hacer un muerto.
  We could have a dummy.

— Más vale buscar un cuarto. Precisamente aquí viene mi compañero de camarote.
  It would be better to look for a fourth. And right here is my roommate.

— Empecemos. Echemos suertes para ver quién da.
  Let's begin. Let's draw to see who deals.

— Usted da, porque tiene la carta más alta.
  You deal, because you have the highest card.

— Ya las barajé. ¿Quiere usted cortar?
  I've already shuffled them. Do you want to cut?

— Ya está. ¿Quien abre (or sale)? ¿Qué dice usted?
  There. Who opens? What do you bid?

— Paso.
  I pass.

— (Jugando) Yo gano esta baza.
  (Playing) I take this trick.

— ¿Qué es eso de fallarme usted[1] el rey de bastos?

> *What do you mean by trumping my king of clubs?*

— Claro. Cuando no puedo servir del mismo palo, echo triunfo.

> *Obviously. When I can't follow suit, I play a trump.*

— Ya me la pagará. Juegue usted.

> *I'll get even with you (lit. "you'll pay me for it"). You play.*

— Ahí va. Ya tenemos diez bazas y me da el corazón que hemos ganado.

> *There. We already have ten tricks and I have a feeling that we've won.*

— ¿Cuántos tàntos (or puntos) tienen?

> *What's your score (lit. "how many points do you have")?*

— No sé, pero tenemos todos los honores.

> *I don't know, but we have all the honors.*

— Aquí donde ustedes nos ven, mi compañero y yo ahora nos desquitamos.[2]

> *Believe it or not (lit. "here where you see us"), my partner and I will now get even.*

— A usted le toca dar.

> *It's your turn to deal.*

NOTAS

1. Some necessary vocabulary: **rey** *m,. king;* **reina** *f.,* *queen;* **sota** *f., jack;* **bastos,** *clubs;* **copas,** *hearts;* **espadas,** *spades;* **oros,** *diamonds;* **baraja** *f., deck* = **mazo de naipes** (Arg.) *m.;* **barajar,** *to shuffle.*

---

[1] **fallar** = **echar triunfo.**   [2] **desquitarse** = **tomar revancha.**

2.   **me da el corazón** = **me late** (Mex.) = **me palpita** or **tengo un pálpito** (Arg.) = **me tinca** (Chile), etc.; **una corazonada**, *a feeling, hunch*.

3.   If the game comes out even, one says it's a tie (**empate** *m.*).

El médico

The Doctor

— ¿Puede usted llamar a un doctor?[1] No me siento bien. Estoy enfermo –a).

> *Can you call a doctor? I don't feel well. I'm sick.*

— Bien, señor. ¿Quiere un especialista?

> *All right, sir. Would you like a specialist?*

— No hace falta. Cualquier médico, pero uno que hable[2] inglés, si es posible.

> *That's not necessary. Any doctor, but one who speaks English, if that's possible.*

— (Llamando por teléfono) ¿Está el doctor Álvarez?

> *(Telephoning) Is Doctor Alvarez in?*

— A sus órdenes (or servidor or para servirle).

> *I am Dr. Alvarez (lit. "at your service").*

— ¿Podría usted pasar por la Calle Mayor, número 20, ahora mismo? Tenemos un (–a) enfermo (–a).

> *Could you call at 20 Main Street right away? We have a sick person.*

— De un momento a otro estará aquí.

> *He'll be here any minute.*

— (Cuando llega el médico) Conteste, por favor, estas breves preguntas preliminares: ¿qué edad tiene? si hay o no incidencia clínica de diabetes o asma en su familia; si es usted

---

[1] **médico** *m.*; *doctor* = **doctor**.   [2] Subjunctive.   § 46.

alérgico a algún antibiótico; si ha sido operado recientemente; si tiene presión alta de la sangre; si ha sufrido de fiebre tifoidea, escarlatina o alguna otra enfermedad usual en su infancia. . . .

> (*When the doctor arrives*). *Could you answer these brief preliminary questions: How old are you? Is there any incidence of diabetes or asthma in your family? Are you allergic to any antibiotic? Have you been operated on recently? Do you have high blood pressure? Have you had typhoid fever, scarlet fever, or any other illness common in childhood?*

— Un momento, doctor. No puedo contestar todas estas preguntas a la vez. Lo único que importa es que tengo treinta y cinco años; estoy algo anémico y las únicas enfermedades infantiles que recuerdo son el sarampión y la amigdalitis.

> *Just a minute, doctor. I can't answer everything at once. The only important thing is that I am thirty-five years old; I am somewhat anaemic and the only childhood diseases that I remember are measles and tonsillitis.*

— Bien, bien, su piel tiene aspecto saludable. Entonces, ¿de qué se trata?

> *Fine, fine. Your skin looks healthy. Well then, what seems to be the matter?*

— En general no me encuentro bien estos días. Tengo náuseas y escalofríos; me siento débil; me duele todo el cuerpo, pero sobre todo tengo dolores en la espalda, en la cabeza y también en la garganta.

> *I don't feel well in general these days. I'm nauseous and have chills; I feel weak; all my body hurts, but mainly I have pains in my back, my head, and my throat.*

— ¿Ha hecho usted gárgaras cada dos horas?

> *Have you gargled every two hours?*

— Sí, pero me siento peor que antes.

> *Yes, but I feel worse than before.*

— ¿También tiene calambres o estreñimiento?

Do you also have cramps or constipation?

— Sí, tengo dolores espasmódicos en el estómago.

Yes, I have spasmodic pains in my stomach.

— ¿Desde cuánto tiempo sufre usted estos dolores inter-
mitentes? ¿Tiene fiebre?

*How long have you had these intermittent pains? Do you
have any fever?*

— Eso no lo sé, porque no tengo termómetro.

I can't tell because I don't have a thermometer.

— Pues, por favor abra la boca y saque la lengua. No, tiene
temperatura normal, treinta y siete grados.[3] Por favor tosa
usted y después respire hondo. Bien, ahora quítese toda la
ropa. Otra cosa: hay que mandarme una muestra de su orina
y sus heces. La sangre la tomaremos ahora mismo.

*Well, then, open your mouth and lower your tongue please.
No, you have a normal temperature, thirty-seven degrees.
Cough please and then breathe deeply. Fine, now take off
your clothing. Another matter: you have to send me a sample
of your urine and your feces. We'll take your blood now.*

— Me va a pinchar, ¿verdad?

You're going to give me a shot, right?

— Sí, pero no es nada. También voy a darle una inyección de
un antiespasmódico.

*Yes, but that's nothing. I'm also going to give you an
antispasmodic injection.*

— ¿No puede usted recetarme una medicina oral — unas
píldoras o comprimidos?

Can't you prescribe an oral medicine — tablets or pills?

— No tenga usted cuidado. Esto no causa ningún dolor. Y
después usted debe acostarse y descansar por lo menos unos

[3] 37° is normal human temperature centigrade.

días. Y sobre todo, no se preocupe. No creo que eso sea[4] nada serio.

> *Don't worry. This doesn't hurt at all. And afterwards you must go to bed. And above all, don't worry. I don't believe that this is anything serious.*

— Entonces, ¿cuándo puedo continuar mi viaje?

> *Then when can I go on with my trip?*

— Le diré cuando lo vea[5] dentro de una semana. Llame a mi consultorio[6] o a la clínica y haga una cita.

> *I'll tell you when I see you within a week. Call at my office or the clinic and make an appointment.*

NOTAS

1.   **horas de consulta**, *office hours*; **despacho** *m.*, *office*; **oficina** *f.*, (*larger*) *office*; **bufete** *m.*, *lawyer's office.*

2.   The following are parts of the body to which you may need to refer, prefixing the words by **tengo dolores en**: **el tobillo** *the ankle*; **el brazo** *the arm*; **el hueso** *the bone*; **los intestinos** *the intestines*; **el seno** *the breast*; **el pecho** *the chest*; **la clavícula** *the collar bone*; **la oreja** *the ear* (*exterior parts*); **el oído** *the ear* (*hearing*); **el dedo** *the finger*; **el pie** *the foot*; **las glándulas** *the glands*; **la mano** *the hand.*

3.   Other useful expressions: **agotamiento** *m.*, *exhaustion*; **artritis** *f.*, *arthritis*; **ataque de corazón**, *heart attack*; **estar acatarrado** (**del pecho, de la cabeza**), *to have a cold* (*in the chest, in the head*) = **tener un constipado** (Spain); **estar embarazada**, *to be pregnant* = **estar esperando un bebé**; **estar a régimen** (**dieta**), *to be on a diet*; **enfermera** *f.*, *nurse*; **microbio** *m.*, *germ*; **perder un período de menstruación**, *to miss a menstrual period*; **pulmonía** *f.*, *pneumonia*; **gripe** *f.*, *flu*; **paperas** *f.*, *mumps*; **sarampión** *m.*, *measles*; **tener una enfermedad** (**leve, grave, crónica, aguda, contagiosa**) *to have a* (*mild serious chronic acute contagious*) *sickness*. **Recetas** *prescriptions* (**tome una, dos, tres cucharaditas cada cuatro horas**, *take one, two,*

---

[4] Subjunctive. § 43*a*.   [5] Subjunctive. § 45*b*.   [6] **consultorio** *m.* = **sala de consulta** = **consulta** *f.*

three teaspoonsful every four hours); **cucharada** *tablespoonsful*; **tome este jarabe con un vaso de agua** *take this syrup with a glass of water*; *usted tiene que ayunar antes del chequeo general* (**reconoci- miento general** Spain) *you must fast before the general check-up.*

Vocabulario médico

Medical Vocabulary

■ **Las partes del cuerpo**   *Parts of the Body*

la rodilla	*knee*	la piel	*skin*
la pierna	*leg*	la espina dorsal	*spine*
el labio	*lip*	el estómago	*stomach*
el hígado	*liver*	el tendón	*tendon*
el pulmón	*lung*	el muslo	*thigh*
la boca	*mouth*	la garganta	*throat*
el músculo	*muscle*	el dedo del pie	*toe*
el cuello	*neck*	la lengua	*tongue*
el nervio	*nerve*	las amígdalas	*tonsils*
la nariz	*nose*	las venas	*veins*
la costilla	*rib*	la muñeca	*wrist*
el hombro	*shoulder*		

■ **Primeros auxilios**   *First Aid Department*

¡Socorro!	*Help!*
Busque un médico (rápido).	*Get me a doctor, (quick).*
Tengo:	*I have:*
una ampolla, un cardenal	*a blister, a bruise*
una quemadura, un hueso roto	*a burn, a broken bone*
una cortadura, una picadura de insecto (avispa, abeja)	*a cut, an insect bite (hornet, bee or wasp)*
una infección, un bulto	*infection, lump*
una inflamación, una herida	*a swelling, a wound*

una ceniza (en el ojo)	*a cinder in my eye*
He tragado (comido) algo venenoso.	*I have swallowed (eaten) something poisonous.*

Usted se ha:	*You have:*
roto, dislocado	*broken, dislocated*
fracturado, distendido	*fractured, pulled*
torcido, herido . . .	*twisted, wounded . . .*

(see previous pages for names of parts of body)

Voy a ponerle:	*I am going to apply:*
una curita, un esparadrapo	*a bandaid, adhesive tape*
una venda, un antiséptico	*a bandage, an antiseptic*
un ungüento	*a salve*
Voy a llevarle (la) al hospital.	*I am going to take you to the hospital.*
Le voy a hacer una radiografía.	*I am going to take an X-ray.*
Se lo voy a enyesar, entablilar.	*I am going to put it in a cast, splint.*
Le voy a recetar un somnífero, un calmante.	*I am going to prescribe a sleeping pill, a sedative.*

El dentista

The Dentist

— Buenos días. Vengo a que me señale hora.
How do you do? I've come to make an appointment.

— Puede usted pasar ahora mismo.
You may come right in now.

— Gracias. Tengo una muela picada (or cariada) que me hace sufrir mucho. No puedo mascar.
Thanks. I have a cavity (lit. "decayed molar") that gives me a great deal of pain. I can't chew.

— Vamos a ver. Eche usted la cabeza para atrás y abra bien la boca.
Let's see it. Put your head back and open your mouth wide.

— Ésta es la que me duele. El dolor me vuelve loco (–a).
This is the one that hurts. The pain is driving me crazy.

— No veo caries. Ah sí, pero es una cavidad (or picadura) muy pequeña.
I don't see any cavity. Oh yes, but it's a very small cavity.

— Entonces no tendrá usted que sacar la muela.
Then you won't have to extract the tooth.

— ¡Qué va! Esto no duele nada. Le voy a poner una inyección para anestesiar la encía.
Oh no! This won't hurt at all. I'm going to give you an injection to deaden the gum.

— ¡Ojalá que no me duela! Estoy muy nervioso (–a).
> *I hope it doesn't hurt. I'm very nervous.*

— ¿Con qué quiere usted que se la tape (or empaste): con porcelana, con oro, con plata, o con platino?
> *What would you like to have it filled with: porcelain, gold, silver, or amalgam?*

— Con lo que a usted le parezca mejor. No quiero que se me caiga[1] el empaste a los pocos días.[2]
> *With whatever you think best. I don't want the filling to fall out in a few days.*

— No se preocupe usted. Le durará diez años.
> *Don't worry. You'll have it ten years.*

— A propósito, aquí traigo la placa[3] provisional de mi mamá para que se la componga.
> *By the way, I've brought my mother's temporary plate for you to fix.*

— Muy bien, ¿sabe usted si ella está cepillándola con la pasta dentífrica que yo recomendé?
> *Fine, do you know if she is brushing it with the toothpaste I recommended?*

— ¿La que tiene fluoruro? En seguida después de cada comida.
> *The one that has fluoride? Right after each meal.*

— Pues debe de[3] tener ahora una sonrisa tan hermosa como cualquier modelo en la televisión.
> *Then she must have a beautiful smile now — like some television model.*

---

[1] Subjunctive of **caer**. § 67, 2.   [2] **a los pocos días**=**después de unos pocos días**.
[3] See also future indicative of probability. § 40*d*

NOTAS

1. **clínica dental** *f.*, *dentist's office*.

2. **tapar,** *to fill* = **empastar** = **emplomar** (Arg.) = **orificar** (*to fill with gold*) = **calzar**.

3. **empaste** = **relleno** = **emplomadura** (Arg.) = **tapadura**; **incrustación** *f.*, *inlay*.

4. **placa** or **dentadura inferior (superior)** *f.*, *lower (upper) plate, set*; **puente movible (fijo)** *m.*, *movable (fixed) bridge*; **dientes postizos,** *false teeth*.

En la relojería

At the Watchmaker's

— ¿Puede usted arreglarme este reloj?
  Can you repair this watch?

— Vamos a ver qué tiene.
  Let's see what's wrong with it.

— No anda bien. Un día se adelanta, otro día se atrasa y ahora está parado.
  It doesn't run well. One day it's fast, another day it's slow, and now it's stopped.

— ¿Le da usted cuerda diariamente?
  Do you wind it every day?

— Todos los días. Pero hace poco se me cayó.
  Every day. But I dropped it a short time ago.

— A ver. El muelle no está roto, pero el minutero está algo torcido.
  Let's see. The spring isn't broken, but the minute hand is a little bent.

— ¿Tardaría mucho en componerlo?
  Would it take you very long to fix it?

— Unos dos minutos. En seguida so lo compongo.
  A couple of minutes. I'll fix it right away.

— ¿Cuánto pide usted por ese reloj?
  What are you asking for that watch?

— Éste se lo dejaré (or pondré) a usted en mil pesos. Es muy barato. Me cuesta eso precisamente.

> *I can let you have this one for a thousand pesos. That's just what it cost me.*

— Entonces, ¿dónde está la ganancia?

> *In that case, where's the profit?*

— En las composturas.

> *In the repairs.*

— Pues no me conviene. Bastante tengo con las composturas del mío.

> *Well, that's no use to me. Repairing mine gives me enough trouble.*

— Sí, pero yo garantizo todos mis relojes por dos años.

> *Yes, but I guarantee all my watches for two years.*

— Bueno, cuando necesite otro, ya pasaré por aquí.

> *Well, when I need another, I'll drop in.*

— Eso es. No vaya a otra parte a dejarse robar; venga aquí. Ya está su reloj. Son setenta pesos.

> *Right. Don't go somewhere else to be robbed; come here. Your watch is ready. That's seventy pesos.*

— Páguese de esto. Hasta otro día.

> *Take it out of that. See you some other day.*

— Servidor de usted. A sus órdenes.

> *I'm always here for business.*

— ¡Ah, por poco se me olvida! ¿Puede usted componerme estos lentes? Se me ha roto un cristal.

> *Oh, I nearly forgot! Can you repair these glasses? I've broken a lens.*

— Aquí al lado hay un óptico muy bueno.

> *There's a very good optician next door.*

— Muchas gracias. Sin lentes no veo nada.
Thank you. I can't see a thing without glasses.

NOTAS

1. **horario** *m.*, *hour hand*; **secundario** *m.*, *second hand*; **cadenita** *f.*, *chain*; **cifra** *f.*, *number*; **cristal** *m.*, *crystal, glass*; **marcha** *f.*, *movement*; **muestra (esfera)** *f.*, *face*; **poner a la hora (en hora)** *to set*; **tocar el registro**, *to regulate*.

2. **garantizar**, *to guarantee*; **garantir** and **garantar** are occasionally heard in Spanish America.

3. Additional vocabulary: **oculista** *m.*, *oculist*; **cristal** or **lente** *m.*, *lens*; **cóncavo**, *concave*; **convexo**, *convex*; **fuerte**, *strong*; **débil**, *weak*; **miope** or **corto (-a) de vista**, *nearsighted*; **présbita** or **largo (-a) de vista**, *farsighted*; **lentes** *m. pl.*, *eyeglasses* = **anteojos** *m. pl.*, or **gafas** *f. pl.*, *spectacles* (with bows); **armazón** *f.* or **armadura** *f.*, *frame*; **de concha**, *of tortoise shell*.

La zapatería

The Shoe Store

—Quiero un par de zapatos como los que están en el escaparate.

> *I want a pair of shoes like those in the (display) window.*

—Muy bien, señor. ¿Qué número calza usted?

> *Very well, sir. What size do you wear?*

—No me acuerdo.[1] No estoy seguro (–a).

> *I don't remember. I'm not sure.*

—En ese caso le tomaré la medida. Número seis.

> *In that case, I'll take your measurements. Size six.*

—El siete sería más cómodo. Así es que déme el ocho. Los zapatos se hacen para los pies y no los pies para los zapatos.

> *Seven would be more comfortable. So give me an eight.*
> *Shoes are made for feet and not feet for shoes.*

—Tiene usted razón. Pruébese este par. Use el calzador.

> *You're right. Try on this pair. Use the shoehorn.*

—Me están un poco estrechos. Me aprietan en el empeine.

> *They're a little narrow. They pinch me at the instep.*

—Haga usted el favor de probarse éstos. Déjeme ponerles polvos.

> *Try these on please. Let me put some powder in them.*

---

[1] no me acuerdo del número = no recuerdo el número.

— Éstos me parecen anchos y me quedan un poco largos.

> *These seem too wide and are a little too long.*

— Menos mal. Así no le saldrán callos.

> *That's good. That way you won't get any corns.*

— En casa tengo unos zapatos de cuero fuerte que me lastiman mucho los pies.

> *At home I have a pair of shoes made of hard leather that really hurt my feet.*

— Eso tiene arreglo. Metiéndolos (or Poniéndolos en) la horma los ensancho[2] en seguida.

> *That can be remedied. By putting them on the last, I can stretch them right now.*

— La próxima vez que venga, los traeré.

> *The next time, I'll bring them.*

— Muy bien. ¿Quiere usted llevarse puestos los zapatos nuevos?

> *Fine. Do you want to leave the new shoes on?*

— Sí. Me los llevo puestos. Haga el favor de enviarme los viejos a esta dirección.

> *Yes. I'll leave them on. Would you send the old ones to this address.*

— Se los envuelvo y se los mando esta misma tarde.

> *I'll wrap them up and send them this afternoon.*

— Adiós. Muy buenas.

> *Good afternoon.*

— A sus órdenes. Que le vaya bien.

> *Good afternoon.*

---

[2] **ensanchar,** *to widen, stretch* = **aflojar** (lit. "to loosen") = **agrandar.**

NOTAS

1. **escaparate** *m.*, (*display*) *window* is used less in Spanish America than **vidriera** *f.*, or **aparador** *m.* (Mex.), or **vitrina** *f.* (Arg., Chile, etc.). In Spanish America **escaparate** is often equivalent to **armario** *m.*, *wardrobe, closet.*

2. **estrecho**, *narrow* = **angosto**; **apretado**, *tight*; ¿**qué ancho?** *what width?*

3. **dedo (del pie)** *m.*, *toe*; **dedo gordo**, *big toe*; **talón** *m.*, *heel* (of foot); **tacón** *m.*, *heel* (of shoe) = **taco** (Arg.).

4. **tela** *f.*, *cloth*, **raso** *m.*, *satin*; **zapatillas plateadas (doradas)**, *silver* (*gold*) *slippers*; **chanclos** (Spain) *m.*, *rubbers, galoshes* = **zapatos de goma** (Span. Am.) = **zapatos de hule** (Mex.); **sandalias** *f. pl.*, *sandals* = **guaraches** *m.* (Mex.) = **caites** *m.* (Cent. Am.) = **ojotas** *f.* (Chile).

Taller de compostura de zapatos

Shoe Repair Shop

— ¿Puede usted componer todos estos zapatos?
Can you repair all these shoes?

— (El zapatero de viejo or el zapatero remendón) Aquí se compone cualquier cosa.
(The cobbler) We can repair anything here.

— Bueno. Ponga usted medias suelas a este par.
All right. Will you put half soles on this pair?

— ¿Las quiere usted delgadas o gruesas?
Do you want them thin or heavy?

— Ni lo uno ni lo otro. Un término medio.
Neither. Just medium.

— «Ni calvo ni con dos pelucas», como decía mi padre.
"Neither bald nor with two wigs," as my father used to say.

— Eso es. Póngales usted tacones de goma.
Right. Put rubber heels on them.

— Mire usted. A éstos les faltan cordones.[1]
And look. These have no laces.

— Ponga usted todo lo que falte. Cuidado con éstos de tacones franceses, que tienen la piel sumamente fina.
Supply everything that's missing. Be careful of the ones with the French heels because the leather is very delicate.

---

[1] **cordones** *m. pl., shoestring, laces* = **cintas** *f. pl., ribbons.*

— Pierda usted cuidado, señora. Aquí se arreglan desde las botas más fuertes y gruesas hasta las zapatillas de raso más finas.

> *Don't worry, madam. We handle everything, from the strongest and heaviest boots to the most delicate satin slippers.*

— Ya me dijo el gerente del hotel que trabaja usted muy bien.

> *The manager of the hotel told me that you do excellent work.*

— Y todos los parroquianos se quedan contentos. Todavía no se ha quejado nadie. Sería usted la primera.

> *And all the customers are satisfied. Nobody has complained yet. You would be the first.*

— ¡Dios me libre! ¿Para cuándo estará todo esto?

> *Heaven forbid! When will all these be finished?*

— Estoy ocupadísimo en estos días. Pero los tendrá usted para el sábado.

> *I'm very busy just now. But you'll have them by Saturday.*

— Sin falta ¿eh? Los necesito a más tardar para el domingo.

> *Don't disappoint me. I need them by Sunday at the latest.*

— No se preocupe, señora. Aquí hay mucha formalidad.

> *Don't worry, madam. We're very reliable here.*

— Eso lo veremos el sábado.

> *We'll see about that on Saturday.*

— Hasta el sábado. ¡Que usted lo pase bien!²

> *I'll see you on Saturday. Good-bye.*

NOTAS

For **formal**, *serious-minded*, *reliable*, **serio, -a** is often used with the same meaning: **es una tienda seria**, *it's a reliable store*; but **traje de etiqueta** *m.*, *formal clothes*; **de mucha etiqueta**, *formal =* **formalista**.

---

² ¡que usted lo pase bien!=¡que usted la pase bien! (Mex.).

En la sastrería

At the Tailor's

— Buenos días. Quiero que me haga usted un traje (a medida).
> *How do you do? I'd like to have a suit made (to order).*

— ¿Qué género desea usted? ¿Género inglés o del país?
> *What material would you like? English or domestic?*

— Quiero género inglés. ¿Se pueden ver las telas importadas?
> *I'd like English material. May I see the imported materials?*

— Tenemos un buen surtido. Mire este paño que acabamos de recibir. Es una tela muy fina y de mucha duración. Es el mejor casimir que tenemos.
> *We have a good stock. Look at this cloth which we've just received. It's excellent material and it wears well. It's the finest worsted we have.*

— Me gusta ésta que es más gruesa. ¿Cuánto cobra usted por un traje de esta tela?
> *I like this heavier stuff. How much do you charge for a suit of this material?*

— Ochocientos pesos por la tela y otros ochocientos por la hechura. Y es una ganga. Un traje de este género no se desforma nunca.
> *Eight hundred pesos for the material and another eight hundred for the tailoring. And that's a bargain. A suit of this material never gets out of shape.*

— ¿Puedo tenerlo dentro de ocho días?
> *Can I have it in a week?*

— Es poco tiempo pero haremos un esfuerzo.

> *That's not long, but we'll make an effort.*

— Entonces ¿quiere usted tomarme la medida?

> *Then do you want to take my measurements?*

— En seguida . . . Ya está. ¿Cómo quiere usted el saco (or la chaqueta)?

> *Right away. . . . There you are. . . . How do you want the coat?*

— Quiero saco recto. No me gusta el saco cruzado.

> *I want it single-breasted. I don't like a double-breasted coat.*

— Muy bien. Como es usted algo gordo, le conviene el saco recto. Y le pondremos forro(s) de seda.

> *Fine. Being a little heavier, you'll look better in the single-breasted. And we'll put in a silk lining.*

— ¿Cuándo vengo a probarme el traje (or para la prueba)?

> *When do I come for the fitting?*

— Puede usted venir el jueves a las siete de la tarde.

> *You can come Thursday at seven in the evening.*

— ¿Cómo quiere usted que se lo pague?

> *How do you want me to pay for it?*

— En cuanto al pago, no corre prisa. Únicamente le ruego que pague un pequeño anticipo.

> *There's no hurry about the payment. Only I'd like to ask you to make a small down payment.*

— Con mucho gusto. Aquí lo tiene usted.

> *Sure. Here you are.*

— Y aquí tiene usted el recibo. Hasta el jueves.

> *And here's your receipt. I'll see you Thursday.*

— ¿Puede usted despacharme? Tengo prisa.
> *Can you wait on me? I'm in a hurry.*

— Sí, señor. ¿Qué es lo que deseaba usted?
> *Yes, sir. What did you want?*

— ¿Tiene usted un traje hecho que me siente (or quede) bien?
> *Have you a ready-made suit that will fit me?*

— Vamos a ver la medida. Treinta y siete. Haga usted el favor de probarse éste.
> *Let's see your size. Thirty-seven. Would you try this one on, please.*

— Éste no me queda bien. Estoy hecho una lástima.
> *This doesn't fit me. I look terrible (in it).*

— ¡Qué va! Mírese al espejo, por favor. Vuélvase usted.
> *Nonsense! Look at yourself in the mirror. Turn around.*

— ¿No ve que aquí detrás me hace muchas arrugas? Y los pantalones están muy ajustados.
> *It wrinkles here in the back, right? And the trousers are too tight.*

— ¿Le gusta este gris rayado?[1]
> *Do you like this gray striped one?*

— No me gusta el dibujo. A ver aquel azul a cuadros.
> *I don't like the design. May I see that blue checked one?*

— Éste sí le va a gustar. Póngase el saco. Voy a abotonárselo. Dése vuelta.
> *You will like this one. Slip on the coat. I'll button it for you. Turn around.*

— Es verdad. Me gusta mucho. ¿Cuánto vale?
> *That's right. I like it very much. What's the price of it?*

---

[1] **rayado** = listado.

— Mil doscientos pesos por el traje completo: pantalones, saco y chaleco.

> *Twelve hundred pesos for the complete suit: trousers, coat, and vest.*

— Las mangas me están un poco largas.

> *The sleeves are a little long.*

— Eso se arregla en media hora. También pondremos un poco más de algodón en esta hombrera.

> *That can be fixed in half an hour. And we'll also put in a little more cotton in this shoulder (pad).*

— ¿Es verdad que mi amigo le debe por un traje que compró hace seis años?

> *Is it true that my friend still owes you for the suit he bought here six years ago?*

— Sí, señor. ¿Quiere usted pagar la cuenta?

> *Yes, sir. Do you wish to settle the account?*

— No, pero quisiera comprar este traje bajo las mismas condiciones.

> *No, but I'd like to buy this suit on the same terms.*

— Eso es imposible, pero le puedo abrir cuenta para que lo pague a plazos.[2]

> *That's impossible, but I can open an account for you, so that you may pay for it in installments.*

— Muy bien. Entonces le pago el anticipo.

> *That's fine. Then I'll make a down payment.*

— En la caja, si me hace usted el favor.

> *At the cashier's desk, if you please.*

NOTAS

1. **traje** *m.* = **terno** *m.*, (*three-piece suit*) = **flux** or, occasionally, **flus** (Span. Am.) *m.*; **americana** *f.*, *coat* = **saco** *m.* = **chaqueta** *f.*,

---

[2] **a plazos = en abonos**.

pantalón or **pantalones** *m.*, *pants*; **chaleco** *m.*, *vest*; **abrigo** *m.*, *overcoat*.

2. **género** *m.*, *goods* = **tela** *f.*, *cloth*, *material* = **paño** = **tejido**; **de color liso**, *of a solid color*.

3. **ganga** = **ocasión** = **pichincha** (Arg.).

4. **anticipo** *m.* = **señal** *f.* = **enganche** (Mex.) *m.*

5. **estoy hecho una lástima** = **estoy hecho una facha** = **un mamarracho**.

6. **abotonar** = **abrochar**; **desabotonar**, *unbutton* = **desabrochar**.

7. **quitarse la americana** (Spain), *to take off one's coat* = **sacarse el saco** (Span. Am.).

En casa de la modista

At the Dressmaker's

— Buenas tardes, señora. Ya ve usted que soy muy puntual.
Good afternoon. I'm very punctual, as you can see.

— Mucho. ¿Me hace usted el favor de esperar un momento?
Aquí tengo otra señorita que está probándose un vestido.
*Very. Would you mind waiting a minute? I have another
young lady here who's trying on a dress.*

— No faltaba más. No corre prisa.
Of course. There's no hurry.

— (Al poco rato) Ahora estoy a su disposición.
(After a short while) Now I'm ready for you.

— A ver cómo me va a quedar mi nuevo vestido.
I wonder how my new dress will fit me.

— Póngaselo. Mire. Le queda como un guante.
Put it on. Look. It fits you like a glove.

— Como un guante quizás, — pero lo que es como vestido . . .
Maybe like a glove — but as for a dress . . .

— Pues mírese usted al espejo y se convencerá.
Well, look into the mirror and you'll agree.

— ¿No puede usted recogerlo un poquito debajo del brazo?
Can't you take it in a little under the arm?

— ¡Cómo no! Permítame. Así, ¿verdad?
Of course. May I? You mean like this, don't you?

— Eso es. El talle podría ser un poco más bajo por delante y más alto por detrás.

Yes. The waist could be lower in front and higher in back.

— Permítame probarle las mangas. Mueva un poco el brazo, por favor.

Just try the sleeves. Move your arm a bit, please.

— ¡Ay! Me están muy estrechas. Hay que ensancharlas.

Oh, they're too tight (or narrow). You'll have to let them out a little.

Los hombros y el cuello están perfectamente.

The shoulders and the neck are perfect.

— La falda cae bien de este lado pero del otro no está pareja.

The skirt hangs well on one side, but it's uneven on the other.

— La voy a prender con estos alfileres. Haré las correcciones (or los arreglos) para pasado mañana.

I'll fasten it with these pins. I'll make the alterations by the day after tomorrow.

— Si estuviera listo ahora, lo podría llevar esta noche.

If it were ready now, I could wear it this evening.

— Lo siento mucho. Pero ¿que le vamos a hacer?

I'm very sorry. But it can't be helped.

NOTAS

1.   en casa de (*at the home of*), a casa de (*to the house of*) = en (or a) la casa de or donde (Span. Am.) = en lo de, a lo de (Arg.): vamos a casa de mi primo, *let's go to my cousin's* = vamos donde mi primo (Span. Am.) = vamos a lo de mi primo (Arg.).

2.   *very* (*much*) when standing alone is mucho: ¿está usted muy cansado? *are you very tired?* mucho, *very.*

3.   me queda bien, *it fits me*; me sienta bien, *it becomes me.*

4.   tener el talle bajo (alto), *to be long- (short-) waisted.*

5. **falda** *f.* = **pollera** (Arg., Chile); **pliegue** *m.*, *pleat*; **adorno(s)** *m.*, *trimming*; **botones automáticos** or **cierre de resorte** *m.*, *snaps*; **cierre automático** or **cierre relámpago** (lit. "lightning") *m.*, *zipper* or **cremallera** *f.*, (Spain); **corchetes** *m. pl.*, *hooks and eyes*; **escotado**, *low-cut* = **descotado**; **figurín** *m.*, *fashion plate*; **patrón** *m.*, *pattern*; **paños (telas) y tejidos**, *materials and fabrics*: **algodón** *m.*, *cotton*; **batista** *f.*, *batiste*; **cretona** *f.*, *cretonne*; **encaje** *m.*, *lace*; **lana** *f.*, *wool*; **lino** *m.*, *linen*; **raso** *m.*, *satin*; **seda** *f.*, *silk*; **terciopelo** *m.*, *velvet*; **ante** *m.*, *suede*; **gasa** *f.*, *chiffon*; **cuero** *m.*, *leather*; **fieltro** *m.*, *felt*; **inarrugable**, *crease-resistant*; **quiero un traje sastre**, *I want a tailored suit*.

En la librería

At the Bookstore

— ¿Cuál es la mejor librería de aquí?
What's the best bookstore here?

— Hay varias muy buenas. Una está muy cerca de aquí.
There are several very good ones. One's auite near here.

— ¿Me podría indicar el camino?
Could you tell me which way to go?

— Con mucho gusto. Cruce usted esta calle y entre usted en el piso bajo de aquel rascacielos de quince pisos.
Sure. Cross this street and it's on (lit. "enter") the ground floor of that fifteen-story skyscraper.

— Muchas gracias. (Cruzando) ¡Ay! Por poco me atropella el auto ese. ¡Qué estúpidos! . . . Aquí estoy.
Thank you very much. (Crossing) Oh! That car there nearly ran over me. The idiots! . . . Here I am.

— ¿En qué puedo servirle, señor?
What can I do for you, sir?

— Quiero la última novela . . . no sé cómo se titula. . . .
I want the latest novel . . . I don't know what the title of it is. . . .

— ¿Quién es el autor?
Who's the author?

— El famoso novelista . . . no sé cómo se llama. . . . Lo tengo
en la punta de la lengua.
> *The famous novelist . . . I don't know what his name is. . . .*
> *I have it on the tip of my tongue.*

— Pues así va a ser algo difícil. Hay tantos novelistas famosos
hoy día. ¿Será alguna novela de Julio Cortázar o Carlos
Fuentes o Ernesto Sábato o Mario Vargas Llosa o Gabriel
García Márquez? ¿Será *Cien años de soledad*? Es la novela
de García Márquez que más se vende.
> *Well, in that case it's going to be rather hard. There are so*
> *many famous novelists nowadays. Could it be a novel by*
> *Julio Cortázar or Carlos Fuentes or Ernesto Sábato or Mario*
> *Vargas Llosa or Gabriel García Márquez? Could it be* One
> Hundred Years of Solitude? *That's García Márquez' novel*
> *that sells best.*

— Exactamente. Es ésa. ¿Qué precio tiene?
> *Exactly. It's that one. How much is it?*

— Sólo nos quedan unos ejemplares en rústica. Los ejemplares encuadernados (or empastados) en tela están agotados.
> *We have only a few paperback copies left. The cloth-bound*
> *copies have all been sold.*

— Pues, en rústica. Cuanto más barata, mejor. ¿Me permite
verla?
> *In that case, (I'll take) a paperback copy. The cheaper it is,*
> *the better. May I see it?*

— Aquí la tiene usted. ¿Algo más?
> *Here it is. Anything else?*

— Sí, quiero una guía y un plano de esta ciudad y un diccio-
nario de bolsillo.
> *I want a guide-book and plan of this city and a pocket*
> *dictionary.*

— Éstos son los mejores y los más baratos.
These are the best and the cheapest.

— (Hojeándolos) Me quedo con éstos. ¿Quiere envolverlos, por favor?
(Glancing through them) I'll take these. Would you wrap them up, please?

— Le pongo también nuestro último catálogo de obras nacionales y extranjeras. Acaba de publicarse.
I'll also put in our latest catalogue of domestic and foreign works. It's just come out.

NOTAS

1.   **librería de ocasión** (or **desegunda mano, de lance**) *f.,* *secondhand bookstore*; **biblioteca** *f., library.*

2.   Other literary vocabulary: **comedia** *f., comedy*; **cuento** *m., short story*; **ensayo** *m., essay*; **historia** *f., history*; **poesía** *f., poetry*; **tomo** (*or* **volumen**) *m. volume*; **la obra ha sido premiada por la Academia,** *the work has been awarded an Academy prize.*

3.   **en rústica = a la rústica**; **lomo** *m., back*; **tipo** *m., type*; **está bien impreso, -a,** *it is well printed*; **ilustrado, -a,** *illustrated*; **edición de lujo** *f., de luxe edition.*

4.   **agotado, -a** (*exhausted*) *sold out, out of print.*

5.   **guía** *f. guidebook,* **guía** *m.,* (personal) *guide.*

6.   **plano** *m., diagram, plan*; **plan** *m., plan, project*: ¿**ha hecho usted algún plan** (or **proyecto**)? *have you made any plan?* **mapa** *m., map.*

7.   **hojear,** *to thumb, glance through*; **dar** (or **echar**) **un vistazo a,** *to glance at.*

La radio y la televisión

Radio and Television

— Esta noche va a hablar nuestro presidente por radio.
Transmiten[1] el discurso por onda corta.

This evening our president is going to speak over the radio.
They're broadcasting the speech by short wave.

— ¿Y no tiene usted ganas de oírle?

You must be anxious to hear him, right?

— Muchas. ¿Me hace usted el favor de poner el aparato?

Right. Would you mind turning on the radio?

— ¿En qué estación radian el programa?

What station is the program being broadcast on?

— En la estación (transmisora)[2] ABC.

(Station) ABC.

— A ver si puedo sintonizar[3] aquella estación (or aquella
emisora).

Let's see if I can get that station.

— ¿Cómo no ha de poder? Es un aparato de seis transistores.[4]

Why shouldn't you be able to? It's a six-transistor set.

— (Dando vueltas a los mandos or botones) Apenas si se oye
al anunciador.[5]

(Turning the controls) You can hardly hear the announcer.

---

[1] transmitir = radiar, emitir.   [2] estación transmisora *f.* = estación emisora or
radio-difusora.   [3] sintonizar = coger (una estración).   [4] transistore = tubo = válvula
f. = lámpara *f.* = bulbo (Mex.) *m.*   [5] anunciador = speaker *m.* = locutor *m.*

— No se alcanza a oír nada. ¿Qué le pasará[6] al aparato?
> *You can't hear a thing. What do you suppose is wrong with the radio?*

— No me diga que está descompuesto.
> *Don't tell me it's out of order.*

— Me temo que nos vamos a llevar un chasco.
> *I'm afraid we're going to be disappointed.*

— Una lámpara se ha quemado[7] y parece que hay mucha estática.
> *One tube is burned out and it seems there's a lot of static.*

— Si le parece,[8] vamos a casa de su vecino.
> *Is it all right with you if we go next door (lit. "if you don't mind, let's go to your neighbor's house")?*

— Tiene grabadora de cinta y televisor.
> *He has a tape recorder and a television set.*

— ¿No es televisor portátil?
> *It's a portable set, right?*

— No, señor. Es una bellísima consola.
> *No, it's a very beautiful console.*

— Ah, sí, una combinación de radio, televisión y tocadiscos automático con alta fidelidad.
> *Oh, yes, a combination of radio, television and automatic high fidelity record player.*

— Tiene veinte válvulas y selector para diez canales.
> *It has twenty tubes and a ten-channel selector.*

— ¿Corriente directa y alterna, y antena interior?
> *Direct and alternate current and built-in aerial?*

---

[6] Future of conjecture. § 40*d*.   [7] **se ha quemado**=**se ha fundido**.   [8] **si le parece** =**si no tiene inconveniente**.

— Exacto. Y con control remoto sin hilos.
Right. And wireless remote control.

— ¡Cuántas horas felices vamos a pasar!
We're going to have a really pleasant time.

NOTAS

1.　**la** or **el radio**, but according to best usage **la radio** is the general term for *radio* (**radiofonía**) and **el radio** means a *radio set*.

2.　**onda larga** *f.*, *long wave*.

3.　**poner (encender)** or **poner en marcha**, *to turn on, put on*; **apagar** or **quitar**, *to turn off*.

Alquilando un departamento

Renting an Apartment

— A usted le va a encantar este departamento. Tiene tres recámaras amplias, cuarto para el servicio en la azotea, agua caliente todo el día y una portera servicial y de confianza. Mantiene la entrada muy limpia.

> *You're going to love this apartment (lit. "this apartment is going to enchant you"). It has three large bedrooms, a maid's room on the roof, hot water all day long, and a building employee who is helpful and dependable. She keeps the entrance very clean.*

— Muy bien, ¿ pero tiene la cocina todo lo necesario? No he traído nada conmigo.

> *Fine, but does the kitchen contain all the essentials? I haven't brought anything with me.*

— No se puede pedir más. Tiene refrigerador, estufa,[1] horno, máquina de lavar platos, otra para la ropa, y naturalmente todos los utensilios tales como sartenes, tetera, cazuelas, cubiertos, y vajilla. Incluso tiene una licuadora.

> *You couldn't ask for more. It has a refrigerator, kitchen range, oven, dishwasher, a washing machine, and naturally all such utensils as frying pans, tea kettle, silverware, and dishes. It even has a blender.*

---

[1] **estufa = hornillo.**

— Pero es importante averigüar si todo funciona bien. No quiero perder tiempo o molestarme en llamar a alguien para hacer arreglos.

> *But it's important to find out if everything works properly. I don't want to waste time or be bothered by calling someone to make repairs.*

— Pues, fíjese en todo antes de firmar el contrato. Apunte todo lo que no le gusta y se lo arreglaremos de antemano.

> *Then look at everything carefully before signing the lease. Write down everything that you don't like, and we'll fix it for you in advance.*

— Muy bien, de todos modos supongo que tendré que hacerlo para el inventario.

> *Fine. In any case I suppose I'll have to do it for the inventory.*

— Sí, es cierto, y antes de olvidarlo, también pedimos un mes extra de renta como indemnización por objetos rotos.

> *Yes, that's true. And before I forget it, we also request an extra month of rent as a deposit against broken articles.*

— Me parece justo. Pero si no rompo nada, supongo que me lo van a devolver.

> *It seems fair to me. But if I don't break anything, I suppose that you are going to return it to me.*

— Claro que sí.

> *Of course.*

— Y el arrendamiento es para seis meses, ¿verdad?

> *And the lease is for six months, right?*

Sí, y es renovable. Pero supongo que usted sabe que va a necesitar un fiador. También, si usted quiere, puede consultar a su abogado.

> *Yes, and it is renewable. But I suppose that you know that you are going to need a guarantor. Also, if you wish, you may consult your lawyer.*

— Buena idea. Pero primero ¿no sería mejor inspeccionar el departmento?

> *Good idea. But first wouldn't it be better to inspect the apartment?*

— ¡Ay, se me olvidó que usted todavía no lo ha visto!

> *Oh, I forgot that you haven't seen it yet (lit. "it escaped me")!*

— (Una hora después) No me gusta la plomería del cuarto de baño. En el lavabo y en la tina el agua se escapa del grifo² y el wáter no funciona bien.

> *(One hour later) I don't like the plumbing in the bathroom. In the washbasin and in the tub water is dripping from the faucet, and the toilet doesn't work very well.*

— Perdone, pero esto no es culpa del departamento. Hay gran escasez de agua por toda la ciudad. Supongo que han cortado el agua como suelen hacer de vez en cuando.

> *I'm sorry, but the fault doesn't lie with the apartment (lit. "it's not the apartment's fault"). There is a severe water shortage throughout the city. I suppose they've shut off the water as they usually do from time to time.*

— ¡Qué lata! Pero además falta ropa de cama: sábanas, fundas, mantas; y los colchones no me parecen bastante duros. Las paredes son tan delgadas que se oye todo de un cuarto al otro. Y los muebles están muy viejos. Fíjese en las quemaduras de cigarrillo en el sofá y en la alfombra.

> *What a nuisance! But besides, there isn't enough bed linen: sheets, pillow cases, blankets; and the mattresses don't seem hard enough to me. The walls are so thin that you can hear everything from one room to another. And the furniture looks very old. Look at the cigarette burns in the sofa and the rug.*

— Señora, todo esto tiene arreglo; podemos cambiar los muebles. Y hay plomeros³ para arreglar el baño. Son detalles

---

² **grifo** = **llave** (Span. Am.).   ³ **plomero** (Span. Am.) = **fontanero** (Spain).

sin importancia. Lo principal es la ubicación del departamento. Está muy céntrico.

> *Madam, everything has a remedy; we can change the
> furniture. And there are plumbers to fix the bathroom.
> They are details without importance. The principal thing is
> the location of the apartment. It is very centrally located.*

— Sí, quizás demasiado. ¿No tiene usted algo en los suburbios,[4] algo limpio, silencioso, moderno, donde no falte[5] el
agua y no chorreen[5] los grifos?

> *Yes, perhaps too much so. Don't you have something in the
> suburbs, something clean, quiet, modern, where there's no
> water shortage and the faucets don't drip?*

— Ay, señora. Usted está pidiendo algo en el paraíso. Por
desgracia está muy lejos de aquí. Y el transporte público
hasta allá es muy deficiente.

> *Ah, madam, you are asking for something in paradise.
> Unfortunately that's quite a way from here. And public
> transportation there is very inadequate.*

NOTAS

1. **azotea**, *flat roof* (a frequent location for maids' rooms
in Latin America).

2. **refrigerador**=**heladera** (Span Am.)= **nevera** (Spain).

3. **cazuela** is usually made of earthenware; certain stews
cooked in a casserole are also called **cazuela** (Sp. Am.).

4. It is customary in many countries to request pros-
pective tenants to have a guarantor (**fiador**) responsible for payment
of rent.

[4] **Suburbios**=**las afueras**=**los alrededores**=**los barrios externos.**   [5] § 46.

5. Other workmen who may be needed for repairs include: **el carpintero** *m.*, *carpenter*; **el electricista** *m.*, *electrician*; **el cerrajero** *m.*, *locksmith*; **el albañil** *m.*, *mason*; **el pintor** *m.*, *painter*; **el jardinero** *m.*, *gardener*. **Agencia de bienes inmobiliarios** or **agencia de bienes raíces**, *real estate agency*.

Un paseo por Buenos Aires

A Drive Around Buenos Aires

— ¿Le parece a usted que demos un paseo en auto esta tarde?
> *What do you say to our taking a car ride this afternoon?*

— Me encantaría. Llamemos a aquel coche.
> *I'd love it. Let's call that taxi.*

— Llévenos por las calles principales para que veamos los monumentos más notables.
> *Take us through the main streets so we can see the most important sights.*

— Yo ya he visto el Jardín Zoológico, la Plaza del Congreso, Palermo, y los subterráneos.
> *I've already seen the Zoological Garden, Congress Square, the gardens of Palermo, and the subways.*

— Pues ha aprovechado bien el tiempo.
> *Well, you've certainly made the most of your time.*

— ¡Qué almacenes más grandes! ¡Y qué lujo!
> *What huge department stores! And the displays (lit. "what luxury")!*

— ¡Mire esos edificios! Aquél es el Teatro de la Ópera. Y ahora es la temporada precisamente.
> *Look at those buildings! That's the Opera House. And this happens to be the (opera) season.*

— Pues mañana saco localidades para la función de la noche.
¿Me acompaña usted?

> *Tomorrow I'll get tickets for the evening performance. Will
> you go with me?*

— Con mucho gusto. Es una cosa que no debemos perder.

> *I certainly will. That's one thing we ought not to miss.*

— Ya estamos en la famosa Avenida de Mayo.

> *Now we're in the famous Avenida de Mayo.*

— ¡Qué larga y ancha! Igual que las de París, Londres, o
Viena.

> *It's really long and wide! Just like the avenues in Paris,
> London, or Vienna.*

— Tiene treinta metros de ancho y más de kilómetro y medio
de largo.

> *It's thirty meters wide and more than a kilometer and a half
> long.*

— Mire aquí a la izquierda.

> *Look here to the left.*

— Es la renombrada calle de la Florida por donde no pueden
pasar coches a esta hora.

> *That's the famous Florida Street where cars aren't allowed
> at this time of day.*

— Pues bajémonos del coche y paseémonos[3] a pie.

> *Well, let's get out and walk.*

— Bien. Me encanta mirar las vitrinas (or las vidrieras) y ver
pasar la gente. Chofer, pare usted aquí. Tome usted.

> *O.K. I like to go window-shopping and watch the people go
> by. Driver, stop here. Here you are.*

NOTAS

1. **dar un paseo**, *to take a walk*; **dar un paseo en auto**, *to
take a drive*; **¿le parece a usted que demos un paseo?** = **si le parece a**

usted, vamos a dar un paseo = si no tiene usted inconveniente daremos un paseo, etc. ¿le parece a usted que regresemos (or volvamos)? *shall we go back?*

2.   metro (Spain) *m.*, *subway* = subte (Buenos Aires) *m.*

3.   bajemos + nos = bajémonos, *let's get out*; paseemos + nos = paseémonos, *let's take a walk*. § 61*a*.

El teatro de la ópera

The Opera House

— ¿Tienen localidades para la ópera de esta noche?
   Do you have seats for tonight's opera?

— (El boletero) Nos quedan muy pocas. Todos las sacan de antemano.
   (The ticket seller) There are very few left. Everyone buys them in advance.

— Y no tardan en agotarse ¿verdad?
   And they'll soon be gone, won't they?

— Eso es. Ya sabe usted que los domingos siempre está atestado el teatro.
   Yes. You know, on Sundays the theater is always filled.

— Quisiera dos butacas. Aquí se llaman plateas (de orquesta) ¿verdad?
   I'd like two orchestra seats. Here they're called plateas, I believe.

— Eso es. ¿En la décima fila o la fila once?
   Yes. In the tenth or the eleventh row?

— La décima. ¿Cuánto valen?
   The tenth. How much are they?

— Tres mil pesos las dos.
   Three thousand pesos for the pair.

— ¡Caramba! ¡Si no traigo tanto dinero encima!
   Well! I haven't that much money with me.

— ¿Entonces quiere usted dos delanteras de la galería, es decir, de la primera fila?

> *Then do you want two front gallery seats; that is, in the first row?*

— Bueno, si me hace el favor.

> *Yes, please.*

— Desde allí se ve bien y no tiene usted que ir de etiqueta.

> *From there you can see well and you don't need to dress.*

— Muy bien. Como soy turista, no tengo traje de etiqueta (smoking).

> *That's fine. I'm a tourist, and I don't have evening clothes (tuxedo).*

— La función empieza a las nueve en punto.

> *The performance begins at nine sharp.*

— Dígame usted, ¿cuándo termina la temporada?

> *Tell me, when does the season end?*

— Terminará de hoy en quince días con una función de gala.

> *It closes two weeks from today with a gala performance.*

— He tenido la suerte de llegar antes que termine.

> *I've been lucky to get here before it ends.*

— Este programa indica todas las funciones y los repartos de esta semana.

> *This program shows all the performances and the casts for this week.*

NOTAS

1. **de antemano** = **con anticipación**; **lo compré con dos días de anticipación**, *I bought it two days in advance.*

2. **butaca** *f.*, *orchestra seat* = **luneta** (Mex.) = **platea** (Arg. and elsewhere). In most Buenos Aires theaters an orchestra seat is called **platea**, and the balcony is referred to as **pullman**. Perfor-

mances are **matinée** (*afternoon*), **vermouth** (*evening* or *cocktail per-formance* beginning 6 to 6:30), **noche** (*night performance* beginning at 9 to 9:30); **camarín** *m.*, *dressing room*; **tramoyista** *m.*, *stage hand.*

3.   Note that ordinal numerals are generally avoided after ten; **primero (-a)**, **segundo (-a)**, **tercero (-a)**, **cuarto (-a)**, **quinto (-a)**, **sexto (-a)**, **séptimo (-a)**, **octavo (-a)**, **noveno (-a)**, **décimo (-a)**. Then **once, doce, trece,** etc.

4.   **reparto** *m.*, *cast* = **elenco** (Span. Am.). **se suspendió la función,** *the performance was canceled*; **se aplazó (se postergó),** *it was postponed.* § 53a.

El cine

The Movies

— ¿Le parece que vayamos al cine[1] esta noche?
   How would you like to go to the movies tonight?

— Encantado. ¿Llegaremos a tiempo?
   Terrific. Are we going to get there on time?

— Creo que sí. La última función es a las nueve.
   I think so. The last show is at nine o'clock.

— Vamos entonces. Pero escojamos[2] uno que tenga[3] aire acondicionado.
   Let's go, then. But let's choose one that's air-conditioned.

— Desde luego. ¡Hace un calor! ¡Uf! Se asa uno vivo.
   Oh, absolutely. It's so hot! Ugh! I'm roasting (lit. "one roasts alive").

— Veamos en el periódico lo que dan.
   Let's find out from the paper what's on (lit. "they're giving").

— Mire. En el Encanto dan *El Cid*, hablada en inglés con títulos en español. Entrada cincuenta pesos.
   Look. At the Encanto they're showing The Cid *(spoken) in English with Spanish subtitles. Admission fifty pesos.*

— ¿Qué más? ¿Hay alguna película francesa?
   What else? Is there a French movie?

---

[1] **cine** = **biógrafo** (Arg., Chile).   [2] **escoger**, *to choose.* § 63, 5.   [3] Subjunctive of **tener**. §§ 46; 67, 19.

— Sí hay. En el Orfeón ponen *Orfeo Negro*, hablada en francés con títulos en español.

> *Yes, there is. At the Orpheum they're showing* Black Orpheus (*spoken*) *in French with Spanish subtitles.*

— Vamos allá. Tomemos un coche para no llegar tarde.

> *Let's go there. Let's take a taxi so as not to get there too late.*

— (En la taquilla[4]) Dos entradas.

> (*At the box office*) *Two tickets.*

— (Acomodador) Es por aquí.

> (*Usher*) *This way.*

— (Pisando el pie a una señora) Perdone usted. Aquí no se ve nada.

> (*Stepping on a lady's foot*) *Excuse me. You can't see a thing here.*

— Llegamos a tiempo de ver las actualidades.

> *We're just in time to see the newsreel.*

— Dicen que los dibujos animados son muy graciosos. Se estrenó la película anoche.

> *They say the cartoon is very funny. The movie began last night.*

— (En el intermedio[5]) Salgamos un momento a fumar un cigarrillo.

> (*During the intermission*) *Let's go out a minute to smoke a cigarette.*

— Bueno. Déme uno. ¿Tiene lumbre? Gracias.

> *O.K. Give me one. Do you have a light? Thanks.*

— Ya sonó el timbre. Entremos.

> *The bell's rung. Let's go in.*

---

[4] **taquilla = boletería** (Span. Am.).   [5] **intermedio = descanso = intervalo.**

NOTAS

1. The opposite of **creo que sí**, is **creo que no**.

2. Another expression: **estoy sudando a mares**, *I'm perspiring all over* (lit. "by oceans").

3. The subjunctive (**veamos**) is used for **vamos a ver**; **¿en qué plana está la sección de espectáculos** (or **la cartelera**)? *what page is the theatrical section on?* **reseña crítica** or **crítica** *f.*, *review*.

4. **entrada**, *admission* (i.e., to downstairs seats)=**luneta** (Mex.)=**platea** or **platea de orquesta** (Arg.); *upstairs seats*=**galería** (*gallery* or *balcony*)=**segundos** (Mex.)=**pullman** (Arg.).

5. **él es muy gracioso** or **tiene mucha gracia**, *he is very funny*; **¡qué gracia!** *how funny!* **me hace mucha gracia**, *it strikes me funny*; **hace morirse** (or **destornillarse**) **de risa**, *you'll split your sides laughing*; **¡qué risa!** *how funny!*

6. **cigarrillo**=**pitillo** (Spain)=**cigarro** (Mex. and elsewhere); **fumar**, *to smoke*=**pitar** (Arg., Chile); **pipa** *f.*, *pipe*=**cachimba** (Span. Am.); **fósforo** *m.*, *match*=**cerilla** (Spain)=**cerillo** (Mex.).

Atravesando los Andes

Crossing the Andes

— (En el tren) ¿Sabe usted a qué hora vamos a llegar a Mendoza?

> *(On the train) Do you know what time we reach Mendoza?*

— Ya falta poco. Allí todos bajamos a tomar los autos que están esperando.

> *We'll soon be there. We all get off there and take the cars that are waiting.*

— ¿Qué le parece este viaje?

> *How are you liking this trip?*

— Pues las inmensas pampas son algo monótonas. Pero no dejan de tener su encanto.

> *The pampas (or plains) stretch on rather monotonously. But they have a certain charm nevertheless.*

— Ya lo creo. Y hoy vamos a ver algo majestuoso cuando atravesemos la cordillera.

> *They surely do. And today we'll have a majestic view when we cross the cordillera (or mountain chain).*

— Primero el trayecto impresionante en auto desde Mendoza a Punta de Vacas.

> *First the imposing stretch by car from Mendoza to Punta de Vacas.*

— Y después por tren hasta el pueblo de los Andes y a Santiago.

> *And then by train to the town of Los Andes and to Santiago.*

—(En el auto) ¡Qué curvas más cerradas! ¡Y cómo corre el chofer!

> (*In the auto*) *What sharp* (*or hairpin*) *curves! And the driver really goes fast!*

—Parece peligrosísimo pero estos choferes saben manejar admirablemente.

> *It seems terribly dangerous, but these chauffeurs are excellent drivers.*

—Ya estamos en Uspallata. Aquí paramos para desayunarnos.

> *We're in Uspallata already. We stop here to have breakfast.*

—Vamos a tomar algo caliente. El café caliente nos hará bien.

> *Let's have something hot. Hot coffee will do us good.*

—(En el tren transandino) ¿Es usted norteamericano (–a), si no es indiscreción (preguntarlo)?

> (*On the trans-Andean train*) *Are you an American, if I may ask?*

—Para servirle. Y usted es chileno (–a), si no me equivoco.

> *Yes I am. And you're Chilean, if I'm not mistaken.*

—A sus órdenes. Mire aquel pico cubierto de nieve. Tiene 23.000 (veintitrés mil) pies de altura.

> *Yes. . . . Look at that snow-covered peak. It's 23,000 feet high.*

—¡Qué imponente! Será el Aconcagua, el pico más alto de los Andes.

> *That's really impressive! That must be Aconcagua, the highest peak in the Andes.*

—Eso es. Lo ha acertado usted. Y esta vía ferroviaria es la más empinada del mundo.

> *That's it. You're right* (*lit. "you have guessed it"*). *And this is the steepest railway in the world.*

— La guía dice que sube 7.774 (siete mil setecientos setenta y cuatro) pies en una distancia de cuarenta millas.

The guidebook says it climbs 7,774 feet in forty miles.

— Eso es subir.

That's real climbing.

NOTAS

1. **peligroso, -a** *dangerous*; **peligrosísimo** = sumamente **peligroso.** § 20.

2. **hacer una excursión,** *to go on an outing*; **hacer alpinismo** (Spain), **andinismo** (Span. Am.), *to engage in mountain climbing*; **alpinista** = **andinista**, *mountain climber.*

3. Some useful items to remember for your outing: **tienda de campaña**, *tent*; **estufa portátil**, *portable stove*; **latas de conserva**, *canned goods*, **hamacas**, *hammocks*; **retrete** (*m.*) **químico**, *chemical toilet*; **abrelatas**, *can opener*; **un hacha**, *axe*; **martillo** *m.*, *hammer*; **sierra** *f.*, *saw*; **una radio de transistores** *f.*, *transistor radio*; **botiquín de primeros auxilios** *m.*, *first aid kit*; **contra-veneno para picadura de serpiente** *m.*, *antidote for snake bite*; **novelas policiales** *f.*, *detective stories*; **encendedor** *m.*, *lighter*; **gasolina para encendedor**, *lighter fluid*; **cuerda** *f.*, *rope*; **lámpara de pilas**, *flashlight.*

4. Some useful expressions: **¿podemos hacer camping aquí?** *can we camp here?* **¿hay agua potable?** *is there drinking water?* **¿cuánto cobran por persona/por coche?** *what do you charge per person/per car?* **¿donde están las duchas/los servicios?** *where are the showers/the toilets?* **¿puede usted llevarme hasta . . . ?** (**¿puede usted darme aventón . . . ?** Mex.) *can you give me a lift to . . . ?* **él pide aventón**; *he is asking for a ride.* Some important signs: **cuidado con el perro**, *beware of the dog*; **prohibido** (**arrojar basuras, entrar, acampar, acampar con caravana, encender hoguera** (Spain) or **fuego** (Span. Am.), *it is prohibited* (*to litter enter, camp, camp with trailer, light fires*).

El almacén

The Department Store

— ¿En qué puedo servirla?
   May I help you?

— Por favor, ¿dónde encuentro ropa interior? Esta tienda es tan grande que me pierdo.
   Where do I find underwear, please? This store is so big that I get lost.

— ¿Ve usted el departamento de guantes y el de medias, a la derecha del elevador?
   You see the gloves and stockings department at the right of the elevator?

— ¿Cerca de donde veo suéteres[1] para señoras?
   Near where I see sweaters for ladies?

— Sí, señorita. Allí venden toda clase de ropa íntima: fajas, sostenes, pantaletas. Y también saltos de cama, camisones, piyamas y fondos.
   Yes, miss. There they sell all kinds of underwear, girdles, bras, panties. And also negligees, nightgowns, pajamas and petticoats.

— Gracias. Y quizá pueda indicarle a mi novio dónde puede encontrar un impermeable.[2] Se le olvidó traer el suyo y ha empezado a llover.
   Thanks. And perhaps you could tell my fiancé where he can find a raincoat. He forgot to bring his and it's begun to rain.

---

[1] suéter = chaqueta de punto.   [2] impermeable = gabardina.

— Al fondo, a la izquierda, está la sección para caballeros. Allí encontrará impermeables, botas de hule, paraguas, y también corbatas, camisas, bufandas, suéteres, pantalones bluyines y trajes.

In the rear to the left is the men's department. There you'll find raincoats, rubbers, umbrellas, and also ties, shirts, scarves, sweaters, blue jeans, and suits.

— Por aquel lado vimos nada más juguetes y utensilios de cocina.

We only saw toys and kitchen articles on that side.

— Sí, pero más a la izquierda encuentra lo que busca, y a la derecha objetos de escritorio y papelería: plumas de todas clases, lápices, papel para escribir, papel carbón, cuadernos, celofán adhesivo, cola de pegar, libretas de direcciones, materiales para artista — pinceles, colores de acuarela y tubos de pintura al óleo, caballetes, lienzos, papel para dibujo — inclusive máquinas de escribir, de sumar, calculadoras electrónicas. Es una papelería muy completa.

Yes, but more to the left you'll find what you're looking for, and to the right are desk supplies and stationery: all kinds of pens, pencils, writing paper, carbon paper, notebooks, scotch tape, glue, address books, artists' supplies — brushes, water colors and tubes of oil paint, easels, canvases, drawing paper — even typewriters, adding machines, and electronic calculators. It's a very complete stationery department.

— Gracias, pero de momento solamente necesita un impermeable de nylon, ligero, de los que se pueden llevar en el bolsillo.

Thanks, but for the moment he only needs a nylon raincoat, a light one, the kind you can carry in your pocket.

— No sé si tenemos de esta clase, pero puede preguntar.

I don't know if we have that kind, but you can ask.

— Carlos, ¿por qué no nos separamos? Yo voy a comprar unas pantimedias y unos pañuelos, quizá también una blusa, y dentro de media hora te busco en la sección para caballeros.

> *Carlos, why don't we separate? I'm going to buy some pantyhose and handkerchiefs, maybe a blouse, too, and in half an hour I'll look for you in the men's department.*

— No, mejor será encontrarnos en la farmacia. Necesito varias cosas: hojas de rasurar, polvos de talco, y un peine.

> *No, it'll be better to meet in the drugstore. I need a few things: some razor blades, talcum powder, and a comb.*

— De acuerdo. Nos vemos en la farmacia dentro de media hora.

> *O.K. We'll see each other in the drugstore in half an hour.*

— (En la sección para caballeros. Carlos, al vendedor) ¿Puede usted atenderme? ¿Qué precio tienen estas camisas?

> (*In the men's department. Carlos, to the salesman*) *Can you wait on me? What price are these shirts?*

— Éstas tienen una rebaja del veinte por ciento. ¿Cuántas le doy? ¿Una docena?

> *These have been reduced twenty percent. How many would you like (lit. "how many shall I give you")? A dozen?*

— Con una camisa me basta. Me quedo con³ esta azul rayada.

> *One shirt is enough. I'll take this blue striped one.*

— ¿No necesita corbatas de seda, calcetines de lana . . .?

> *Do you need any silk ties, any woolen socks . . .?*

— No sé si traigo bastante dinero.

> *I don't know whether I have enough money with me.*

— Es muy poco lo que se necesita.

> *Very little is needed.*

---

³ **me quedo con,** *I'll take* = me llevo.

— (Abriendo la cartera) No tengo. Si tuviera dinero, compraría más.[4] ¿Puede usted abrirme cuenta?

> (*Opening his billfold*) *No, I haven't. If I had money, I'd buy more. Can you open an account for me?*

— Lamento no poder hacerlo. No vendemos a crédito sino solamente al contado.

> *I'm sorry I can't do that. We don't make credit sales, only cash sales.*

— Muy bien. Pago en la caja ¿verdad? ¿Por dónde se sale?

> *O.K. I pay the cashier, right? How do you get out?*

— Por aquí, señor. La salida está a la derecha al lado de la escalera mecánica.

> *This way, sir. The exit is to the right next to the escalator.*

— Muchas gracias.

> *Thanks very much.*

NOTAS

1. Some vocabulary connected with **rebaja**: **rebajar**, *to reduce the price*; **regatear**, *to haggle*; **saldo** *m.*, = **ocasión** *f.* = **barata** *f.* (Mex.), *sale*; **ganga** *f.*, *bargain*.

2. **traer dinero**, *to have money with one, on one's person* = **tener dinero encima**; **tener dinero**, *to have money*; **dinero** *m.* = **plata** *f.* (Span. Am.) = **pisto** *m.* (Cent. Am.).

3. **¿puede usted cargármelo en cuenta?** *can you charge it to my account?* **comprar al fiado**, *to buy on credit*; **mandar C. O. D.**, (**cobrar o devolver**), *to send C. O. D.* = **contra reembolso** (for parcel post).

4. **subir (bajar) por la escalera mecánica**, *to go up (go down) on the escalator*; **escaparate** *m.*, *display window*.

En la farmacia

At the Pharmacy (Drug store)

— (Tres cuartos de hora más tarde) ¿Se puede saber qué has comprado en todo este tiempo, querida? Hace veinte minutos que te estoy esperando aquí.

> (*Three quarters of an hour later*) *What on earth* (*lit. "may one know what"*) *you've been buying all this time, darling? I've been waiting here for you for twenty minutes.*

— Habrás llegado temprano. Y además no tuviste que probarte nada. Mientras que yo tuve que probarme un montón de cosas: una combinación de medio cuerpo, una bata para el bano, un cinturón . . . un sombrero. ¡Y cuanta dificultad en encontrar mi tamaño!

> *You must have arrived early. And besides, you didn't have to try anything on. While I had to try on a whole lot* (*lit. "heap"*) *of things: a half slip, a bathrobe, a belt . . . a hat. And I had real trouble finding my size!*

— Bueno, veo que no debí preguntar nada. Por lo menos supongo que has terminado tus compras.

> *O.K., obviously I shouldn't have asked anything. At least I suppose you've finished your shopping.*

— Me falta ahora comprar un regalo para los vecinos.

> *I (still) need to buy a present for the neighbors.*

— A lo mejor lo puedes encontrar aquí, en la farmacia.

> *Maybe you can find it here in the drugstore.*

— Lo dudo. Me parece que en esta farmacia no venden más que medicinas. Tendré que ir a una perfumería para comprar

crema para la piel, agua de colonia, desodorante y toda clase
de maquillaje.

> *I doubt it. It seems to me that in this pharmacy they sell
> only medicines. I'll have to go to a perfume store to buy
> facial cream, toilet water, a deodorant, or any kind of
> make-up.*

— Si es así, ¿qué es lo que vas a comprar aquí?

> *O.K., then, what are you going to buy here?*

— Todos los artículos que se me olvidó meter en mi maleta . . .
gotas para los ojos, más gotas para los oídos, jarabe y pastillas
para la tos.

> *All the things I forgot to pack in my suitcase . . . eye drops,
> drops for my ears, a syrup, and some cough lozenges.*

— A lo mejor encuentras unas gotas maravillosas que sirven
para todo.

> *Maybe you'll find some marvelous, all-purpose drops.*

— No seas absurdo. Necesito tres medicinas en tres frascos
diferentes. También necesito una crema contra las quemaduras del sol, una crema antiséptica, unas compresas[1] y unas
pastillas para la garganta . . . y un laxante.

> *Don't be silly. I need three kinds of medicine in three
> different bottles. I also need a cream (that protects) against
> sunburn, an antiseptic cream, some sanitary napkins, and
> some throat pills . . . and a laxative.*

— ¿No crees que vas a necesitar una receta para alguna de
estas medicinas?

> *You're going to need a prescription for some of these
> medicines, aren't you?*

— No lo creo. Todo está a la mano.

> *I don't think so. Everything's handy (within arm's reach).*

— Señores, ¿puedo ayudarles en algo?

> *May I help you with something?*

---

[1] **compresas** *f.* = **paños higiénicos, toallas sanitarias** (Span. Am.).

— Sí, por cierto. Mi novio necesita un calmante ahora mismo.

Yes, actually. My fiancé needs a sedative right away!

NOTAS

1. Some cosmetic articles: **delineador** *m.*, *eye liner*; **lápiz de ojos** *m.*, *eye pencil*; **crema** *f.* **(bronceadora, limpiadora, nutritiva, para cutículas)**, (*suntan, cleansing, cold, cuticle*) *cream*; **broches para el pelo**, *bobby pins.* Other useful words: **anti-ácido** *m.*, **alka-soda** (Spain), *antacid pill*; **leche** *f.* (or **pastillas**) **de magnesia**, *magnesia milk* or *pills*; **antibióticos** *m.*, *antibiotics*; **penicilina**, *penicillin*; **inyección** *f.*, *injection*; **inyección intravenosa**, *intravenous injection*; **aspirina** *f.*, *aspirin*; **enjuagadientes** *m.*, *mouthwash*; **gasa** *f.*, *gauze*; **yodo** *m.*, *iodine*; **callicidas** *f.*, *corn plasters*; **tabletas de cloro** *f.*, *chlorine tablets*; **papel higiénico** *m.*, *toilet paper*; **pañuelos de papel** or **kleenex** *m.*, *tissue.*

2. For baby supplies: **baberos** *m.*, *bibs*; **pañales desechables** *m.*, *disposable diapers*; **talco** *m.*, *talcum powder*; **aceite** *m.*, *oil*; **imperdibles** *m.*, *safety pins*; **bragas** *f. pl.* (Spain) or **pantaletas de plástico** *f.*, *plastic pants.*

3. Other bathroom supplies: **jabón** *m.*, *soap*; **esponja** *f.*, *sponge*; **brocha de afeitar** *f.*, *shaving brush*; **polvos para los pies** *m.*, *foot powder*; **cepillo de dientes** *m.*, *toothbrush*; **toallas** *f.*, *towels*; **pinzas** *f.*, *tweezers*; **tijeras de uñas** *f.*, *manicuring scissors*; **lima de uñas** *f.*, *nail file*; **limas de cartón**, *emory boards.*

Una llamada a la policía

A Call to the Police

— Por favor, señorita, comuníqueme usted con la policía. Es una emergencia.
> *Put me through to the police, please. This is an emergency.*

— ¿Desde dónde habla usted?
> *Where are you calling from?*

— Estoy hablando desde un teléfono público, al lado de la Farmacia Insurgentes.
> *I'm calling from a public telephone beside the Insurgentes Pharmacy.*

— Entonces le comunicaré con la 4a. (cuarta) Delegación.
> *Then I'll connect you with the fourth district.*

— Por favor, ¿puede atenderme alguien?
> *Can someone help me please?*

— Al habla[1] el sargento Ramírez Arellano. Por favor, deme su nombre y su dirección, y exponga su problema.
> *Sergeant Ramírez Arellano speaking. Please give me your name and address and explain your problem.*

— Me llamo Carlos O'Donnell. Soy turista norteamericano, hospedado en el hotel Hilton. Estoy frente a la Farmacia Insurgentes. Mi automóvil, con placas del Estado de Texas SN-3749, quedó estacionado frente a la farmacia, hace unas dos horas, y ahora ha desaparecido.

---

[1] also: **al aparato**.

My name is Carlos O' Donell. I'm an American tourist staying at the Hilton. I'm in front of the Insurgentes Pharmacy. My car, with Texas plates SN-3749, was parked in front of the pharmacy about two hours ago, and now it has disappeared.

— No se preocupe. El carro grúa se lo habrá[2] llevado. Tendrá que venir a recogerlo y pagar una multa. A ver . . . aquí tengo la lista de los carros: acaba de llegar. Es un Ford color café, ¿no? Tiene usted mucha suerte. No tiene que pagar más que doscientos pesos de multa por esta infracción. El capitán Gómez Ovando, encargado del carro grúa, encontró algo sospechoso en su auto: unos cigarrillos que parecían de marijuana, y unos polvos en un paquetito de celofán. Creyó que podían ser cocaína o heroína, quizá opio en polvo. . . .

Don't worry. The tow truck must have taken it away. You'll have to come pick it up and pay the fine. Let's see . . . I have the list of the cars here: it's just come in. It's a Ford, color brown, right? You're very lucky. You only have to pay a two-hundred pesos fine for this infraction. Captain Gómez Ovando, who was in charge of the tow truck, found something suspicious in your car: some cigarettes that seemed to be marijuana and some powder in a cellophane package. He thought that it could be cocaine or heroin perhaps opium in powder form. . . .

— ¡Qué error! ¡Qué estupidez! ¡Qué locura! Esto es una barbaridad, un atropello, una injusticia. . . . ¿O es que es ésta una forma de pedirme una mordida?[3] Pero yo no soy culpable de nada; soy inocente, y no voy a pagar.

What a mistake! How stupid can you get! This is crazy (lit. "what stupidity! what insanity")! Plain uncivilized, an outrage, an injustice. . . . Or is this a form of asking me for a bribe? But I'm not guilty of anything; I'm innocent, and I'm not going to pay.

[2] § 40d.   [3] **mordida** = **soborno** *m.* = **cohecho** *m.* (Spain).

—Cálmese, por favor. Aquí no ha sucedido nada. En seguida vimos que los cigarros eran de tabaco, liados a mano, y que los polvos eran azúcar. Aquí no somos tontos . . . ni explotamos a los turistas.

> *Calm down, please. Nothing has happened here. We saw right then and there that the cigarettes were tobacco, rolled by hand, and the powder was sugar. We're not fools here . . . and we don't exploit tourists.*

—Bueno, perdone mi exaltación. Estoy algo nervioso. Mañana salgo de regreso para Estados Unidos. Pagaré la multa, ¿qué remedio? De todos modos . . . me voy contento y feliz, y espero regresar pronto.

> *O.K., I'm sorry to have got so excited. I'm a bit nervous. Tomorrow I'm leaving and going back to the United States. I'll pay the fine. What else can I do? Anyway, I'll leave content and happy, and I hope to return soon.*

NOTAS

Marijuana is also called idiomatically: **la mota**, **la juanita**, **la yerba** (*grass*).

APPENDIX

1. The Definite Article *the*

	SINGULAR	PLURAL
Masculine	**el**	**los**
Feminine	**la**	**las**
el libro the book	**los libros** the books	
la casa the house	**las casas** the houses	

Contraction:

a + el = al   to the
de + el = del   of (from) the

2. **El** is used instead of **la** before a feminine noun beginning with stressed **a** (or **ha**):

el **agua**   the water   But: **las aguas**   the waters
el **ala**   the wing   But: **la aleta**   the fin

3. The neuter definite article **lo** is used with adjectives (and past participles) with the meaning of *what is* or *the part of it*, etc.:

lo malo   the bad part of it, what is bad
lo hecho   what is done

   a) **Lo** + adjective or adverb + **que** = **qué** + adjective or adverb with the meaning of *how*:

No sabe usted *lo* contenta que está ella.   You do not know *how* glad she is.

4. The definite article is used

a) With nouns denoting all of a class:
Los soldados llevan uniforme.   Soldiers wear a uniform.

b) With abstract nouns:
El valor es necesario.   Courage is necessary.

c) With adjectives denoting a language:
El español es fácil.   Spanish is easy.
Except after **hablar** and **en:**
Hablo francés.   I speak French.
Dígalo usted en inglés. Say it in English.

d) With certain geographical names (**el Perú, el Ecuador, el Canadá, el Brasil, el Japón,** etc.):
Voy *al* Perú.   I am going to Peru.
Soy de *la* Habana.   I am from Havana.

e) With a title not in direct address:
El general «Blanco» está aquí.   General "White" is here.
El señor «Verde» es español.   Mr. "Green" is a Spaniard.

f) With nouns of weight and measure:
Cuesta un dólar *la* libra.   It costs one dollar a pound.
Paga dos dólares *el* metro.   She pays two dollars a meter.

g) Instead of the possessive adjective with parts of the body and articles of clothing when meaning is clear:
¿Qué tiene usted en *la* mano?   What have you in your hand?
Póngase usted *el* sombrero.   Put on your hat.

h) With names of days, seasons, meals, expressions of time, etc.:
Iré *el* lunes próximo.   I shall go next Monday.
La primavera es hermosa.   Spring is beautiful.
Vino *el* año pasado.   He came last year.

5. The Indefinite Article *a, an*

	SINGULAR	PLURAL	
Masculine	**un**	**unos**	⎫
Feminine	**una**	**unas**	⎬ means *some*
un libro a book		**unos libros** (some) books	
una casa a house		**unas casas** (some) houses	

6. The indefinite article (**un, una,** etc.) is omitted

   a) Before certain unmodified predicate nouns:

   Es soldado. He is a soldier.

   Soy español. I am a Spaniard.
   But: **Es un aviador famoso.** He is a famous aviator.

   b) Before *ciento, cierto, mil, otro*:

   cien (mil) hombres a hundred (a thousand) men
   otro avión another plane

   c) After ¡**qué!** (= *what a*) and after certain verbs especially when negative:

   ¡**Qué mujer!** What a woman!
   No tengo fusil. I haven't a gun.

7. Nouns are masculine or feminine. If a noun denotes a male being, it is masculine; if it denotes a female being, it is feminine:

el hombre the man	**la mujer** the woman
el padre the father	**la madre** the mother

   a) The masculine plural of certain nouns may denote both genders:
   los padres the parents (father and mother)
   los reyes the king and queen
   mis hermanos my brothers and sisters

8. Nouns ending

   a) in –**o** are generally masculine:

el cielo the sky	**el dinero** the money

   EXCEPTION: **la mano,** *the hand*

   b) in –**a** (also –**dad,** –**tad,** –**ción** and –**sión**) are generally feminine:

la casa   the house   **la ciudad**   the city
la libertad   liberty   **la nación**   the nation

EXCEPTIONS: **el día,** *the day,* and most nouns in **ma (pa):**

el clima   the climate   **el problema**   the problem
el mapa   the map

9. Plural of Nouns. If a noun ends

a) In a vowel, add **–s:**

el libro   the book   **los libros**   the books

EXCEPTIONS: **el rubí,** *the ruby*; **los rubíes,** *the rubies*

b) In a consonant, add **–es:**

el avión   the plane   **los aviones**   the planes

c) In **z,** change **z** to **c** before adding **–es:**

el lápiz   the pencil   **los lápices**   the pencils

10. Possession is expressed by the preposition **de:**

el hermano *del* **cabo**   the corporal's brother

11. The Personal **"a."** The preposition **a** is used before a direct object denoting a definite person or personified thing, or geographical name, and before **nadie, alguno, quien,** etc., and sometimes to distinguish object from subject:

Veo *a* **Juan.** I see John.
Visité (*a*) **México.** I visited Mexico.
¿*A* **quién ve usted?** Whom do you see?
El otoño sigue *al* **verano.** Autumn follows summer.

12. Adjectives agree in gender and in number with the nouns they modify:

un hombre alto   a tall man
una mujer alta   a tall woman
dos hombres altos   two tall men
dos mujeres altas   two tall women

a) An adjective modifying two nouns of different genders is generally masculine:

las manos y los pies limpios   the clean hands and feet

13. The Feminine of Adjectives

  a) If the ending is –**o,** change –**o** to –**a:**

  alto, alta high, tall   **bajo, bajo** low

  b) Otherwise there is no change:

  un libro azul a blue book
  una casa azul a blue house
  un muchacho cortés a polite boy
  una muchacha cortés a polite girl

Except that

  c) Adjectives of nationality add –**a:**

  español, española Spanish
  francés, francesa French

  d) The endings –**án,** –**ón,** and –**or** (except comparatives) add –**a:**

  holgazán, holgazana lazy
  preguntón, preguntona inquisitive
  encantador, encantadora charming
  But: **el mejor libro** the best book
        la mejor pluma the best pen

14. The plural of adjectives is formed like that of nouns (see § 9).

15. Position

  a) Descriptive adjectives generally follow the noun, unless the quality is inherent:

  un libro blanco a white book
  But: **la blanca nieve** the white snow

  b) Articles, possessives, and other common and limiting adjectives precede the noun:

  muchas personas many persons
  un buen muchacho a good boy

c) A few adjectives change meaning according to position:

una mujer pobre   a poor woman
una pobre mujer   an unfortunate woman
un hombre grande   a large man
un gran hombre   a great man

d) In a question, the predicate adjective is placed before a noun subject:

¿Es fácil la lección?   Is the lesson easy?

16. Comparison of Adjectives.   Place **más** (more) or **menos** (*less*) before the adjective:

fácil   easy   **más fácil**   easier   **el más fácil**   the easiest

Irregular:

bueno	good	**mejor**	better, best
malo	bad	**peor**	worse, worst
grande	large	**mayor**	(larger) older, etc.
pequeño	small	**menor**	(smaller) younger

17. Comparison of Equality: **tan . . . como,** *as* (*so*) *. . . as*:

tan fácil como   as easy as

18. Comparison of Inequality: **más (menos) . . . que,** *more* (*less*) *. . . than*:

El español es más fácil que el inglés.   Spanish is easier than English.

19. *a*) But *than* is **de lo que** when followed by a clause in which the adjective is understood:

Es más inteligente de lo que parece.   He is more intelligent than he seems.

b) And *than* is **del que** (**de los que, de la que, de las que**) when followed by a clause in which a noun is understood:

Tengo más libros de los que tenía.   I have more books than I had.

c) Than is **de** before numerals (except when negative):

Tengo más de diez.   I have more than ten.

20. The absolute superlative in **–ísimo** denotes an extreme degree without definite comparison:

muchísimo   very much   **carísimo**   very dear

21. Other Comparisons:

a) **tanto, –a . . . como**   as much as
   tantos, –as . . . como   as many as

b) **cuanto más . . . (tanto) más**   the more . . . the more
   cuanto menos . . . (tanto) menos   the less . . . the less
   Cuanto más estudio, (tanto) más aprendo.   The more I study, the more I learn.

22. Apocopation

a) The following adjectives drop the final **–o** before a masculine singular noun:

bueno	**uno**	**ninguno**	**tercero**
malo	**alguno**	**primero**	**postrero**

un buen hombre   a good man

b) **Santo** becomes **San** except before **To–** and **Do–**:

San Juan   But: **Santo Tomás**

c) **Grande** may become **gran**:

el gran hombre   the great man

d) **Ciento** becomes **cien** immediately before a noun:

Tengo cien dólares.   I have a hundred dollars.

23. Possessive Adjectives

SINGULAR	PLURAL	
mi	**mis**	my
tu	**tus**	your (*familiar*)

su	sus	his, her, its, your (*polite*)
nuestro, –a	**nuestros, –as**	our
vuestro, –a	**vuestros, –as**	your (*familiar in Spain*)
su	**sus**	their, your (*polite and familiar in Spanish America*)

24. To avoid confusion one may say instead of **su libro** (*his, her, your, their*, etc., *book*): **el libro de (él, ella, usted, ellos, ellas, ustedes)**.

25. Possessive Pronouns:

SINGULAR	PLURAL	
(el) **mío**, (la) **mía**	(los) **míos**, (las) **mías**	mine
(el) **tuyo**, (la) **tuya**	(los) **tuyos**, (las) **tuyas**	yours (*familiar*)
(el) **suyo**, (la) **suya**	(los) **suyos**, (las) **suyas**	his, her, its, yours (*polite*)
(el) **nuestro**, (la) **nuestra**	(los) **nuestros**, (las) **nuestras**	ours
(el) **vuestro**, (la) **vuestra**	(los) **vuestros**, (las) **vuestras**	yours (*familiar in Spain*)
(el) **suyo**, (la) **suya**	(los) **suyos**, (las) **suyas**	theirs, yours (*polite and familiar in Spanish America*)

26. Demonstrative Adjectives:

SINGULAR		PLURAL		
Masc.	*Fem.*	*Masc.*	*Fem.*	
este	**esta**	**estos**	**estas**	this, these (*near speaker*)
ese	**esa**	**esos**	**esas**	that, those (*near person spoken to*)
aquel	**aquella**	**aquellos**	**aquellas**	that, those (*away from both*)

The adverb **aquí** (*here*) corresponds to **este**; **ahí** (*there*) to **ese**; and **allí** (*there*) to **aquel**.

27. Demonstrative pronouns are the same but bear a written accent:

> **éste** this one   **aquélla** that one

In addition we have the neuter forms **esto,** *this*; **eso,** *that*; **aquello,** *that*, referring to unnamed objects or to an idea.

28. Adverbs may be formed by adding **–mente** to the feminine singular of the adjective:

> **rápido, –a** rapid   **rápidamente** rapidly
>
> EXCEPTIONS:
> **bueno** good   **malo** bad
> **bien** well   **mal** badly

29. Comparison as for Adjectives (see §16).

> EXCEPTIONS:
> **bien** well   **mejor** better, best
> **mal** badly   **peor** worse, worst
> **poco** little   **menos** less, least
> **mucho** much   **más** more, most

30. Negatives

a) **No,** *not*, is placed before the verb:

> **Veo.** I see.   **No veo.** I do not see.

b) If negative words are used after the verb, **no** must precede:

> *No* **veo nada.** I see nothing.
> *No* **voy nunca.** I never go.
> But: **Nada veo.** I see nothing.
> **Nunca voy.** I never go.

a) Subject pronouns are used only for emphasis or contrast or to avoid ambiguity. The subject neuter pronoun *it* is generally not expressed in Spanish.

PERSON	SUBJECT	INDIRECT OBJECT	DIRECT OBJECT	REFLEXIVE	OBJECT OF A PREPOSITION
1	yo I	me (to) me	me me	me (me) myself	(para) mí*
2	tú you (*familiar*)	te (to) you	te you	te (you) yourself	(para) ti*
	usted you (*polite*)	le (to) you	le, lo, la you	se (you) yourself	(para) usted**
3	él he (it)	le (se) (to) him	le, lo him***	se ⎰ himself	(para) él
	ella she (it)	le (se) (to) her	la her, it	se ⎨ herself	(para) ella
	(it)	le (se) (to) it	lo it	se ⎱ itself	(para) ello
1	nosotros, –as we	nos (to) us	nos us	nos ourselves	(para) nosotros, –as
2	vosotros, –as you (*familiar*)	os (to) you	os you	os yourselves	(para) vosotros, –as

This form is used only in Spain.   Elsewhere **ustedes** is used both for familiar and polite second person plural.

PERSON	SUBJECT	INDIRECT OBJECT	DIRECT OBJECT	REFLEXIVE	OBJECT OF A PREPOSITION
3	ustedes you	les (se) ⎰ (to) you	los (les), las ⎰ you	se ⎰ yourselves	(para) ustedes
	ellos, –as they	les (se) ⎱ (to) them	los, las ⎱ them	se ⎱ themselves	(para) ellos, –as

*With the preposition **con**, **mí** and **ti** become **conmigo** and **contigo**.

The reflexive prepositional form of the third person of both numbers is **sí; with **con** it becomes **consigo**.

***In Spain **le** is preferred to **lo**; in Spanish America **lo** is commoner.

32. Object pronouns are placed before the finite verb or are attached to an infinitive or a gerund:

> **Le veo.** I see him.
> **Quiere verle.** I want to see him.
> **Estoy mirándole.** I am looking at him.

33. Object pronouns follow affirmative commands but precede negative commands (these are always subjunctive):

> **Dígamelo Vd.** Tell me (it).
> **No me lo diga Vd.** Don't tell me (it).

34. When there are two object pronouns

a) The indirect precedes the direct:

> **Me lo dice.** He tells it to me.

b) If both begin with **l**, the indirect (**le, les**) becomes **se:**

> **Se lo digo** (not **le lo digo**). I tell it to him (to her, to them, to you, etc.)

35. To avoid ambiguity and for stress, third person object pronouns (especially indirect object pronouns) are generally repeated with the prepositional form:

> **¿Qué le pasa (a usted)?** What is the matter with you?
> **Le doy el libro.** I give him (her, you) the book.
> **Le doy el libro a él.** I give *him* the book.
> **Le doy el libro a ella.** I give *her* the book.
> **Le doy el libro a usted.** I give *you* the book.

Repetition is used for stress with other persons:

> **Me gusta el libro.** I like the book.
> **A *m*í me gusta el libro.** *I* like the book.

36. Relative Pronouns

> **que** who, which, that
> **a quien, a quienes** whom (*direct or indirect object*)
> **quien, quienes** who (*subject*)

el (la) cual, los (las) cuales   which, who
lo que, lo cual   which (*referring to a statement*)
el (la) que, los (las) que   the one(s) who (which)

37. Interrogative Pronouns

¿qué?   what? (*pronoun*)
¿qué?   what? which? (*adjective*)
¡qué!   how! what a!
¿cuál(es)?   what? which? (*pronoun*)
¿quién(es)?   who
¿a quién(es)?   whom?
¿de quién(es)?   whose?
¿cuánto, –a?   how much?
¿cuántos, –as?   how many?

38. **Para,** *for* (*in order to*), expresses purpose, destination, proximity of an act:

Estudio para aprender.   I study in order to learn.
La carta es para usted.   The letter is for you.
Está para llover.   It is about to rain.

39. **Por,** *for*, expresses *by, for the sake of, through, in exchange for, rate*:

Pagué un dólar por el libro.   I paid a dollar for the book.
Por ella lo he hecho.   I did it for her (sake).
Dos mil pies por minuto.   Two thousand feet a minute.

40. Tenses of the Verb (that differ from English)

a) The present indicative is often· used for a future

To indicate a definite or immediate act:

Mañana voy.   I (shall) go tomorrow.

To ask for orders:

¿Qué hago?   What shall I do?

b) The imperfect indicative expresses a descriptive act or condition or a customary act:

Él escribía **una carta cuando entré.**   He was writing a letter when I entered.

c) The preterite (indicative) expresses a single (accomplished) act in the past:

Ayer escribí una carta.   Yesterday I wrote a letter.
Fuimos a verla.   We went to see her.

NOTE: **Ya** + the preterite has the force of **ya** + the present perfect:

Ya lo ví.   I have already seen it.

d) The future (indicative) may be used idiomatically to express conjecture or probability in the present:

¿Qué hora será?   What time can it be?
Estará en la casa.   He is probably in the house.

e) The conditional may be used similarly to express conjecture or probability in the past:

¿Qué hora sería?   What time could it have been?
Estaría en la casa.   He was probably in the house.

f) The perfect indicative sometimes expresses a simple past like the more usual preterite:

He comido.   I have eaten *or* I ate.

41. The subjunctive is used in polite affirmative commands:

Dígamelo usted.   Tell me (it).
Póngaselo usted.   Put it on.

And in all negative commands:

No me lo digas.   Don't tell me (*familiar sing.*).
No me lo diga (usted).   Don't tell me (*polite sing.*).
No me lo digáis.   Don't tell me (*familiar pl. in Spain*).
No me lo digan (ustedes).   Don't tell me (*polite, and familiar pl. in Spanish America*).

The affirmative commands of the second person singular and plural are the true imperatives:

habla (*sing.*)   **hablad** (*pl.*)   speak

42. The subjunctive is used in wishes and exhortations:

> **¡Ojalá que lo haga!**   I wish he would do it.
> **¡Ojalá lo supiera!**   Would that I knew it!
> **¡Que vengan!**   Let them come.
> **Entremos.**   Let us go in.

And in softened statements:

> **Quisiera verle.**   I should like to see him.

43. In noun clauses, the subjunctive is used

a) When the main-clause verb expresses volition, emotion, doubt, etc.:

> **Quiero que lo haga.**   I want him to do it.
> **Temo que él no llegue.**   I'm afraid he won't (may not) arrive.
> **Duda que lo sepamos.**   He doubts that we know it.

b) After verbs of knowing and believing when negative:

> **No creo que lo sepa.**   I don't think he knows it.

44. The subjunctive is used after impersonal expressions, except those denoting certainty:

> **Es preciso que lo diga.**   It is necessary that he say it.

The infinitive is sometimes used:

> **Me es imposible salir.**   It is impossible for me to go out.

45. The subjunctive is used in adverbial clauses expressing

a) Purpose:

> **Se lo diré (a usted) para que lo sepa.**   I will tell you so that you may know it.

b) Time or manner when futurity is implied:

> **Cuando la vea, se lo diré.**   When I see her, I shall tell her.
> **Esperaré hasta que llegue Vd.**   I shall wait until you come.
> **Como quiera usted.**   As you (may) like.
> But **antes (de) que**, *before*, always takes the subjunctive.

c) Concession when a statement is not a fact, and exception:

Aunque llueva mañana, iremos a verle. Although it may rain tomorrow, we shall go to see him.

But: **Aunque llovía, fuimos a verle.** Although it was raining, we went to see him.

No iré a menos que vaya él. I shall not go unless he goes.

d) Condition clauses contrary to fact:

Si tuviera el dinero, compraría (*or* **comprara**) **la casa.** If I had the money, I would buy the house.

Si lo hubiera (*or* **hubiese**) **sabido, no hubiera ido.** If I had known it, I wouldn't have gone.

46. The subjunctive is used in adjective relative clauses that refer to an indefinite or negative antecedent:

Busco un muchacho que sepa hablar español. I am looking for a boy who can speak Spanish.

No conozco a nadie que haya estado allí. I don't know anyone who has been there.

47. When the main verb and the subordinate verb have the same subject, the infinitive is generally used instead of a subjunctive clause:

Siento haber llegado tarde. I am sorry that I have arrived late.

A few verbs allow the use of the infinitive even when there is a change of subject:

mandar	**obligar**	**permitir**
dejar	**hacer**	**prohibir** *etc*.

Me permitió hacerlo. He allowed me to do it.

48. Sequence of Tenses. When the action of the subordinate verb takes place at the same time or after that of the main verb, the subjunctive tenses to be used are as follows:

$$\text{Le}\begin{cases}\textbf{digo}\\\textbf{diré}\\\textbf{he dicho}\end{cases}\textbf{que se vaya.}\quad(\textit{present subj.})$$

$$\text{Le}\begin{cases}\textbf{decía}\\\textbf{dije}\\\textbf{diría}\\\textbf{había dicho}\end{cases}\textbf{que se fuera } \textit{or} \textbf{ fuese.}\quad(\textit{imperfect subj.})$$

When the action of the subordinate verb is prior to that of the main verb, the present subjunctive in the above cases is replaced by the perfect subjunctive or the imperfect subjunctive, and the imperfect subjunctive is replaced by the pluperfect subjunctive:

Temo que lo $\begin{cases}\textbf{haya oído.}\\\textbf{oyera } \textit{or} \textbf{ oyese.}\end{cases}$ I am afraid he (has) heard it.

Temía que lo hubiera (hubiese) oído. I was afraid that he had heard it.

49. The infinitive is used instead of the English present participle

   a) After a preposition:

   Salió sin hablarme. He went out without speaking to me.

   Al + the infinitive is *on* + the present participle:

   Al salir de la casa, cerró la puerta. On leaving the house, he closed the door.

   b) As the subject of a verb:

   El comer mucho es malo. Eating (too) much is bad.

   c) After **ver, oir, sentir,** etc.:

   Le veo venir. I see him coming.

50. The present participle is used to express manner (with no preposition):

   Aprendemos estudiando. We learn by studying.

51. There are two verbs meaning *to be*: **ser** and **estar.**

a) **Ser** is used with an adjective to denote inherent or permanent quality:

La nieve es fría.   Snow is cold.

b) **Estar** is used to denote temporary quality, location, and the result of an act (often **ir, venir,** etc., when motion is expressed):

Esta sopa está fría.   This soup is cold.
El libro está en la mesa.   The book is on the table.
La ventana está cerrada.   The window is closed.
Va mal vestida.   She is badly dressed.

c) **Estar** is used with the present participle to form progressive tenses:

Estábamos **comiendo cuando usted entró.**   We were eating when you came in.

52. The true passive voice is formed with the verb **ser** (occasionally **ir, quedar,** etc.) and the past participle (the agent is expressed by **por**):

El fusil fue limpiado por el soldado.   The gun was cleaned by the soldier.

53. The true passive is replaced by a reflexive construction which may assume the following forms:

a) When the subject is not a person the verb agrees in number:

Aquí se habla inglés.   English is spoken here (*lit.* "English speaks itself here").
Se quemaron dos casas.   Two houses were burned.

In this construction the verb generally precedes the subject.

b) When the subject is a person, the verb is put in the third person singular and the person becomes the object:

> **Se mató al hombre.** The man was killed.
> **Se le mató.** He was killed.
> **Se mató a los hombres.** The men were killed.
> **Se les mató.** They were killed.

In this construction **les** (not **los**) is generally used as the third person plural object pronoun.

c) When the subject is impersonal ("one," "people") the verb is always singular:

> **Se come bien aquí.** The food is good here (One eats well here).
> **Se paga en la caja.** One pays at the (cashier's) desk.

54. The reflexive pronouns are used

a) As in English:

> **Me engaño.** I deceive myself.

b) With no reflexive meaning:

> **Se fue.** He went away.
> **Nos dormimos.** We fell asleep.
> **No nos atrevimos a hablar.** We did not dare to speak.

55. Idiomatic Uses of **tener,** *to have*

a) **Tener que** + the infinitive = *to have to* or *must* + the infinitive:

> **Tengo que irme.** I have to (must) go.
> **Tengo mucho que hacer.** I have much to do.

b) **Tener** + the noun = *to be* + the adjective:

	hambre		hungry
	sed		thirsty
	sueño		sleepy
Tengo	miedo	I am	afraid
	vergüenza		ashamed
	razón		right
	prisa		in a hurry

c) With parts of the body:

Tengo los ojos azules.   My eyes are blue.
Tengo las manos limpias.   My hands are clean.

d) To express age:

Tengo veinte años.   I am twenty years old.

56. Idiomatic Uses of **haber,** *to have*

a) **Hay** (**había, hubo, habrá,** *etc.*), *there is* or *are* (*was* or *were*, *will be*, etc.) denoting existence:

Hay muchos soldados aquí.   There are many soldiers here.
Hubo una huelga.   There was a strike.

b) *Hay que* + the infinitive = *to be necessary to* + the infinitive:

Hay que torcer a la derecha.   It is necessary to (one must, you must, etc.) turn to the right.

c) **Haber de** + the infinitive = *to be to* or *to be going to* or *shall* (*will*) + the infinitive:

Ha de hacerlo mañana.   He is to (is going to, will) do it tomorrow.

d) In expressions of visible aspects of weather (see §57*a*):

	barro *or* lodo.		muddy.
Hay	polvo.	It is	dusty.
	niebla.		foggy.

Hay una niebla espesa.   There is a dense fog.

But: **Está** { **nublado.** / **encapotado.** / **despejado.** }   It is { cloudy. / overcast. / clear (*or* fair). }

57. Idiomatic Uses of **hacer,** *to do* or *make*

a) In expressions of weather (see §56*d*):

Hace { **buen tiempo.** / **mal tiempo.** / **calor.** / **frío.** / **fresco.** / **viento.** / **sol.** }   It is { good weather. / bad weather. / warm. / cold. / fresh. / windy. / sunny. }

b) In expressions of time (note tenses in both Spanish and English):

Hace dos años que *estoy* aquí.
Estoy aquí desde *hace* dos años.
(Also: *Llevo* dos años aquí.) } I *have been* here two years.

Hacía dos años que *estaba* aquí.
Estaba aquí desde *hacía* dos años.
(Also: *Llevaba* dos años aquí.) } I *had been* here two years.

c) **Hace** + the time element = the time element + *ago* (note tenses):

Se murió hace tres años.   He died three years ago.
Mañana hará dos meses que se fue.   Tomorrow it will be two months since he went away.

58. Regular Verbs: three conjugations

	I		II		III	
			INFINITIVE			
habl ar	(to) speak	**com er**	(to) eat	**viv ir**	(to) live	
			PRESENT PARTICIPLE			
habl ando	speaking	**com iendo**	eating	**viv iendo**	living	
			PAST PARTICIPLE			
habl ado	spoken	**com ido**	eaten	**viv ido**	lived	

59. The Simple Tenses

INDICATIVE MODE

PRESENT

habl o I speak, am speaking, do speak
habl as you (*familiar*) speak, *etc.*
habl a you (*polite*), he, she, it speak(s), *etc.*
habl amos we speak, *etc.*
habl áis you (*fam. in Spain*) speak, *etc.*
habl an they, you (*polite and fam.*) speak, *etc.*

com o I eat, am eating, do eat, *etc.*

com es
com e
com emos
com éis
com en

viv o I live, am living, do live, *etc.*

viv es
viv e
viv imos
viv ís
viv en

IMPERFECT (Past Descriptive)

I

habl aba I was speaking,
habl abas used to speak,
habl aba spoke, *etc.*
habl ábamos
habl abais
habl aban

II and III (endings identical from here on)

com ía I was eating, used to
com ías eat, ate, *etc.*
com ía
com íamos
com íais
com ían

PRETERITE (Past Absolute)

I

habl é I spoke, did speak, *etc.*
habl aste
habl ó
habl amos
habl asteis
habl aron

II and III

com í I ate, did eat, *etc.*
com iste
com ió
com imos
com isteis
com ieron

FUTURE

I, II, and II (endings identical, added to infinitive)

hablar é I shall (will) speak,
hablar ás *etc.*
hablar á
hablar emos

comer é
comer ás
comer á
comer emos

vivir é
vivir ás
vivir á
vivir emos

hablar éis	comer éis	vivir éis
hablar án	comer án	vivir án

CONDITIONAL

I, II, and III (endings identical, added to infinitive)

hablar ía	I should (would) speak, *etc.*	hablar íamos
hablar ías		hablar íais
hablar ía		hablar ían

SUBJUNCTIVE MODE*
PRESENT

I	II and III (endings identical)
(que) habl e	com a
habl es	com as
habl e	com a
habl emos	com amos
habl éis	com áis
habl en	com an

IMPERFECT (two forms)

I	II and III (endings identical)
habl ara *or* ase	com iera *or* iese
habl aras *or* ases	com ieras *or* ieses
habl ara *or* ase	com iera *or* iese
habl áramos *or* ásemos	com iéramos *or* iésemos
habl arais *or* aseis	com ierais *or* ieseis
habl aran *or* asen	com ieran *or* iesen

60. The Compound Tenses (perfect tenses)**

PERFECT INFINITIVE

haber { hablado / comido / vivido }   to have { spoken / eaten / lived }

PRESENT PARTICIPLE

habiendo { hablapo / comido / vivido }   having { spoken / eaten / lived }

* The uncommon future subjunctive is omitted.

** The uncommon second past perfect is omitted.

INDICATIVE MODE

PRESENT PERFECT (Present of **haber** + past participle)

he ⎤ I have spoken, been speaking, *etc.*, eaten, lived
has |
ha | **hablado**
     ⎬ **comido**
hemos | **vivido**
habéis |
han ⎦

PLUPERFECT (Past perfect = imperfect of **haber** + past participle)

había ⎤ I had spoken, been speaking, *etc.*, eaten, lived
habías |
había | **hablado**
     ⎬ **comido**
habíamos | **vivido**
habíais |
habían ⎦

FUTURE PERFECT

habré ⎤ I shall have spoken, eaten, lived
habrás |
habrá | **hablado**
     ⎬ **comido**
habremos | **vivido**
habréis |
habrán ⎦

CONDITIONAL PERFECT

habría ⎤ I should (would) have spoken, eaten, lived
habrías |
habría | **hablado**
     ⎬ **comido**
habríamos | **vivido**
habríais |
habrían ⎦

SUBJUNCTIVE MODE

PRESENT PERFECT		PLUPERFECT	
haya		hubiera *or* hubiese	
hayas		hubieras *or* hubieses	
haya	hablado	hubiera *or* hubiese	hablado
	comido		comido
hayamos	vivido	hubiéramos *or* hubiésemos	vivido
hayáis		hubierais *or* hubieseis	
hayan		hubieran *or* hubiesen	

61. Imperative Mode

		I	II	III
Familiar singular		habl a	com e	viv e
Familiar plural		habl ad ⎱speak	com ed ⎱eat	viv id ⎱live
(used only in Spain)				
Polite singular		habl e (usted)	com a	viv a
			(usted)	(usted)
Polite plural (Spain)	⎱			
Polite and familiar	⎰ habl en	com an	viv an
plural (Spanish		(ustedes)	(ustedes)	(ustedes)
America)				

a) Note that **vamos + nos = vámonos** (*let's go*); **sentemos + nos = sentémonos** (*let us sit down*); **sentad + os = sentaos,** *etc*.

b) The infinitive is sometimes used as an imperative:

¡**(A) trabajar!**   Get to work!

62. Progressive Tenses. The various tenses of **estar** (sometimes **ir, seguir,** *etc.*) combine with the present participle to form the progressive tenses of other verbs:

estoy (estaba, *etc.*) **hablando, comiendo, viviendo,** *etc.*   I am (was, *etc.*) speaking, eating, living, *etc.*

63. Orthographic (Spelling) Changes in Verbs

Verbs whose infinitives

End with	Change Before	Examples
1. –car	c to qu ⎫	buscar, sacar, tocar
2. –gar	g to gu ⎬ e	llegar, pagar
3. –guar	gu to gü ⎭	averiguar
4. –zar	z to c	alzar, empezar, comenzar
5. –ger or gir	g to j ⎫	coger, dirigir
6. –quir	qu to c	delinquir
7. –guir	gu to g	seguir
8. consonant before	⎬ o and a	
–cer and –cir	c to z	vencer, torcer
9. vowel before	⎭	
–cer and –cir	c to zc	conocer, lucir

PRETERITE   busqué, buscaste, etc.; llegué, averigüé, alcé

PRES. SUBJ.   busque, busques, etc.; llegue, llegues, etc.; averigüe, alce, etc.

PRES. IND.   cojo, coges, etc.; dirijo, diriges, etc.; delinco, delinques, etc.

sigo, sigues, etc.; venzo, vences, etc.; conozco, conoces, etc.; luzco, luces, etc.

PRES. SUBJ.   coja, cojas, etc.; dirija, etc.; delinca, etc.; distinga, etc.; venza, etc.; conozca, etc.; luzca, etc.

10. An unstressed **i** between two strong vowels is written **y**:
     creyó he believed; **leyeron** they read, etc.
11. Verbs whose stem ends in **ñ** or **ll** lose the **i** (in spelling) of the
     diphthongs **ie** and **io**:
     reñir: riñó, riñeron

64. Radical- (Stem-) Changing Verbs

Class	Conjugation	Change	When	When o or e is unstressed and followed by a stressed –ió, ie and a:
I.	⎧ –ar	e to ie ⎫ stressed		no change
	⎩ –er	o to ue ⎭		
II.	–ir	e to ie ⎫ stressed		e to i
		o to ue ⎭		o to u
III.	–ir	e to i	stressed	e to i

EXAMPLES:

I. **cerrar,** to close; **contar,** to tell; **entender,** to understand; **volver,** to return
II. **sentir,** to feel; **dormir,** to sleep
III. **pedir,** to ask; **vestir,** to dress; **seguir,** to follow

PRESENT INDICATIVE

cierro, cierras, cierra, cerramos, cerráis, cierran
cuento, cuentas, cuenta, contamos, contáis, cuentan
entiendo, entiendes, entiende, entendemos, entendéis, entienden
siento, sientes, siente, sentimos, sentís, sienten
duermo, duermes, duerme, dormimos, dormís, duermen
pido, pides, pide, pedimos, pedís, piden

PRETERITE

sentí, sentiste, sintió, sentimos, sentisteis, sintieron
dormí, dormiste, durmió, dormimos, dormisteis, durmieron
pedí, pediste, pidió, pedimos, pedisteis, pidieron

PRESENT PARTICIPLE

sintiendo, durmiendo, pidiendo, etc.

PRESENT SUBJUNCTIVE

sienta, sientas, sienta, sintamos, sintáis, sientan
duerma, duermas, duerma, durmamos, durmáis, duerman
pida, pidas, pida, pidamos, pidáis, pidan

IMPERFECT SUBJUNCTIVE

durmiera, durmiese; sintiera, sintiese; pidiera, pidiese, etc.

IMPERATIVES

cierra, cuenta, entiende, vuelve, siente, duerme, pide

65. Verbs ending in –**uir** (except –**guir** and –**quir**) insert y after the stem vowel **u** before all vowels except **i**:

> **concluir:** concluyo, concluyes, concluye, concluimos, concluís, concluyen, etc.

66. Certain verbs in –**iar** and –**uar** have a stressed **i** or **u** with written accent in the present indicative and subjunctive

(except the first and second persons plural) and in the imperative singular:

enviar, to send

PRES. IND.   envío, envías, envía, enviamos, enviáis, envían, etc.

continuar, to continue

PRES. IND.   continúo, continúas, continúa, continuamos, continuáis, continúan, etc.

67. The Irregular Verbs

1. **andar, andando, andado,** to go, walk

PRETERITE   anduv–e, –iste, –o, –imos, –isteis, –ieron
IMP. SUBJ.   (1st form) anduviese, etc. (2nd form) anduviera, etc.

2. **caer, cayendo, caído,** to fall

PRES. IND.   caigo, caes, cae, caemos, caéis, caen
PRES. SUBJ.   caig–a, –as, –a, –amos, –áis, –an
PRETERITE   caí, caíste, cayó, caímos, caísteis, cayeron
IMP. SUBJ.   (1st form) cayese, etc. (2d form) cayera, etc.

3. **traducir, traduciendo, traducido,** to translate

PRES. IND.   traduzco, traduc–es, –e, –imos, –ís, –en
PRES. SUBJ.   traduzc–a, –as, –a, –amos, –áis, –an
PRETERITE   traduj–e, –iste, –o, –imos, –isteis, –eron
IMP. SUBJ.   (1st form) tradujese, etc. (2d form) tradujera, etc.

4. **dar, dando, dado,** to give

PRES. IND.   doy, das, da, damos, dais, dan
PRES. SUBJ.   dé, des, dé, demos, deis, den
PRETERITE   di, diste, dió, dimos, disteis, dieron
IMP. SUBJ.   (1st form) diese, etc. (2d form) diera, etc.

5. **decir, diciendo, dicho,** to say, tell

PRES. IND.   digo, dices, dice, decimos, decís, dicen
PRES. SUBJ.   diga, –as, –a, –amos, –áis, –an
FUT. IND.   diré, dirás, etc.; COND. diría, dirías, etc.
PRETERITE   dij–e, –iste, –o, –imos, –isteis, –eron
IMP. SUBJ.   (1st form) dijese, etc. (2d form) dijera, etc.
IMPERATIVE   (sing.) di

6. **estar, estando, estado,** to be

PRES. IND.	estoy, estás, está, estamos, estáis, están
PRES. SUBJ.	esté, estés, esté, estemos, estéis, estén
PRETERITE	estuv–e, –iste, –o, –imos, –isteis, –ieron
IMP. SUBJ.	(1st form) estuviese, etc. (2d form) estuviera, etc.

7. **haber, habiendo, habido,** to have

PRES. IND.	he, has, ha, hemos, habéis, han
PRES. SUBJ.	haya, hayas, haya, hayamos, hayáis, hayan
FUT. IND.	habré, habrás, etc.; COND. habría, etc.
PRETERITE	hub–e, –iste, –o, –imos, –isteis, –ieron
IMP. SUBJ.	(1st form) hubiese, etc. (2d form) hubiera, etc.

8. **hacer, haciendo, hecho,** to make, do

PRES. IND.	hago, haces, hace, hacemos, hacéis, hacen
PRES. SUBJ.	hag–a, –as, –a, –amos, –áis, –an
FUT. IND.	haré, harás, etc.; COND. haría, etc.
PRETERITE	hice, hiciste, hizo, hicimos, hicisteis, hicieron
IMP. SUBJ.	(1st form) hiciese, etc. (2d form) hiciera, etc.
IMPERATIVE	(sing.) haz

9. **ir, yendo, ido,** to go

PRES. IND.	voy, vas, va, vamos, vais, van
PRES. SUBJ.	vaya, vayas, vaya, vayamos, vayáis, vayan
IMP. IND.	iba, ibas, iba, íbamos, ibais, iban
PRETERITE	fui, fuiste, fue, fuimos, fuisteis, fueron
IMP. SUBJ.	(1st form) fuese, fueses, fuese, fuésemos, fueseis, fuesen
	(2d form) fuera, fueras, fuera, fuéramos, etc.
IMPERATIVE	(sing.) ve; (1st plural) vamos

10. **jugar, jugando, jugado,** to play

PRES. IND.	juego, juegas, juega, jugamos, jugáis, juegan
PRES. SUBJ.	juegue, juegues, juegue, juguemos, juguéis, jueguen
PRETERITE	jugué, jugaste, jugó, etc. IMPERATIVE juega, jugad

11. **oír, oyendo, oído,** to hear

PRES. IND.	oigo, oyes, oye, oímos, oís, oyen
PRES. SUBJ.	oig–a, –as, –a, –amos, –áis, –an
PRETERITE	oí, oíste, oyó, oímos, oísteis, oyeron
IMP. SUBJ.	(1st form) oyese, etc. (2d form) oyera, etc.
IMPERATIVE	(sing.) oye

12. **oler, oliendo, olido,** to smell

PRES. IND.	huelo, hueles, huele, olemos, oléis, huelen
PRES. SUBJ.	huela, huelas, huela, olamos, oláis, huelan
IMPERATIVE	huele, oled

13. **poder, pudiendo, podido,** to be able

PRES. IND.	puedo, puedes, puede, podemos, podéis, pueden
PRES. SUBJ.	pueda, puedas, pueda, podamos, podáis, puedan
FUT. IND.	podré, podrás, etc.; COND. podría, etc.
PRETERITE	pud–e, –iste, –o, –imos, –isteis, –ieron
IMP. SUBJ.	(1st form) pudiese, etc. (2d form) pudiera, etc.

14. **poner, poniendo, puesto,** to put, place

PRES. IND.	pongo, pones, pone, ponemos, ponéis, ponen
PRES. SUBJ.	pong–a, –as, –a, –amos, áis, –an
FUT. IND.	pondré, pondrás, etc.; COND. pondría, etc.
PRETERITE	pus–e, –iste, –o, –imos, –isteis, –ieron
IMP. SUBJ.	(1st form) pusiese, etc. (2d form) pusiera, etc.
IMPERATIVE	(sing.) pon

15. **querer, queriendo, querido,** to wish, be willing

PRES. IND.	quiero, quieres, quiere, queremos, queréis, quieren
PRES. SUBJ.	quiera, quieras, quiera, queramos, queráis, quieran
FUT. IND.	querré, querrás, etc.; COND. querría, etc.
PRETERITE	quis–e, –iste, –o, –imos, –isteis, –ieron
IMP. SUBJ.	(1st form) quisiese, etc. (2n form) quisiera, etc.

16. **saber, sabiendo, sabido,** to know, know how

PRES. IND.	sé, sabes, sabe, sabemos, sabéis, saben
PRES. SUBJ.	sep–a, –as, –a, –amos, –áis, –an
FUT. IND.	sabré, sabrás, etc.; COND. sabría, etc.
PRETERITE	sup–e, –iste, –o, –imos, –isteis, –ieron
IMP. SUBJ.	(1st form) supiese, etc. (2d form) supiera, etc.

17. **salir, saliendo, salido,** to go out, leave

PRES. IND.	salgo, sales, sale, salimos, salís, salen
PRES. SUBJ.	salg–a, –as, –a, –amos, –áis, –an
FUT. IND.	saldré, saldrás, etc.; COND. saldría, etc.
IMPERATIVE	(sing.) sal

18. **ser, siendo, sido,** to be

PRES. IND.	soy, eres, es, somos, sois, son
PRES. SUBJ.	sea, seas, sea, seamos, seáis, sean
IMP. IND.	era, eras, era, éramos, erais, eran

PRETERITE   fui, fuiste, fue, fuimos, fuisteis, fueron
IMP. SUBJ.   (1st form) fuese, fueses, fuese, fuésemos, fueseis,
              fuesen   (2d form) fuera, fueras, fuera, fuéramos,
              fuerais, fueran

19. **tener, teniendo, tenido,** to have

PRES. IND.   tengo, tienes, tiene, tenemos, tenéis, tienen
PRES. SUBJ.   teng–a, –as, –a, –amos, –áis, –an
FUT. IND.   tendré, tendrás, etc.; COND. tendría, etc.
PRETERITE   tuv–e, –iste, –o, –imos, –isteis, –ieron
IMP. SUBJ.   (1st form) tuviese, etc. (2d form) tuviera, etc.
IMPERATIVE   (sing.) ten

20. **traer, trayendo, traído,** to bring

PRES. IND.   traigo, traes, trae, traemos, traéis, traen
PRES. SUBJ.   traig–a, –as, –a, –amos, –áis, –an
PRETERITE   traj–e, –iste, –o, –imos, –isteis, –eron
IMP. SUBJ.   (1st form) trajese, etc. (2d form) trajera, etc.

21. **valer, valiendo, valido,** to be worth

PRES. IND.   valgo, vales, vale, valemos, valéis, valen
PRES. SUBJ.   valg–a, –as, –a, –amos, –áis, –an
FUT. IND.   valdré, valdrás, etc.; COND. valdría, etc.

22. **venir, viniendo, venido,** to come

PRES. IND.   vengo, vienes, viene, venimos, venís, vienen
PRES. SUBJ.   veng–a, –as, –a, –amos, –áis, –an
FUT. IND.   vendré, vendrás, etc.; COND. vendría, etc.
PRETERITE   vin–e, –iste, –o, –imos, –isteis, –ieron
IMP. SUBJ.   (1st form) viniese, etc. (2d form) viniera, etc.
IMPERATIVE   (sing.) ven

23. **ver, viendo, visto,** to see

PRES. IND.   veo, ves, ve, vemos, veis, ven
PRES. SUBJ.   vea, veas, vea, veamos, veáis, vean
IMP. IND.   veía, veías, veía, veíamos, veíais, veían
PRETERITE   vi, viste, vió, vimos, visteis, vieron
IMP. SUBJ.   (1st form) viese, etc. (2d form) viera, etc.

24. Irregular Past Participles. The following verbs and their compounds, which are regular in other respects, have only irregular past participles.

abrir	to open	**abierto**	**escribir**	to write	**escrito**
cubrir	to cover	**cubierto**	**imprimir**	to print	**impreso**

68. Cardinal Numerals

1 un(o), una	32 treinta y dos
2 dos	40 cuarenta
3 tres	41 cuarenta y un(o),
4 cuatro	cuarenta y una
5 cinco	50 cincuenta
6 seis	51 cincuenta y un(o),
7 siete	cincuenta y una
8 ocho	60 sesenta
9 nueve	61 sesenta y un(o),
10 diez	sesenta y una
11 once	70 setenta
12 doce	71 setenta y un(o),
13 trece	setenta y una
14 catorce	80 ochenta
15 quince	81 ochenta y un(o),
16 diez y seis (dieciséis)	ochenta y una
17 diez y siete (diecisiete)	90 noventa
18 diez y ocho (dieciocho)	91 noventa y un(o),
19 diez y nueve (dieci-	noventa y una
nueve)	100 cien(to)
20 veinte	101 ciento un(o), ciento una
21 veintiún, veintiuno, –a	102 ciento dos
22 veintidós	200 doscientos, –as
23 veintitrés	300 trescientos, –as
24 veinticuatro	400 cuatrocientos, –as
25 veinticinco	500 quinientos, –as
26 veintiséis	600 seiscientos, –as
27 veintisiete	700 setecientos, –as
28 veintiocho	800 ochocientos, –as
29 veintinueve	900 novecientos, –as
30 treinta	1,000 mil
31 treinta y un(o),	2,000 dos mil
treinta y una	1,000,000 un millón

69.

1 centimeter (**centímetro**) = .393 inches (**pulgadas**)
1 inch = 2.54 centimeters
1 meter (**metro**) = 39.37 inches or 3.28 feet or 1.093 yards
1 foot = .304 meters

1 yard = .914 meters
1 kilometer (km.) = .621 miles
1 mile (**milla**) = 1.609 kilometers

1 liter (**litro**) = 2.113 pints or 1.056 quarts or .264 gallons
1 pint = .473 liters
1 quart = .946 liters
1 gallon = 3.785 liters

1 gram (**gramo**) = .035 ounces (**onzas**)
1 ounce = 28.35 grams
1 kilogram (**kilo**) = 2.204 pounds (**libras**) or 35.273 ounces
1 pound = .453 kilograms

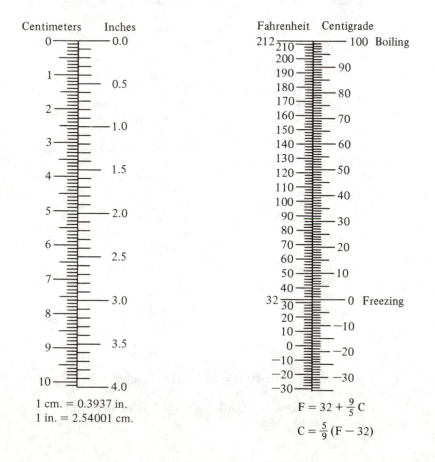

1 cm. = 0.3937 in.
1 in. = 2.54001 cm.

$$F = 32 + \frac{9}{5}C$$

$$C = \frac{5}{9}(F - 32)$$

32 degrees (**grados**) Fahrenheit (F) = 0° centigrade (**centígrado**)
100° C = 180° F

To change degrees F to degrees C, subtract 32 and multiply
by $\frac{5}{9}$. $(F - 32) \times \frac{5}{9} = C$

To change degrees C to degrees F, multiply by $\frac{9}{5}$ and add 32.
$(C \times \frac{9}{5}) + 32 = F$

1 cm. = 0.3937 in.

1 in. = 2.54001 cm.

$$F = = 32 + \frac{9}{5} C$$
$$C = \frac{5}{9} (F - 32)$$

70.   A few place names and their derivation adjectives. (The
English equivalent is omitted when meaning is apparent.)

Alemania (*Germany*)	alemán (*German*)
la Argentina	argentino
Bolivia	boliviano
el Brasil	brasileño
el Canadá	canadiense
Chile	chileno
China	chino
Colombia	colombiano
Costa Rica	costarricense, costarriqueño
Cuba	cubano
el Ecuador	ecuatoriano
España (*Spain*)	español
Europa	europeo
Francia	francés
Grecia	griego
Guatemala	guatemalteco
la Habana	habanero
Holanda	holandés
Honduras	hondureño
Inglaterra (*England*)	inglés
Islandia (*Iceland*)	islandés, islándico
Italia	italiano
el Japón (*Japan*)	japonés
Méjico *or* México	mejicano *or* mexicano
Nicaragua	nicaragüense
Noruega (*Norway*)	noruego
Panamá	panameño
el Paraguay	paraguayo
el Perú	peruano

Polonia (*Poland*)	polaco
Portugal	portugués
Puerto Rico	puertorriqueño
Rusia	ruso
El Salvador	salvadoreño
Santo Domingo	dominicano
Suecia (*Sweden*)	sueco
Suiza (*Switzerland*)	suizo
Turquía (*Turkey*)	turco
Uruguay	uruguayo
Venezuela	venezolano

Important Signs and Notices

abierto   *open*
alto   *stop*
arriba   *up*
caliente or "C"   *hot*
carretera particular   *private road*
cerrado   *closed*
completo   *filled up*
cuidado   *caution*
empujar   *push*
libre   *vacant*
no obstruya la entrada   *don't block the entrance*
no tocar   *don't touch*
ocupado   *busy, occupied*
peligro   *danger*
prohibido   *forbidden*
prohibido el paso   *no entrance*
prohibido escupir, fumar, estacionarse (aparcar)   *forbidden to
  spit, smoke, park*
reservado   *reserved*
salida   *exit*
se alquila   *to rent*
servicios   *toilets*
tire   *pull*

71. Cartas   Letters

ENCABEZAMIENTO	HEADING	
Muy señor mío:	*Dear Sir:*	⎫ *business letters*
Muy señores míos:	*Gentlemen:*	⎭

Muy estimado Sr. A:	*Dear Mr. A:*
(Mi) querido amigo:	*(My) dear friend:*
(Muy) recordado amigo A:	*(My) dear friend A:*

FINAL	ENDING
Atentamente	*Yours truly*
Reciba Vd. mis afectuosos sa-ludos	*Sincerely yours*
(Reciba) un abrazo de su amigo	
No olvide a su afmo. amigo que le estima	
Su afectísimo servidor y amigo	*Cordially yours, etc.*
Le estrecha la mano cordial-mente su amigo que le apre-cia	
Cordialmente	

10 de enero de 19—	*January 10, 19—*
Sres. López, Gómez y Cía.	*López, Gómez and Company*
Madero, 53	*53 Madero Street*
México, D.F.	*Mexico City*
Muy señores míos:	*Gentlemen:*
Sírvanse mandarme (*or* enviarme) lo antes posible (*or* a la mayor brevedad posible) por tren rápido (por tren de carga, a vuelta de correo) lo siguiente:	*Please send me as soon as possible by express (by freight, by return mail) the following:*
Cárguenme Vds. en cuenta el valor de este pedido.	*Charge the amount of this order to my account.*
Quedo de Vds. muy atento y S.S.	*Yours truly,*
Muy señor mío:	*Dear Sir:*
Hemos recibido su atenta (*or* su grata) del 10 del co-rriente. Tenemos el gusto de remitirle a Vd. por correo:	*We have received your letter of the 10th (of this month). We are forwarding you today by mail:*

Por separado le mandamos nuestro catálogo.	*Under separate cover we are sending you our catalog.*
En espera de sus gratas órdenes, nos repetimos de Vd.	*Awaiting your appreciated orders, we are*
Atentos y S.S.	*Yours truly,*

72. National Holidays and Dates of Independence

Argentina	July 9 (1816)
Bolivia	August 5–7 (1825)
Brazil	September 7 (1822)
Central America	September 15 (1821)
Chile	September 18 (1810)
Colombia	July 20 (1810)
Cuba	May 20 (1902)
Dominican Republic	February 27 (1844)
Ecuador	August 10 (1809)
Mexico	September 16 (1821)
Panama	November 3 (1903)
Paraguay	May 14–15 (1811)
Peru	July 28–30 (1821)
Uruguay	August 25 (1825)
Venezuela	July 5 (1811)

IMPORTANT ABBREVIATIONS

A.C.	año de Cristo	A.D.
a/c	al cuidado de	c/o
apdo.	apartado de correos	post office box
Av., Avda.	avenida	avenue
C., Cia.	compañia	company
C/	calle	street
cta.	cuenta	account
cte.	corriente	this month
D.	don	title of respect (sir)
Da. Dª	doña	title of respect (madame)
E.E.U.U.	(los) Estados Unidos	United States (U.S.)
f.c.	ferrocarril	railroad
G.C.	guardia civil	police (Spain)
N.ª S.ʳª	Nuestra Señora	Our Lady (the Virgin)
n.º, núm.	número	number
P.P.	porte pagado	postage paid
pta.	peseta	peseta (Spain)
$	peso	peso (Mex.)

RENFE	Red Nacional de Ferrocarriles Españoles	Spanish National Railway
S., Sta.	San, Santa	Saint
S.A.	Sociedad Anónima	Inc.
Sr.	Señor	Mr.
Sra.	Señora	Mrs.
Sres., Srs.	Señores	gentlemen
Srta.	Señorita	Miss
Ud. Vd.	usted	you
Uds., Vds.	ustedes	you (plural)
v. g., v. gr.	verbigracia	viz., namely

INDEX TO APPENDIX

311

direct object: preceded by **a,**
  § 11
el que, la que, etc., § 36
estar: uses of, § 51*b* and § 51*c*

future ind. of probability, § 40*d*

gender: of nouns, §§ 7, 8; of
  adjs., §§ 12, 13
grande: apocopation of, § 22*c*

haber: idiomatic uses of, § 56
hacer: idiomatic uses of, § 57

imperative mode, § 61
imperfect ind. tense, § 40*b*
indefinite: *see* article
infinitive: used instead of subj.,
  § 47; uses of, § 49; forms of,
  § 58
interrogative adjs. and pronouns, § 37
–ísimo: use of, § 20

lo: neuter article, § 3

malo: apocopation of, § 22*a*
mode: indicative of regular
  verbs, §§ 59, 60; subjunctive,
  §§ 59, 60; imperative, § 61

necessity: expressions of, § 56*b*
  (hay que), § 55*a* **(tener que)**
negatives, § 30
ninguno: apocopation of, § 22*a*
noun clauses: subj. in, § 43
nouns: pl. of, § 9; gender of,
  §§ 7, 8
numerals: cardinal, § 68

orthographic changes in verbs,
  § 63

para: uses of, § 38
passive voice, §§ 52, 53; impersonal reflexive, § 53*c*
perfect ind. as simple past,
  § 40*f*
personal pronouns: forms of,
  § 31; position of, §§ 32–34;
  use of prepositional forms,
  § 35; relative, § 36; interrogative, § 37
plural: of nouns, § 9; of adjs.,
  § 14
por: uses of, § 39
position: of adjs., § 15; of personal pronouns, §§ 32–34
possession: with **de,** § 10
possessive: adjs., §§ 23, 24; pronouns, § 25
present ind. tense used for future, § 40*a*
present participle: to express
  manner, § 50; forms of, § 58
preterite ind. tense, § 40*c*
primero: apocopation of, § 22*a*
progressive tenses: **estar** used to
  form, § 51*c,* § 62
pronouns: *see* Demonstrative,
  Interrogative, Personal, Possessive, Reflexive, Relative
purpose: subj. in adv. clauses
  expressing, § 45*a*

radical-changing verbs, § 64
reflexive passive construction,
  § 53
reflexive pronouns, § 31; uses
  of, § 54
relative pronouns, § 36

sequence of tenses, § 48
ser: uses of, § 51*a,* § 52